Tipping the Sacred Cow

The Best of *LiP: Informed Revolt*, 1996–2007

edited by Brian Awehall

AK Press · Oakland, California · 2007

Tipping the Sacred Cow: The Best of *LiP: Informed Revolt*, 1996–2007

© 2007 All copyrights rest with the individual contributors
© 2007 This edition copyright AK Press

ISBN 978-1-904859-73-4
Library of Congress Control Number: 2007928388

Printed in Canada

Front cover art by Mona Caron (monacaron.com)
Cover and interior design by Brian Awehali

Published by

AK Press
674-A 23rd Street
Oakland, CA 94612
U.S.A
www.akpress.org
akpress@akpress.org

AK Press
PO Box 12766
Edinburgh, EH8 9YE
Scotland
www.akuk.com
ak@akedin.demon.co.uk

All of us at AK Press would be delighted to send you our distribution catalog, which features the several thousand books, pamphlets, zines, audio and video products, and stylish apparel published and/or distributed by AK Press. Alternatively, visit our website(s) for the complete catalog, latest news, and secure ordering.

This book was printed using vegetable-based inks and a union printer.

ENVIRONMENTAL IMPACT STATEMENT

This book was made with 100% post-consumer waste, acid- and chlorine-free paper. By using this paper, the following resources were saved:

trees	water	energy	solid waste	greenhouse gases
32 fully grown	11,682 gallons	22 million BTU's	1500 pounds	2814 lbs. CO_2 equiv.

Calculated using PaperCalculator.org, a service provided by Environmental Defense, in partnership with the Paper Task Force, a peer-reviewed study of the lifecycle environmental impacts of paper production and disposal.

"Children's Games," by Eric Drooker | drooker.com

This painting appeared on the back cover of *LiP* 2.1 (Spring 2004), the Oddly Dangersome "First" Issue

TiPPiNG THE SACRED COW

Table of Contents

Greetings, dear reader.

You hold in your hands a literary fusillade devoted to a marvelous revolt for the overthrow of miserabilism. We could also describe our target as the crippling mass apparatus of dichotomized*, linear (p. 193), alienating, and anthropocentric, white supremacist patriarchal capitalist oligarchy, but doesn't *miserabilism* more succinctly, poetically—more *sufferably*—evoke the same complex of ideas, in a vastly simpler way? We need justice, equity, and peace, but we need it in a creative, ecstatic, natural, and diversely liberatory framework. We need the marvelous as we struggle.

I invoke this florid Surrealist language not because it appeared often in *LiP* (it didn't), but because it was the guiding editorial spirit I tried to bring to our efforts, even—especially—when those efforts involved delving into some of the more horrifying and demoralizing aspects of our present reality.

* *See Glossary of Terms, p. 240.*

1. **The Oddly Dangersome "First" Issue** (2.1 - Spring 2004) 2. **The Flabbergastingly Larcenous "Theft" Issue** (2.2 - Winter 2005) 3. **The Vaguely Apocalyptic "Waste" Issue** (2.3 - Spring 2005)

From the Gregorian years 1996 through 2007, *LiP: Informed Revolt*, a quirky Chicago-, then Seattle-, then northern New Mexico-based print and online zine,[a] ripened into an award-winning Oakland-based online and print sporadical distributed throughout the U.S. and Canada. Concocting an imaginative mix of politics, culture, sex, and humor, the project took motley, divergently coherent aim at the essential topics of our day and place. All-volunteer and never for profit, *LiP* was produced by a diverse and ever-shifting crew of editors, writers, artists, and administrative contributors (roughly 600 in all), quasi-organized by an itinerant editor, who devoted themselves to articulating an entertaining vernacular radicalism unencumbered by the more obvious limitations of self-marginalizing radical chic subculture or lifestylism.[b]

[a] *A small, self-produced publication, created primarily for self expression, often by a single person, and rarely with a commercial purpose in mind. LiP began as a zine, then grew into something between a zine and a magazine, though not primarily because of a growth in circulation (100 copies of issue #1 in January 1996 to 8,000 copies of issue #4 in June 2005.) The more significant shift occurred with the advent of the second iteration of LiP (#2.1) in the Spring of 2004, when our focus broadened and the number of editors and contributors expanded.*

[b] *Speaking of which, the illustration on this cover of this collection is intended as a humorous comment on the cartoonish and self-satirizing aspects of predominantly white U.S. radical-left chic subculture, and is meant to pose an inflammatory, yet important question: What distinguishes a subculture from a movement? ("Movements for social justice would be a lot better off if we could laugh at the absurdity of our own craft, and the absurdity of what goes on in this society as a way to penetrate and to change it."—Tim Wise. See p. 208 for more on this matter.)*

4. **The Constructively Negative Sacred Cows Issue** (2.4 - Summer 2005) 5. **The Relentlessly Persuasive Propaganda Issue** (2.5 - Winter 2006) 6. **The Curiously Unflinching Futures Issue** (2.6 - Summer 2006) 7. **The Grossly Unexpected Bugs Issue** (2.7 - Winter 2007)

1. **The Scattershot "Atrociously Designed" Issue** (1.1 - January 1996) 2. **The Polemical "Thoroughly Earthy" Issue** (1.2 - February 1997) 3. **The Provocative "My Other Bludgeon is a Nike" Issue** (1.5 - May 1997) 4. **The Opinionated "Get Whitey" Issue** (1.6 - August 1997)

There were two print iterations of *LiP*, which you may read about in the History appendix of this book, if you're so inclined. The first iteration spanned three years and 11 issues, and was produced by the cheapest available means. The second, expanded iteration of *LiP (see Appendix: Editor's Letters)* spanned three years and seven issues, and was produced entirely using post-consumer waste recycled paper, vegetable-based inks, and local worker-owned or union print shops.

This change came about because I realized it was counterproductive for a magazine with our systemic political focus to engage in a production process that took money from advertisers, subscribers, and private donors, and gave most of that money to printers operating in ecologically unsound ways, and using alienating labor practices. It does cost more to produce a print publication in an ecologically sound manner,[c] but the more publications make this move, the more we help create a viable economy for green (or anyway greener) printing practices. The second iteration of *LiP* put our production where our politics were, and AK Press, an Oakland-based worker-run collective, agreed to use the same practices for the publication of this anthology.

---

[c] *There probably isn't a truly ecologically sound way to produce a print magazine, since even the use of postconsumer-waste paper has limitations, due to downcycling (the successive breakdown of substances as they're recycled and re-recycled), and the externalized energy costs associated with the recycling of materials and the shipping of magazines.*

LiP evolved during its run, but I always intended for it to be a *divergent* undertaking. It was meant to be a medium for talking about how to imagine and get a better world, using a variety of premises, especially unfamiliar or unusual ones, while avoiding common limiting assumptions. The point wasn't necessarily to critique existing independent media, though that was sometimes a byproduct, but to do something unique, that might spur different conversations, generate different frames, and attract people who frankly, feel stultified by a lot of U.S. progressive and radical media. *LiP* did not cultivate a *programmatic* focus. We concerned ourselves instead with asking good questions, challenging unfounded assumptions, and examining the propositional content of contemporary political discourse. Rather than focusing on the specific details of a discourse, we focused our energies on the often coercive framing and underlying logic of those discourses.[d]

> *"People know what they do; frequently they know why they do what they do; but what they don't know is what what they do does."*
> —French philosopher, historian, and occasional pedant Michel Foucault

[d] *If that's unsatisfyingly nebulous for you, please do read through the Editor's Letters collected in the Appendix of this collection. They're short; they're informative; They frame.*

Despite being an expressly "political"ᵉ publication at a dramatic time in U.S. electoral history, *LiP* rarely used the trees, ink, labor, time, and money that went into making our pages to talk about electoral politics or the purview of elected officials. Why? For one thing, because a lot of publications were already expending quite a lot of resources covering that boondoggled realm of guaranteed disappointment, and I, as the editor, simply found it boring. But the deeper reason was that we were more interested in talking about how to get a world we *really* want, and posited in our editorial framework that the way to that world is direct, not mediated or representative, and that individuals are prey to institutions in modern mass societies. Our analysis was radical, not liberal or progressive: We were interested in exploring the root causes of current problems, and we presumed in our analysis that structure trumps individual agency in the political realm. Individuals can struggle mightily against institutionalized conditions, but without changing the institutions themselves, those efforts will be largely for naught, since people tire, lose focus, forget, and, eventually, give up their ghosts, while institutions share no such limitations. We were trying to advance a more fundamental understanding, about power, and about the manipulation of perception.

That's the basic explanation of what *LiP* was, and what we were trying to achieve with it. My earnest hope is that it served a useful and uplifting purpose, and that this collection proves to be a stimulating and entertaining medium for you, dear reader. Making media for liberatory political purposes involves having a certain dogged faith and hope, which Jennifer Whitney sums up perfectly in her article, "Make Media, Make Real Trouble," (p. 44):

ᵉ *What is "political," anyway? More to the point, what's not? One of several operational definitions given for "politics" is "the total complex of relations between people living in society," yet the obvious interconnectedness and interdependence of human beings and the natural and animal world makes it reasonable to expand the definition of politics from the prevailing anthropocentric model, to a more ecocentric model that's inclusive of the animal and natural world.*

Making media is a bit like scattering seeds, in that we never know where our work will end up—if it will germinate, take root, and spread; if it will survive fire or drought; if others will notice and propagate it. We should put out the hardiest and healthiest seeds that we can, so the information stored within will have a better chance at survival.

It was a sometimes arduous pleasure producing *LiP*, and many people gave a lot of their passion and many moments of this life to producing it. I hope we have sown some good seeds.

Onward & upward,

Founder, Editor, and Creative Director

If Women Ruled the World, Nothing Would be Different

Lisa Jervis

FALL 2005

illustrations by
Hugh D'Andrade

The biggest problem with U.S.-American feminism today is its obsession with women.

Yes, you heard me: It's time for those of us who care deeply about eliminating sexism within the context of social justice struggles to stop caring so damn much about what women, as a group, are doing. Because a useful, idealistic, transformative, progressive feminism is not about women. It's about gender, and all the legal and cultural rules that govern it, and power—who has it and what they do with it.

But much of the contemporary U.S.-American feminist movement is preoccupied with the mistaken belief—call it *femininism*—that female leadership is inherently different from male; that having more women in positions of power, authority, or visibility will automatically lead to, or can be equated with, feminist social change; that women are uniquely equipped as a force for action on a given issue; and that isolating feminist work as solely pertaining to women is necessary or even useful.

The influence of femininist thinking is broadly in evidence today, from casual conversations in which arrogant know-it-alls are described in shorthand terms like "typically male" and "how very boy" to nonprofit groups that exist to promote the leadership of women—any women—in business and politics. It manifests itself in the topics that are considered most central to feminism. The problems feminists should be trying to solve are not caused primarily by a dearth of women with power. The overwhelming maleness of the U.S.-American population of congressional representatives and physics professors, CEOs and major-newspaper op-ed columnists, is a symptom, sure, of a confluence of economic, political, and cultural forces that devalue women's work, denigrate our ideas as less important than men's, and discourage us from aiming high.

Would more women in high places signify a change in that? Yeah. And that would be nice.

> Much of contemporary U.S.-American feminist thought is preoccupied with the belief that having more women in positions of power, authority, or visibility will automatically lead to, or can be equated with, feminist social change.

But any changes would likely be superficial: More women in high-paying corporate jobs might mean that women would finally be making more, on average, than 76 cents to the male dollar, but it would do nothing about the 35.8 million people under the poverty line—and it's definitely not going to transform the structural forces that keep them there. It wouldn't even necessarily mean that large numbers of women were being paid wages closer to their male counterparts'. Like the wage gap itself, it would be a symptom of power at work, a signal that women are being allowed more access to the benefits of a destructive economic and political system. If we're fighting just for that access on behalf of women, without mounting a challenge to it, then feminism is, to borrow a phrase from Barbara Smith, nothing more than female self-aggrandizement.

Furthermore, the most pressing issues facing women worldwide—slave wages, inadequate health care systems, environmental degradation, the endless war and surveillance society of Bush-era neo-conservatism, and rampant corporate profiteering involved in all of the above—are a) no less important to feminists just because they also happen to be the most pressing issues facing men and b) directly related to the particularly ruthless brand of global capitalism we're currently living under.

This vulture capitalism would not magically disappear if women were in charge of more stuff. Racism would not go away. Hell, sexism itself would probably be alive and kicking. God knows the gender binary would be stronger than ever. In short: The actual workings of power will not change with more chromosomal diversity among the powerful.

Even if, to stick with our example, the wage gap were eliminated through genuine equal pay for equal work, without a radical challenge to the economic system that structures all of our lives, it would most likely mean that men would be paid as badly as women. (In fact, the narrowing of the wage gap since 1979 can be largely attributed to decreases in men's wages.) And while that certainly seems fair on its face—if we all have to live under a shitty system, the burdens of shit should at least be shared as equally as possible—as a political goal it's an admission of defeat.

Let's take a quick look at some history. Femininism is an outgrowth of the deeply flawed and largely debunked philosophy of gender essentialism: the belief that biology is destiny and that men and women's bodily differences translate into universal and unchanging/unchangeable gender roles and traits. Essentialist thought dates back at least to the ancient Greeks, who saw men (of a certain class) as smart, strong, noble citizens and women as unfit to take part in intellectual exchange. Eighteenth-century philosophers laid down the natural law, which dictated that women's childbearing bodies rendered them natural caretakers and little else. To this effort, scientists at the time contributed their data on things like skull size to confirm women's lack of intellectual capacity. Similar modes of data interpretation were also useful in "proving" that black people were fit only for the hard physical labor of slavery and that poor immigrant folks' criminal tendencies were evident in the shapes of their heads. Today's version of this argument—with the same flaws in evidence and interpretation—comes from the evolutionary psychologists and brain researchers who assert all kinds of neurobiological explanations for supposed gender differences in everything from verbal skills to the propensity to cheat on a partner.

The first feminist activists, the suffragists and temperance women of the 19th and early 20th centuries, sought to use essentialist thinking to their benefit: Women, as the raisers of children and caretakers of home and hearth, had a natural morality that could be brought to bear in politics and against the social ills caused by excessive drinking. Feminist essentialism grew up along with the movement as a whole, as thinkers and activists in the '60s and '70s sought much-needed recognition for undervalued "feminine" attributes like cooperation and caretaking and as part of the struggle for gender equality. Feminist essentialism reached full flower in the backlash-laden '80s, as rigorous intellectual work exploring the behavioral effects of gendered socialization—most famously, Carol Gilligan's *In a Different Voice*—was broadly popularized, misinterpreted, and oversimplified as nothing more than a call for the essential male and female natures to switch places in our value sytem, elevating the supposed, culturally determined feminine over the supposed, culturally determined masculine. Thus certain political and intellectual circles came to valorize women as inherently nurturing, peaceful, connected to nature, and noncompetitive, and to demonize men as bellicose, unfeeling, and destructive.

It's important for me to pause for a minute and make a few things crystal clear. First of all: Yes, gender difference exists. Of course men and women often behave differently, see the world differently, and have different political views—when you've been raised with sugar-and-spice-and-everything-nice expectations and the knowledge that if you choose to sleep with men you're just a broken condom away from a lifelong responsibility, it tends to make you

both more empathetic and more likely to favor things like safe, legal, accessible abortions. Duh. But such differences are neither automatic (as the evolutionary biologists would have us believe) nor universal (as the cultural essentialists assert).

Second of all, the forces I'm referring to as those that have led to the problem of femininism have been essential to both concrete feminist political gains and to feminism's intellectual development. I am not at all suggesting it's unimportant to call attention to the fact that the Senate is only 13% female, to encourage society to recognize the value of women's unpaid childcare labor, or even to rescue politically neutral traditionally female pursuits like knitting from the pink ghetto.

Acknowledgement and discussion of culturally produced gender differences is essential to dismantling sexism—but the line between acknowledging cultural differences that demand examination and allowing them to persist unchallenged is a fine one indeed. Femininism crosses it constantly.

And some of those alleged gender differences are easily disproved. If women's maternal instincts and natural compassion will bring about a kinder, more peaceful world, what's up with Condoleezza Rice? (It's also worth noting that Madeleine Albright didn't exactly transform the Clinton administration's foreign policy into a bastion of benevolence, either.) If women were truly sympathetic to and cooperative with each other, Ann Coulter's journalistic achievements would have made the media less misogynist, not more. A woman was in charge of Abu Ghraib when Iraqi prisoners were tortured by U.S.-American soldiers; three of the seven charged with perpetrating the abuse are female. Inherently nurturing? Sisterly? Yeah. Sure.

More important, however, is that femininist thinking threatens to drain feminism of progressive politics—and, in many cases, of any politics at all. Take, for example, a 2004 book called *If Women Ruled the World*. The changes this slim volume predicts would result from such ruling are both serious ("we would all have health care") and silly ("business would be more fun!"). A few might even be accurate ("equal parenting would be the norm, not the exception"). But they are all assumptions based on a fallacy: that (as the book's foreword asserts) "empathy, inclusion across lines of authority, relational skills, [and] community focus" are "values that women uniquely bring to the table." This line of reasoning urges us to forget about forging the argument that our current health care system is inhumane, profit-driven, and inefficient. It gives us a pass on making the case for universal health care as the best solution to skyrocketing costs and 44 million of us without insurance. We won't need to do that if we can just get more women in on that ruling-the-world game.

This tactic is taken up by quite a few feminist groups seeking to influence the political landscape. One of these is the White House Project, "a national, non-partisan organization dedicated to advancing women's leadership across

sectors and fostering the entry of women into all positions of leadership, including the U.S. presidency." A female president is a tempting goal to pursue, an important symbol of gender equality, and, yes, someone whose inauguration will surely make me kvell even if I find her policies repugnant. But having a woman in the White House won't necessarily do a damn thing for progressive feminism. Though the dearth of women in electoral politics is so dire as to make supporting a woman—any woman—an attractive proposition, even if it's just so she can serve as a role model for others who'll do the job better eventually, it's ultimately a trap. Women who do nothing to enact feminist policies will be elected and backlash will flourish. I can hear the refrain now: "They've finally gotten a woman in the White House, so why are feminists still whining about equal pay?"

Other groups carry the "if only women ruled the world" belief to a wistful, apolitical extreme. Take the organization (and I use that term loosely) Gather the Women. GTW is "a gathering place for women and women's organizations who share a belief that the time is now to activate the incredible power of women's wisdom on a planetary scale." One of its purported goals is to "celebrate women as global peacemakers." However, they "seek not to change minds but to connect hearts." Just how anyone is supposed to be a global peacemaker without trying to change anyone's mind is never articulated. Then again, neither is anything these folks do, except have an annual conference with panels such as "Divine Goddess and Leadership."

If the problem were confined to fringe, mushy-thinking non-organizations, it wouldn't even be worth writing about. But even groups doing effective, important, progressive feminist work often fall prey to essentialist thinking. Code Pink's Call to Action contradictorily declares that women organize for peace "not because we are better or purer or more innately nurturing than men but because the men have busied themselves making war. Because…we understand the love of a mother in Iraq for her children and the driving desire of that child for life." Translation: It's not that women are naturally more nurturing and peaceful than men—it's just that women are naturally more nurturing and peaceful than men.

This covert embrace of essentialist thinking (and the intellectual dishonesty that it requires) manifests in many of Code Pink's central tactics. One of the group's major activities has been sending delegations of parents and others close to either 9/11 victims or enlisted folks to Afghanistan, Iraq, and Iran. The delegations have brought humanitarian aid and drawn attention to horrific conditions caused by U.S.-American military activities. But their very premise—that being a mother of a soldier is the best platform from which to speak out against the war—ensures that the resulting arguments are a plea not to cause unhappiness by sending a kid off to die rather than a principled stance against unjust and corrupt use of force. The former

isn't even a compelling moral argument, much less any kind of a political analysis. And when real political analysis is slipped into a femininist framework, it's easily neutered: In a keynote speech at the 2005 Center for New Words Women and Media Conference, Code Pink cofounder Medea Benjamin detailed the ways in which their peace delegates' comments to the media were edited to remove commentary critical of the war and of the Bush administration so that only worry over their children remained.

Women's eNews, a news service that, in the words of its mission statement, "cover[s] issues of particular concern to women and provide[s] women's perspectives on public policy," is yet another promising project that would be far more effective if it weren't thoroughly mired in femininism. While it is indeed imperative for the news media to recognize women as sources, experts, and commentators more than they currently do, an approach like Women's eNews' is patently unhelpful. Its May 9, 2005, cover story is indicative. Headlined "Mothering From Afar Extracts Heavy Price," and accompanied by introductory text noting that "as a growing number of Latin American women migrate to the U.S., many of these women will spend the [Mother's Day] holiday far from their children—some of whom have forgotten them," the piece does little more than tug at readers' heartstrings. When Women's eNews defines "women's concerns" as Ana and her plans to migrate north to better support her and 8- and 10-year-old sons, but not the issues of globalization and capital flows that make her unable to earn a living in her home country, it actually works to shore up the "feminine" realm of home, hearth, and kids.

Likewise, stories like "Female Dems Say Social Security Is Their Fight," "Women Pioneer Biofuel to Save Mother Earth," and "Record Number of Female Soldiers Fall" tightly circumscribe what women are supposed to care about. If Social Security were gender neutral, it would hardly be any less of a women's issue. It's not because "we've got kids and we are thinking generations ahead of ourselves," as one of the sources in the biofuels article asserts, that feminists bring an important perspective to the environmental movement. And it's damn sure not primarily because female soldiers are dying that we should be paying attention to the war.

But the problem with feminism goes even deeper than these strategic missteps. Because it's founded on gender difference, it retains a strong investment in gender divisions. Not only will we never dismantle gender discrimination as long as gender divisions are philosophically important to feminism, but we'll end up reproducing the gendered oppression we're supposedly fighting against.

Femininism seeks a circumscribed set of qualities for womanhood the same way that conservative, gender-traditional patriarchy does. Gender conservatives see motherhood as women's natural role; feminists see motherhood (or the capacity for it) as the ultimate

political motivator. Gender conservatives prefer to see women in the role of helpmate; feminists see women as uniquely equipped with superior relational skills. Gender conservatives justify male aggressive behavior by virtue of its being an inherently male character trait; feminists criticize male aggressive behavior for the same reason. But what about those women (and there are many) who have no interest in parenting, who have crappy communication skills, who would rather compete than cooperate? Are they not women? More to the point, are they bad feminists?

This sort of gender essentialism can be particularly divisive when it comes to women's and feminist activism, because it polices the boundaries of womanhood; implicitly or overtly, femininist organizations, groups, and events require a certain degree of "femininity" for participation. Nowhere is this problem more apparent than in the tension between certain corners of the feminist world and trans and genderqueer movements. Femininist thinking practically demands distrust of, and even hostility toward, gender-variant people. There's simply no room in a movement overinvested in cherished notions of who women are and how they behave for the myriad gender identities that exist in our world: transsexual women who know they were born as women even if their genitals said otherwise; biologically female butch dykes who prefer male pronouns; intersex folks who choose not to check any F or M box; and many, many others.

But it's the obliteration of rigid gender categories themselves, not any kind of elevation of the feminine, that is our best hope for an end to gender discrimination. Progressive trans and genderqueer folks are, for obvious reasons, feminist allies in this fight (and, not incidentally, cisgender* feminists should be allies to trans and genderqueer folks as well—but that's a tad beyond the scope of this essay). Furthermore, trans and genderqueer movements are forcing us to ask deeper questions about what woman- and manhood are, how femininity and masculinity are defined and determined—that stands to enrich feminist thought and action immeasurably.

In spite of my generalizations, feminism as I've been discussing it here is far from monolithic, and, like feminism as a whole, encompasses people and ideas with disagreement and contradictions aplenty. It includes folks as wide-ranging as liberal feminist organizations such as the White House Project and separatist crowds like those who attend the Michigan Womyn's Music Festival. There are valuable aspects of each of these branches of feminism, and critiquing their femininist tendencies does not have to mean rejecting everything about them. But it's equally important to recognize that those femininist tendencies are deeply antithetical to where feminism needs to go in order to stay effective and vibrant, to eliminate gender discrimination at its core, and to fight for a broad-based social justice.

If we continue to believe, hope, or even suspect that women, simply because they are women, will bring pro-feminist policies with them into the corridors of power, we will be rewarded with more powerful women in the mold of our aforementioned warmongering secretary of state; anti-choice, anti-civil rights, anti-minimum wage DC Circuit Court of Appeals nominee Janice Rogers Brown; and business-as-usual corporate execs like the women occupying top slots at Avon, Xerox, Citigroup, ChevronTexaco, Pfizer, MTV, Procter & Gamble, Genentech, the New York Times Company, and more. If we allow the fact of our femaleness to motivate our objection to, say, the war on Iraq, we are forced into asserting that a feminist position is one of simple concern for the deaths of civilian women and children, and we will have to abandon opposition to the war on more substantive grounds.

If we cling to any gender categories at all, we lose out on tremendous liberatory potential. In other words, the half-witted, sentimental obsession with women that is femininism causes sloppy thinking, intellectual dishonesty, and massive strategic errors. Thanks to the tremendous feminist work of the last century, we have the opportunity to leave that obsession behind. If vital feminist work is going to continue, we need to seize it.

Cisgender: "not transgender," that is, having a gender identity or performing in a gender role that society considers appropriate for one's sex. The prefix cis- is pronounced like "sis."

I Love to Burn the Flag

One beautiful summer day, when I was ten years old, my father called me outside. He was barbecuing ribs in the backyard. "Son," he said, "there's something I want to give you."

Dad handed me a long cardboard box. I opened it to find a full-sized handmade American flag inside. I pressed it against my face. It felt soft and fresh.

"Dad," I gasped. "This is…*incredible!*"

"Read the note," he said.

Attached to the box was a little card.

"Throw the flag on the grill," it read.

"Very funny, Dad," I said.

"I'm serious, son," he said. "I want you to put the flag on the barbecue."

Neal Pollack

FALL 1998

"But…" I said. "The flag will burn!"

"That's the point," he said.

"I can't burn the flag! It's the symbol of everything our country stands for! My ancestors fought and died for this flag! It represents the hopes and dreams of—"

"Save the grade-school propaganda for later, son, " Dad said. "And do what I say…"

Tears in my eyes, I placed the Star Spangled Banner over the burning coals. Soon, it was completely aflame, red-white-and-blue consumed in a blistering blaze of orange.

Dad had his hand over his heart. He was softly humming God Bless America.

"That's what this country is all about," he said. "That flag is worth nothing if a man can't burn it in his own backyard. It is a sacred American right."

I stared at the wisps of smoke coming off the grill in wonder, and in my heart, knew my dad was right.

After that, my family barbecued at least one flag every year, and I grew to love the ritual. Sometimes the stars would ignite first, sometimes the stripes. Sometimes, the whole thing would go up in a blaze of Old Glory. When it was all done, we'd have a picnic of burgers, fresh corn, and cole slaw and laugh well into the night. One summer, all our neighbors came over with their own flags and we had a big community flag bonfire, melting marshmallows over the flames and making s'mores.

When I left home and went to college, I started burning my own flags.

My friends and I would spend hours listening to jazz, talking about Russian novels, and burning flags in our dorm rooms. I became politically active and joined several radical organizations. But when these groups to which I belonged would burn a flag in protest, my stomach would churn. To me, flag-burning was a private, family affair. It was about friendship and trust. I didn't want it sullied by vitriol against the U.S. government.

Now I hear Republicans in Congress are again threatening to deny Americans one of their most cherished freedoms—burning the flag. I think about my father, older now but still dedicated to crisping a flag in the backyard at least once a year. I think about how I want to raise a family of my own, how I want my sons and daughters to know the pleasure of burning a flag along with their dad. Most of all, I think about the millions of Americans, young and old, rich and poor, black and white, who love burning the flag as much as I do. I urge our senators and congressmen to think about my story before they vote yes for a Constitutional amendment to ban flag-burning. Please don't hurt America's families. Please don't take away our sacred right.

I'll always remember what my father said to me that summer afternoon so many years ago. "Son," he said, his voice constricting into a sob, "there's only one thing more American than burning a flag…and that's choking a bald eagle with your bare hands."

Whiteness and the Future of the Planet

Trying to divine the future of anything, much less the future of something as multifarious as institutionalized white supremacy, is always risky, but it's still a worthwhile endeavor, if for no other reason than to get us thinking about how things might be different than they are now; to examine the kind of world we hope to create and how we might go about getting there.

I have absolutely no idea if white world supremacy is capable of being abolished, or even significantly reformed. Fact is, people of color have been trying to solve the riddle of ending this system for hundreds of years, so if a white guy like me comes along, claiming to have answers, you should probably run like your ass was on fire.

Tim Wise

SPRING 2006

Yet I can surely offer up at least a few suggestions about what must be done in order to put us closer to creating a society where inequity on the basis of so-called race is a thing of the past.

The Primacy of Self-Interest

Traditionally, those in the civil rights and antiracism movements have sought to appeal to the decency and morality of U.S.-America's majority—that is to say, white folks—in order to secure legislative and policy changes that would promote equal opportunity. While these approaches, combined with the force of social movements amassed in the streets, have secured certain reforms, the truth remains (as legal scholar Derrick Bell has argued), that white U.S.-America has mostly responded not to its inner decency but rather our sense of self-interest. Only when whites have found ourselves menaced by the status quo, and decided that its maintenance would be a considerably worse idea than acceding to change, has change happened. So during the key period of the 1950s and 1960s civil rights movement, absent the pressure generated by the Cold War to present itself as a bastion of democracy and liberty, it is unlikely that white U.S.-America would have capitulated to change as quickly as it ultimately did.

Likewise—and as John David Skrentny notes in his book, *The Ironies of Affirmative Action*—absent the urban rebellions of the 1960s, which ultimately

> The idea that white America (as a corporate entity, not as individuals) gives a rat's ass about doing what's right, flies in the face of more than a couple hundred years of experience.

scared white U.S.-America shitless, it is doubtful that affirmative action programs (however limited they may be in securing true racial equity and justice) would have been implemented at all.

In other words, whatever moral conscience white U.S.-America as a collective entity may or may not possess (and I wouldn't suggest placing too large a bet on locating such a social commodity anytime soon), it has not traditionally been that, but rather self-interest that has finally made whites, at least some of us, wake up to the need for a different direction.

Liberals might not like the sound of this. I'm certain they won't. They would prefer to believe that a really well-written position paper, explaining why racism and poverty are bad, will finally persuade policymakers to do the right thing. Maybe Congress just hasn't seen the latest missive from the Children's Defense Fund, they speculate. Maybe a few more letters to one's representative. Maybe another demonstration with really catchy placards. Maybe another bumper sticker slapped on one's car, reading something like, "It will be a great day when schools have all the money they need, and the military has to hold a bake sale to buy another bomber." Sure, that should do it.

But who are we kidding? The idea that white U.S.-America (again, as a corporate entity, not as individuals) gives a rat's ass about doing what's right, flies in the face of more than a couple hundred years of experience. In 1963, about three-quarters of white U.S.-Americans, according to Gallup polls, believed that the civil rights movement was moving "too fast" and asking for "too much." What can be honestly expected from a population as ethically moribund as that? A group that, at the dawning of the Civil Rights Act in 1964, told Gallup that the new anti-discrimination law should be phased in gradually, and should rely mostly on voluntary compliance? A group that, as recently as the mid-1990s said that although everyone should have equal opportunity to obtain any job, without regard to race, the government shouldn't actually do anything to ensure equal opportunity in practice?

No, for persons such as this—persons who couldn't be bothered with more than a split-second glance at race and racism in the wake of Hurricane Katrina—the truth, however painful, is clear: White U.S.-America, in the main, has no moral center to which one can appeal any longer, if it in fact ever did. We have been staking everything on the contrary

hope for a long time, with very little to show for it. Whatever changes we now celebrate rarely (if ever) stemmed from white folks waking up to the hell we had made for persons of color (whether in the U.S., Africa, colonial Southeast Asia, or anywhere else) and realizing the moral cost of continued oppression.

There have always been ulterior and much more self-interested motives for advances in racial equity in the U.S.. Lincoln, by his own accounting, went to war not to free black folks (whom he considered inferior and contemplated sending back to Africa had it only been feasible), but to preserve the federal system. White soldiers certainly didn't slaughter their blood brothers out of love for the sons and daughters of Africa. Indeed, the suggestion that the conflict might be about slavery, so enraged whites in New York (particularly Irish and German immigrants), that they responded to Lincoln's draft order by rioting—first attacking government buildings, but inevitably moving on to black neighborhoods, burning a black orphanage to the ground in the process.

Thus, as a matter of strategic concern, antiracists will have to do far more than make the moral case for equity. While such a case is still worth pressing, it cannot, alone, be expected to do very much—a fact that, although perhaps not terribly comforting, really shouldn't bother us in the least. After all, why do folks of color fight racism? Surely it is not out of the goodness of their hearts, or for some altruistic or charitable reason.

Rather, it is because racism is deadly, and harms them: Fighting it is a matter of self-interest for people of color. And so what if it is? Do we really wish to suggest that whites should aspire to more noble motives—as if we should be expected to be more selfless than others—in our struggle against racism? Surely not.

So starting with the assumption that whites will not likely sever their attachment to existing systems of privilege and advantage for the "right" reasons, is it at least possible that they might be made to understand how those systems menace them too, every bit as much, if not more, than the former Soviet Union ever did, or more than any urban revolt led by the dispossessed? Again, far be it from me to speculate as to what is or is not possible, let alone likely. Figuring out what will and will not motivate white U.S.-Americans to head to the barricades so as to push for social change is probably a fool's enterprise in any event. But if such motivation is possible to come by, conjuring it must surely require a healthy dose of what follows.

Understanding the Roots of Modern Crises

While most of the left has long argued that capitalism is the primary impediment to peace and stability—whether economic, ecological, or otherwise—in fact, white world supremacy may be at least as critical, if not more so. Indeed, the extent to which capitalism is itself an outgrowth of European/white supremacy has been underappreciated by most on the left (particularly the white left, for reasons that are probably easy to understand). Marimba Ani, in her classic work *Yurugu: An African Centered Critique of European Cultural Thought and Behavior,* and Charles Ephraim, in *The Pathology of Eurocentrism,* (among others), have argued persuasively that competitive systems of economics did not simply develop naturally, as if by some Marxian edict of logical progression. Rather, they grew principally out of the dualistic mindset so common to European cultural thought and systems, stemming from Platonic and Aristotelian ethics. The splitting off of reason from emotion, now to be seen as conflicting human characteristics, or the splitting of nature from humanity, whereby the latter is seen as in need of controlling the former, and other such dyads, led to the creation of market systems, as well as racism and patriarchy.

Ani explains that Plato laid the groundwork of "an elaborate trap":

> Once the person was artificially split into conflicting faculties or tendencies, it made sense to think in terms of one faculty "winning" or controlling the other(s). And here begins a pattern that runs with frighteningly predictable consistency throughout European thought...The mind is trained from birth to think in terms of dichotomies or "splits," (which) become irreconcilable, antagonistic opposites... one is considered "good," positive, superior; the other is considered

"bad," negative, inferior. And unlike the Eastern conception of the Yin and the Yang, or the African principle of "twinness," these contrasting terms are not conceived as complementary and necessary parts of a whole. They are, instead, conflicting and "threatening" to one another...it is this dichotomized perception of reality on which the controlling presence (imperialistic behavior) depends.

To clarify: I am not saying that racism, in modern terms, preceded capitalism or patriarchy. Rather, I am suggesting that a particular way of viewing reality and the world—a dominant cultural paradigm, or what scholars call cosmology—emanating from Europe, having first taken root in ancient Greece and Rome, is what made the class system (ultimately capitalism), the gender system (patriarchy) and the race system (white supremacy) inevitable. All three are essentially European.

What began as a system of cultural imperialism, and Christian religious imperialism, later became racialized, with the creation of the concept of the white race. Although this concept was, as Theodore Allen has noted, largely crafted so as to rationalize oppression of African peoples, and to divide and conquer economically oppressed persons from one another, what Marxist theorists have often ignored is the origin of class conflict itself, which was necessary for either capitalism or racism to blossom. Most Marxists view capitalism as an inevitable stage of development, and thus, see no need to delve

further into its culturally specific roots. But can we really view as merely coincidental the fact that the class system and capitalism as we know it developed in and was exported from Europe? Or should we recognize in this something specific, something unique (and uniquely dangerous) about the European worldview?

As Euro/white supremacy developed into a full-blown system of now racialized and color-coded exploitation, it gained new life in the colonies of what would become the United States, and then the U.S. itself, even as the old European empires were beginning to crumble. Thus, white supremacy increasingly came to be a U.S.-American product: after all, being expelled from one's colonial outposts, as happened with the British, the French, the Belgians, the Dutch, and the Portuguese, made it increasingly difficult for Europeans to cling to the fantasies of their own inherent superiority. That dream had begun to die, for them, at the hands of Toussaint Louverture and Jean-Jacques Dessalines' leadership of the Haitian Revolution (1791–1804), and would continue its slow demise throughout the 19th and 20th centuries. Likewise, the visible depravity with which Europeans treated one another—with Nazi Germany being only the most extreme example—made the idea of European supremacy harder to swallow, for those actually embedded in the cultures that had brought forth such monstrosities.

But in the U.S., second thoughts have been harder to come by, if for no other reason than the relative insularity, provincialism, and even security that being bound by two oceans has long provided and encouraged. It is the U.S.-American form of white supremacy, still, as with its predecessor rooted in the dichotomization of peoples into good/bad, responsible/irresponsible, which leads a nation such as the U.S. to believe itself entitled to the resources of the earth, be they oil reserves beneath the sands of Iraq, or coal deposits in a West Virginia mountainside. That entitlement mentality precedes the drive for profit, and helps to place it in its proper context. That same mentality then contributes to the world's ecological predicament, including global climate change, soil and wetland erosion, polluted drinking water and air, and the related health effects of all these.

It is the same white supremacist mindset that leads such a nation to believe itself worthy of dictating which nations around the globe can and cannot have weapons of mass destruction, or develop nuclear energy programs "responsibly." White nations can, as can Israel—which although not quite as "white" as the lands of Northern Europe, nonetheless is led by mostly European-descended Jews, in contradistinction to the region's darker, Arab majority. On the other hand, the black and brown are presumed incapable of possessing such munitions, and are to be stopped whenever possible in their quest to do so.

White supremacy, American-style —which has become the dominant form on the planet today—is what led U.S. policy elites not only to believe an invasion of Iraq on false pretenses was justified, but also to assume it would be a smashing success. The hubris and self-congratulatory narcissism that led to predictions that U.S. troops would be met in the streets by grateful flower-throwing Iraqis—and which now cannot seem to fathom how badly things are going for the U.S.-American empire—stems from the mindset of racial and cultural supremacy that simply fails to see oneself through the eyes of others. After all, privilege and domination has allowed that same culture to never really care, or need to care, what others think. The result of such willed ignorance, is, sadly, now proving disastrous.

And it was only white U.S. Americans who seemed not to envision such a disaster, or to consider the moral implications of such a course of action. After all, prior to the March 2003 invasion, persons of color were largely opposed to the war in Iraq—especially when the prospect of large-scale civilian death there was raised—while whites, especially white men, remained resolute that the slaughter must go on, no matter how many Iraqis had to perish in the process. While black and brown folks, and even white Europeans, took a more nuanced and critical view of American war plans, that special breed of white person who we might call Caucasoid Americanus—who, unlike our European counterparts haven't (yet) had their attachment to white supremacy tempered by the crumbling of our own version of colonialism—pushed forward, convinced in the righteousness of our cause, and the invincibility of our gung-ho military.

This same mindset has regularly allowed the brushing off of mass death, so long as those doing the dying weren't white like us. Five hundred thousand Iraqis dead from U.S. sanctions, according even to former Secretary of State Madeleine Albright? No problem. At least 50,000 Iraqi civilians dead because of the current war, even according to Bush? Again, no problem. It's worth it.

Even the Cold War was seen by many U.S.-American war planners as a racial, and not merely economic or ideological conflict. Consider what General Edward Rowney, who would become President Reagan's chief arms negotiator with the Soviets, told Manning Marable in the late 1970s, and which Marable then recounted in his book *The Great Wells of Democracy*:

> One day I asked Rowney about the prospects for peace, and he replied that meaningful negotiations with the Russian Communists were impossible. "The Russians," Rowney explained, never experienced the Renaissance, or took part in Western civilization or culture. I pressed the point, asking whether his real problem with Russia was its adherence to communism. Rowney snapped, "Communism has nothing to do with it!" He looked thoughtful for a moment and then said simply, "The real problem with Russians is that they are Asiatics."

In other words, even the struggle with the Soviet Union, which drained vast resources from both nations, helped squander monies that could have been used for human needs, and led to millions of deaths in Africa, Asia, and Central America (and the deaths of more than a few U.S. and Russian citizens as well, in places like Korea, Vietnam, and Afghanistan) was in large measure predicated on a desire to maintain white supremacy. Quite a cost, this system.

White supremacy also cannot prepare for, though it is directly implicated in, the coming energy crunch facing the West. Largely unwilling to move toward renewable energy—the West ambles into unsustainable and irrational energy policies (like drilling in the Arctic National Wildlife Refuge, or building more refineries and drilling platforms in the hurricane-ravaged Gulf of Mexico). So, too, we maintain our dependence on Middle East oil reserves, not realizing that given a few more years of U.S.-American imperialism abroad, OPEC may decide they've had enough, and choose to stop trading in dollars as their main currency. A shift to the euro on the part of the oil producing nations (something a few of those states have already talked about) would literally cripple the American economy, demonstrating the limits of white supremacy, American style.

In other words, and to put it in colloquial terms, this cowboy shit won't work for much longer. At some point, the Indians fight back: economically, militarily, socially, and culturally. For those seeking an answer to the eternal (and almost exclusively white) question, "Why do they hate us?" you couldn't do much better than to come to understand the way in which racism and white supremacy, with capitalism and militarism as its primary transmission belts, has been experienced by brown-skinned people of the planet.

A fraction of our culture's military budget could save millions of lives if redirected to people's immunization needs; less than a couple of weeks of spending on the war in Iraq could guarantee sanitary water supplies for everyone in the world. That the U.S. in this way could save millions of children from death every year and yet chooses not to do so, speaks volumes about the fundamental evil of the white supremacist mindset, and fairly guarantees the kind of hatred, instability, and even terrorism down the line, that U.S. Americans have come to fear.

So, for those concerned about terrorism; upset by how the war is going in Iraq; pissed off at the price of gasoline, or worried about the melting of the polar ice caps, extreme weather events, and related environmental catastrophes: Blame white supremacy. For those upset about the unavailability of health care in the U.S., and the unwillingness of this nation to make such a thing a birthright rather than a commodity, blame white supremacy too. After all, the difference between the U.S. and Europe when it comes to providing a wide array of social services has long been the sense that in U.S.-America "those people" (meaning the black and brown) would suck

up too many taxpayer dollars under such initiatives. Racist backlash to welfare programs has then, ironically, limited benefits for whites as well.

And for those concerned about their wages being too low, don't just lash out at corporations and capitalism: blame white supremacy, too. After all, it is the sense that persons working in sweatshops abroad or harvesting our food here at home are not fully human (and certainly not the intellectual or cultural equals of white U.S.-Americans) that feeds our unwillingness to push for higher wages and better working standards globally, not just the desire for mega-profits in a vacuum.

Likewise, how else (except as a product of a deeply supremacist mind) can we rationalize the words of former World Bank chief economist (and most recently President of Harvard University) Lawrence Summers, who said in a 1991 memo that the West should encourage polluting industries to locate in "less developed countries," because "health impairing pollution should be done in the country with the lowest cost, which will be the country with the lowest wages." He went on to explain, "I think the economic logic behind dumping a load of toxic waste in the lowest wage country is impeccable and we should face up to that," and that, in his estimation, "underpopulated countries in Africa are vastly underpolluted." While such sentiment poses as mere economic hard-headed rationality, in fact it demonstrates a racist contempt for the victims of such policies, which, whether deliberate and thought out, or merely so taken for granted as to approach the level of the banal, results in the same thing: dead brown people for the benefit and glory of whites.

Ironically, by keeping the world's black and brown poor in a state of destitution (or even making it worse, as Summers would prescribe), we guarantee the kind of economic hardship that will encourage businesses to take advantage of their labor—desperate people, after all, will work for shitty wages and in awful conditions—to the detriment of wage rates and benefits in the U.S. as well. And anyone who has a problem linking such cavalier dismissals of human life and worth on the one hand, to "anti-Americanism" and terrorism on the other, demonstrates a profound inability to connect even the most basic of dots.

At some level, perhaps we already know the linkages are real, even as we are loathe to say so out loud. Consider, just for a moment the meaning of a 2004 study in the *Journal of the American Medical Association,* noting that U.S.-America has a diagnosed rate of mental illness roughly double the global average, and five times higher than conflict and corruption-torn Nigeria. And not just for any mental disorders, but specifically for "anxiety related" disorders and substance abuse maladies. Why, pray tell would such a thing be true? Why should the most powerful people on the planet—and we can rest assured that as with all clinical studies, whites were likely oversampled and make up the dis-proportionate bulk of those examined in the U.S.—have more anxiety and feel more stressed than the world's poor?

Perhaps it is precisely the privilege and power that remains so tightly in our hands, which generates the anxiety, the sense of dread, the fear that provokes such ludicrous concepts as "preventative war," so as to get them before they get you. Add to the disproportionate power the mindset of competition and greed nurtured by both white supremacy and capitalism and you have the perfect recipe for mass paranoia. White supremacy is crazy-making, and not only for its targets.

What it all Means for Social Justice Movements

Only by connecting a wide array of global crises to the overriding system of racism and white supremacy can we hope to persuade white folks to kick their addiction to privilege and power. Even that may not work for most, but it certainly stands a better chance than hoping against hope that white U.S.-America is going to undergo some moral awakening anytime soon. For movement activists and organizers, this means infusing all of our existing projects with an antiracist analysis that seeks to explore the white supremacist roots of the various single-issue and multi-issue crises we face. By forsaking the exposure of this common thread, we risk continuing the isolated and atomistic efforts that make movements weaker, by allowing activists to conceive of their issues as separate and distinct from others. In addition, by focusing only on the economic linkages, as white leftists often do, we fail to account for why so many non-ruling class, and even working class whites, continue to support regressive and reactionary politicians and their policies—war in Iraq, budget cuts for social services, tax policy favoring the rich, and so on.

The reason for their fealty to such efforts is, of course, that in the short run it makes sense: their interests as whites are furthered by policies that denigrate, locally or globally, the world's black and brown. So explaining the underlying, albeit destructive rationality to white conservatism on the part of working people is the first step: otherwise, we risk sounding like intellectual scolds, who insist on explaining to the lower classes their "false consciousness," which to most sounds like an effete way of saying stupidity. They are not stupid. Rather, they are playing the hand as it was dealt to them. But then, by demonstrating that playing that hand is, in the long run, self-destructive—in other words, that there are absolute interests that are sacrificed by maintaining relative advantage and privilege—we might convince a large enough number to trade in one form of rational behavior for another, more lasting one.

Not to mention, stressing the racist roots of our current predicaments will also likely allow a much broader coalition building than we see now. If people of color, who are usually far ahead of white folks in their commitment to equality and social justice, see whites willing to take up these issues of racial supremacy and privilege, and connect those to issues of war, peace, ecology, and economics, they will be far more willing to work with whites on projects of joint concern. At present, white liberal and left dismissal of the role of race and privilege in antiwar and environmental work often fractures would-be alliances and prevents movements from gaining in both strength and militancy, with obvious poor results.

I would suggest that we must utterly reconstruct our existing movements for social change, from the bottom up, so as to make them antiracist in both analysis and action. This means refusing to work with activists and organizations unwilling to bring an understanding of white supremacy and privilege to their work: quitting, not going to the meetings, not attending the marches, not giving such efforts your money or your time, no matter how much you support their goals. This means insisting so long as you are in such contingencies that a comprehensive discussion of the racial roots of these problems be brought to the fore. It means insisting on following leaders of color in local and national groups who are struggling with daily issues of survival, and assisting with their efforts, in any way they deem necessary: prioritizing their issues, and demonstrating ones commitment to racial justice and equity as a first order of business. It means standing up as whites and challenging white supremacy and privilege, in ones community and one's activist groups, even at the risk of being ostracized, criticized, and ignored.

The key is doing this in a way that makes clear one is acting not so as to save folks of color, but because one sees that racism and white supremacy are at the root of the crises that menace all of us. Making this argument clearly will allow us to avoid the anger/guilt response so common to whites when racism is discussed—in other words, the feeling that one is being blamed for hurting others and asked to make amends only for their benefit—and instead focus on self-interest (in the broad, communal sense of the term) as a motivator for action.

In short, the project is to pathologize whiteness, white privilege, and institutional white supremacy. It is to make white culture—the dominant cultural form on the planet today—the problem, the enemy, not only of folks of color, but of whites too. It is to demonstrate that white supremacy is not only homicidal to the black and brown but suicidal to those of us who are members of the club that created it. For thirty years or more we've been subjected to one or another analysis, policy paper, or best-selling book that sought to pathologize black folks, black culture, and black behavior. Blaming the victim has been elevated to high art in such a short time as this. Only by flipping that script and demonstrating that we have not a "Negro problem" (as it used to be said in the 1960s) but rather a "white problem," are we likely to have a future at all, let alone one to which we should look forward.

On the bright side, we can always take heart in the realization that former white empires, imbued with every bit as messianic and self-assured mentalities of supremacy (and the wealth and power in each case to back up that mindset), ultimately crumbled. They overreached, planted the seeds of their own destruction with their hubris, and ultimately bumped up against the limits of their own ambition, and the immovable will of their victims to finally stop dying en masse.

On the far less bright side, we must recall that the end of those empires came at the expense of many millions of gallons of human blood and tons of human bones, whether spilled and stacked by King Leopold, Hitler, Stalin, or the South African Boers. One can hope that the end of the U.S.-American empire will come with fewer spasms of orgiastic violence than these past collapses, that somehow the end will come more peacefully. But the willingness of fading tyrants to bring others down with them is so great, such hope may be more wishful thinking than anything else.

If we wish to see the end of this empire (and surely we should know that others around the globe are literally dying for such an outcome, and quickly), we must do all in our power to make clear its dangers to others and ourselves. We must attack it from within, not because we hate our country, (whatever, at long last, that is supposed to mean), but because we love ourselves, our children, and the children of the world more. Because we are tired of being afraid.

by Timothy Kreider

Native Energy Futures
Renewable Energy, Actual Sovereignty, and the New Rush on Indian Lands

Huge investments in electrical power grids, highways, and telecommunications would help Colombia open up its vast gas and oil resources and its largely undeveloped Amazonian territories; the projects, in turn, would generate the income necessary to pay off the loans, plus interest. That was the theory. However, the reality, consistent with our true intent around the world, was to subjugate Bogota, to further the global empire. My job...was to present the case for exceedingly large loans.

—John Perkins,
Confessions of an Economic Hit Man

The ability for tribes to obtain bonds in the hundred-million-dollar range to finance energy projects is now a reality. And $20 million a year for an Indian energy office at the Department of Energy is something that we started working on years ago under Energy Secretary Bill Richardson.

—Chris Stearns, former Indian Affairs Director at the U.S. Department of Energy

Brian Awehali

SPRING 2006

It all started with a single 750kW wind turbine built by the Rosebud Sioux in South Dakota in 2003. At the time, the *Business Journal* called the turbine "a four-way transcontinental deal in which everyone makes money while fighting global warming, generating clean electricity and helping Native Americans." In other words, the *Journal* gushed, the wind project was "a 'green capitalist's' dream." The editors at the *Business Journal* might have been a tad hyperbolic in their assessment, but energy on Indian land is certainly big business. In 2004, some $400 million was split between 41 tribes for the sale of oil, gas, and coal on their lands. According to the Indigenous Environmental Network, 35% of the fossil fuel resources in the U.S. are within Indian country; The Department of the Interior estimates that Indian lands hold undiscovered reserves of almost 54 billion tons of coal, 38 trillion cubic feet of natural gas, and 5.4 billion barrels of oil. Indian lands also contain enormous amounts of alternative energy: "Wind blowing through Indian reservations in just four northern Great Plains states could support almost 200,000 megawatts of wind power," Winona LaDuke told *Indian Country Today* in March 2005. "[And] tribal landholdings in the southwestern U.S....could generate enough power to eradicate all fossil fuel burning power plants in the U.S.."

Now imagine, if you can, that you run a U.S.-based energy company at a time when increasing resistance to U.S. imperialism, coupled with rising business costs related to political instability, has made getting the oil, coal, and gas from foreign sources more difficult. Imagine that you're savvy enough to know that your fossil fuel-based business model is about to get dramatically less lucrative. If you didn't already have them, you'd probably want to start setting up operations in the more business-friendly, less regulated Wild West of Indian Country. If you were really devious—or maybe just smart—you might want to have your cake and eat it too, by getting tax subsidies and favorable terms for developing your next business model while greenwashing your ongoing fossil fuel operations. Wouldn't you?

"Consistent with the President's National Energy Policy to secure America's energy future," testified Theresa Rosier, Counselor to the Assistant Secretary for Indian Affairs, "increased energy development in Indian and Alaska Native communities could help the Nation have more reliable home-grown energy supplies. [The Native American Energy Development and Self-Determination

> Are cooperative energy projects with Native American tribes a beacon of eco-capitalist light, or just more corporate greenwashing?

Act of 2003] promotes increased and efficient energy development and production in an environmentally sound manner."

The bill did not ultimately pass, but the idea that "America's energy future" should be linked to having "more reliable home-grown energy supplies" can be found in other native energy-specific legislation that has passed into law. What this line of thinking fails to take into consideration is that Native America is not actually U.S.-America, and that the "supplies" in question belong to sovereign nations, not to the United States or its energy sector.

Rosier's statement conveys quite a lot about how the government and the energy sector intend to market the growing shift away from dependence on foreign energy, and how they plan to deregulate (by using "efficiency" as a selling point) and step up their exploitation ("development") of "domestic" native energy resources: by spinning it as a way to produce clean energy while helping Native Americans gain greater economic and tribal sovereignty.

Of course, if large companies can establish lucrative partnerships with tribes, largely free of regulation and federal oversight, then so much the better. In this regard, a look at the Alaska Native "communities" Rosier mentioned is instructive.

In 1971, Alaskan tribal companies were set up by Congress with roughly $1 billion and 44 million acres of land to divide. Although the real reason for establishing these companies had to do with breaking down largely unified tribal opposition to the construction of an oil pipeline, they were pitched at the time as a way to help stimulate tribal economies and mitigate the scale of poverty on tribal lands. "Tribal companies [can] be considered small businesses even after winning billions of dollars in contracts, and there is no limit to the size of the no-bid awards they can win," reported Michael Scherer in an excellent 2005 *Mother Jones* article entitled "U.S.: Little Big Companies."

The Alaska tribal companies have, according to Scherer, "become a way for large corporations with no Native American ownership to receive no-bid contracts, an avenue for federal officials to steer work to favored companies, and a device for speeding privatization." Evidence for this assertion abounds. From 2002 through the end of 2004, the Olgoonik Corporation, owned by the Inupiat Eskimo tribe, garnered revenues in excess of $225 million for construction work on U.S. military bases around the world. Because of its tribal status, Olgoonik procured this work without having to bid against others for it. It then subcontracted most of the work to the infamous multinational corporation Halliburton.

A November 2004 article in the *News & Observer* (UK) further reported that "Procurement rules allow native American-owned company, Alutiiq, to provide favored entrée to government contracts and then outsource them to British-owned multinational, Wackenhut." The article also went on to note that the Chugach Alaska Corp., owned by 1,900 Alaska natives, "was ranked ahead of IBM, Motorola, Goodrich, Goodyear and AT&T in total value of defense contracts in 2003."

Apologists and professional flak catchers, of course, claim that this state of affairs is nothing more than an unfortunate, and unforeseen accident. But Michael Brown, a major player in the formation of Alaskan tribal companies and the so-called "godfather of tribal contracting," told *Mother Jones* that this explosion in federal work was "exactly what he hoped for" when he went to work as the chief executive for a subsidiary of the Arctic Slope Regional Corporation in 1982 and pioneered such practices. Arctic Slope is the state's largest tribal corporation, and the single largest company in Alaska.

Now jump forward with me, to April 2003, and the completion of the first large-scale native-owned wind turbine in history—the aforementioned Rosebud Sioux project, built in partnership with NativeEnergy, LLC. During the preceding 21 years, reports ranging from the cautionary to the apocalyptic about carbon emissions and global warming have piled up, and all but the most pig-headed of carbon-emitting industrialists now concede that a fossil fuel-based business model is soon going to be a lot less lucrative.

NativeEnergy, which wants to help consumers "enjoy a climate neutral lifestyle," was founded in 2000 with a mission "to get more wind turbines and other renewable energy systems built." There were no Native Americans present in the

management of NativeEnergy at the time of its founding. The multiphase wind development initiative, which began in earnest with the completion of the first wind turbine in 2003, was billed as a way to bring renewable energy-related jobs and training opportunities to the citizens of this sovereign nation, who are among the poorest in all of North America.

NativeEnergy's President and CEO Tom Boucher is an energy industry vet who formerly worked at Green Mountain Energy, a subsidiary of a company now controlled by oil industry giant BP and Nuon, a Netherlands-based energy company. Boucher was convinced there was profit to be made in alternative energy, and the Rosebud project was his test case. Boucher financed the project by selling, of all things, air. More specifically, he took advantage of the new "flexible emissions standards" created by the Kyoto Protocol. Essentially, the standards created tax-deductible pollution credits (or "green tags") for ecologically responsible companies, which can then be sold to polluters wishing to "offset" their carbon dioxide generation without *actually* reducing their emissions.

As you might expect from a company staffed largely by energy industry vets, NativeEnergy was fiscally crafty. In a novel accounting move, they bought from the Rosebud Sioux, at deep discount, all the green tag pollution credits that they speculated would be accrued over the lifespan of the Rosebud wind project—a total of 50,000 tons of carbon dioxide—then made a lump-sum, one-time funding commitment to the construction of the project.

Since their first test case proved successful, NativeEnergy has moved forward with plans to develop a larger "distributed wind project," located on eight different reservations. NativeEnergy also became a majority Indian-owned company in August 2005, when the pro-development Intertribal Council on Utility Policy (yes, Intertribal COUP), purchased a majority stake in the company on behalf of its member tribes.

Pat Spears, the President of COUP and a member of the lower Brule Sioux tribe, described the purchase as "a great day for Native American people everywhere, because we are demonstrating that living in harmony with our Mother Earth is not only good for the environment, it is also good business. We look forward," he added, "to bringing in more tribes as equity participants and taking NativeEnergy to the next level."

It's probably no coincidence that this purchase coincided with that month's passage of the 2005 Energy Policy Act, which contains Native energy–specific provisions in its Title V. Supporters like Tex Hall, president of the National Congress of American Indians, touted the act as "one of the most important tribal pieces of legislation to hit Indian country in the past 20 years. [It] provides real incentives for energy companies to partner with Indian tribes in developing tribal resources." Keeping in mind that tribal-owned companies are exempt from a great deal of the regula-

tion, oversight, and competitive bidding stipulations that apply to other businesses, and that the legislation increases subsidies for wind energy in particular, the act leaves NativeEnergy ideally situated to exploit its tribal status.

But there are a host of alarming provisions in the act. For starters, Section 1813 of Title V gives the U.S. the obviously dangerous power to grant rights of way through Indian lands without permission from Indian tribes, if deemed to be in the strategic interests of an energy-related project. Other critics have derided the act as a fire sale on Indian energy, characterizing various incentives as a broad collection of subsidies for U.S. energy companies, particularly those in Texas. And, according to a 2005 *Democracy Now!* interview with Clayton Thomas-Muller, Native Energy Organizer for the Indigenous Environmental Network, the act "rolls back the protections of the National Environmental Policy Act and the protections of the National Historic Preservation Act, both of which are critical pieces of legislation that grassroots indigenous peoples utilize to protect our sacred sites."

Most importantly, under the guise of promoting tribal sovereignty (leaving out those aspects of sovereignty that have little or nothing to do with economics), the act also releases the government from its trust responsibility to tribes where "resource development" is concerned.

The trust relationship between the U.S. and Native tribes has been a crucial way for Native Americans to hold the government accountable, as evidenced by the string of losses suffered by the Department of the Interior and Treasury during the years-long Indian Trust Case filed by Eloise Cobell on behalf of more than 500,000 Native American landholders. Dating back to about 1887, the government was supposed to disburse to Native landholders the royalties generated by the (forced) leasing of Native lands to timber, mining, livestock, and energy companies. But the government didn't disburse most of the money, and now admits that at least $137 billion is simply missing. Without the trust relationship, Cobell and her coplaintiffs could not have sued.

The Energy Policy Act also shifts responsibility for environmental review and regulation from the federal to tribal governments. This, too, was promoted under the auspices of increasing tribal sovereignty, but it doesn't take a genius to know that Native Americans won't be any more successful in regulating the energy industry than the U.S. government, a host of well-funded environmental groups, and the UN have been. In fact, it probably only takes a village-variety idiot to comprehend the predictably disastrous outcome of this shift for Native Americans

It's hard to believe, in light of the relevant history, that an ever-avaricious energy industry—which has been all too willing to play a game of planetary ecological brinksmanship in the name of profit—places any value on tribal sovereignty unless there's a way to exploit it. It's hard to believe, after hundreds of years of plunder and unaccountability, that further deregulation, coupled with

economic incentives, and even with the participation of some well-meaning "green" players on the field, is going to deliver anything but the predictable domination of Native Americans by white European economic powers.

In fact, I'll go out on a limb and say that the emerging Native American energy infrastructure looks more like the beginnings of a new rush on Indian lands than it does the advent of any kind of brave new sovereign era.

But don't take my word for it. Take it from Billy Connelly, the senior advisor on marketing and communications for NativeEnergy, the company, you'll recall, that helped usher in the dawn of this renewable energy rush. When asked during a March 2006 phone interview why the demonstration of a potentially viable renewable energy economy on Native American lands wasn't simply an example of small businesses laying the groundwork for the eventual control and megaprofits of major corporations, Connelly sighed and said simply, "I'd be pleasantly surprised if this didn't follow that age-old pattern."

Perhaps, at a minimum, tribes can attain a modicum of energy independence from the development of wind, solar, and other renewable energy infrastructure on their lands. And there may well be a way to ride Native American renewable energy resources to a future of true tribal sovereignty. But it won't come from getting into bed with, and becoming indebted to, the very industry currently driving the planet to its doom.

The First Thanksgiving

The cities were a terrible mistake for humanity. That mistake is evident to a lot of people now, but most of them are trapped. They don't have the money or the education to escape, even temporarily—and we learned, once we took our rose-colored glasses off and actually started building this place, that sustainable living really requires both. Someday it may be different, it may be accessible to everyone, and of course we all pray for that day, and focus our ceremonies on the hope that humanity is moving toward that understanding, but in the meantime we simply try to serve as an example of what is possible.

Later, I'll give you the full tour, so you can see all our beautiful straw bale and cob houses, and Irv will explain the water system and the solar system—heating, I mean— it's really quite fascinating!

Christy Rodgers

SPRING 2006

After a long day of spirit-seeking, settle into the comfort and rejuvenation of sun-dried linens prepared each day by our highly skilled all-Native staff.

It required a lot of planning and resources to set it all up, and this was happening right around the time of the coup, just after the Crash, so we had to work out all sorts of exotic deals with the contractors, some of which were almost like guerrilla actions, since everybody was being ordered to spend money in certain places in order to keep the economy going, and people's bank accounts were all being frozen if there wasn't enough of the right kind of activity, or if they were suspected of stockpiling durable goods, and, well, you remember. It was chaos. But we'd been predicting something like that would happen, so we were readier than most. It helps to have a financial analyst or two in your core group, let me tell you.

How did we find this place? Well, you noticed the old sign on the road in from the airstrip? So you know that this is—well, was—"reservation" land. You see, during the crisis, a number of measures were imposed, for economic reasons, of course; well, one of them actually opened up Native reservation lands for development! And through some contacts that one of our group had—he used to come up here to hike and fish—we offered the tribal people a deal. We would buy up the land, take a small piece for our community, and of course the Native people already there would retain the right to inhabitation in perpetuity—it was all in a contract, and the lawyer who drew it up was even part Native American!

We thought it was a really perfect solution. Especially because, while we had all the technological ideas of sustainable construction and solar power, and composting toilets, and permaculture and so on, we had all been city dwellers for so long—generations, in some cases—and we had all had our separate careers, and our own apartments, and so we really had no idea how to actually live *in community*, you know? We thought we would need to learn from the ancient tribal people in our midst just to survive in this new context. So we saw having them here as, really, an asset for us.

Well, as it turns out, it was a much more complicated situation. There were only about ten Native families left living on the land when we came here. Three of them had all their young men in prison or the National Guard. Ironically, one of the mothers told me her son was actually patrolling the city where I lived during the riots just before the coup. The Crash and all the fighting basically cut him off from going back home, although at least he was still able to send some money. But, frankly, I have never seen people living in poorer conditions than the families here, and I've been to India. And the drinking! It seemed like everybody who was still there was drunk all the time. And the fighting—well, *how naïve I was*. I wondered if we could learn anything from them at all?

But you can't push the river, as they say. The land was bought, and we'd gotten out of our city lives just in time, and couldn't go back; now we had to make this work. We had to deal with what was there. We had to see what would come from it.

So we started out meeting with the families, just to try to make friends, you know, and letting them know, in spite of our reservations—no pun intended!—that we really respected their culture and wanted to learn about it. It was a terribly slow process. We hit a lot of walls just trying to find out who were the right people in the tribe to talk to; one person would tell us one thing, and one person another. It really got tiring. We couldn't find anyone who was interested in helping us with spiritual knowledge, or ancient wisdom, or anything like that. Everybody we talked to just wanted to complain to us about something somebody else in the tribe had done, and tell us not to give them any money—it was horrible. Then the first winter came, and suddenly things changed.

With what was going on around the coup, I don't think we realized how totally cut off we were going to be, and the builders still hadn't built much, and were working out a lot of kinks in terms of the techniques they were trying that, of course, no one anticipated at the time.

That was when, in an odd sort of way, the Indians really came to our rescue. I mean, they had learned to survive with nothing for so long. For example, there was the Dramatic Rescue, as I call it, when five of our little group of pioneers went ice fishing and totally miscalculated the depth of the ice! My goddess! These two old men we'd never seen doing anything but sitting in front of their broken-down trailer drinking beer appeared from nowhere and got them all out before they had time to feel the cold, as my husband said. And they never said a word the whole time, just disappeared after they'd built a fire, dried them out, and dropped them off back at our log house.

And meanwhile, their grandsons pulled enough fish out of the hole in the lake to feed us all dinner that night! There must have been a dozen other little incidents like that that winter. We got through, miraculously! And we were very grateful to them, of course, and tried to pay each time they helped us. They wouldn't take anything, so we didn't know what else to do.

But I think in the end we realized that we'd been on the wrong track with the idea that we could learn about community from the Native people. Because what we saw was that the community only kicked in when you were on the verge of real catastrophe. Then everybody put aside their differences and helped out. Once we learned that, we saw there was really nothing else they could teach us. It made more sense to focus on trying to follow our sustainability plan and manage our assets well so that this place could give us all a good income. That was something we did know how to do. I mean, it seems obvious, perhaps, but who wants to live on the verge of catastrophe all the time? Our aim was to be sustainable and comfortable.

After that winter, things improved. We learned from our mistakes, believe me! By the time the government and business situation stabilized enough, with the whole Govcorp reorganization, and martial law was lifted so people could travel, and money was circulating again, we were ready to open the retreat.

Anyway, that was when we finally figured out how to work out a mutually beneficial relationship with the Native people here. We needed staff, to take care of the guests; they needed jobs. At first, we said, we could only pay room and board, but as things picked up there would be good jobs, and more jobs—tending the permaculture gardens, repairing the lodge, keeping the vehicles running, and so on. And laundry, of course, there's always a lot of laundry. Being a laundress here is skilled labor! We sun-dry everything, there's a real art to the way our sheets are done that you will experience for yourself.

So that's our story. I hope I haven't tired you out—I know how dreary that flight over the Wasteland is. So sad, to think of all that land poisoned by one reactor in a single incident. At least it makes you truly appreciate havens like this one, yes? And that is what we are here for. To make sure you get the healing and rejuvenation you need during your time with us. Just leave all your worries behind! You're in the Running Brook house, I believe? You just follow that path over the little bridge. I'll have Akwesane bring your bags.

Make Media, Make Real Trouble
What's Wrong (and Right) With Indymedia

Jennifer Whitney

SUMMER 2005

photos by
Andrew Stern

In the last week of November 1999, a news website run entirely by volunteers was launched. "Don't hate the media; be the media" was the battle cry of hundreds of people who converged in Seattle to bring about the birth of the Independent Media Center (IMC, or Indymedia). The project promised the democratization of the media, and more: "Imperfect, insurgent, sleepless and beautiful, we directly experienced the success of the first IMC in Seattle and saw that the common dream of 'a world in which many worlds fit' is possible," wrote media activist and City Lights Press editor Greg Ruggiero. The idea was contagious. Almost 8 years on, there are 169 Indymedia websites in about 45 countries on 6 continents.

The newborn IMC provided the most in-depth and broad-spectrum coverage of the historic direct actions against the World Trade Organization that fall. Despite having no advertising budget, no brand recognition, no corporate sponsorship, and no celebrity reporters, it received 1.5 million hits in its first week—more than CNN got in the same time. Its innovative "open publishing" newswire meant that anyone with computer access could be a reporter. The user-friendly software allowed people to publish directly online, and since more than 450 people got IMC press passes (and scores more reported from their homes), they provided coverage of the historic protests from every block of downtown Seattle. Audio, video, photos, and articles were uploaded at a breathtaking pace. The site embraced the do-it-yourself ethic completely, meaning that there were no restrictive site managers, editors, or word-count limits. At the time, such restrictions seemed dictatorial, oppressive—counterrevolutionary, even. Now, I find them rather appealing.

The open publishing newswire, once filled with breaking stories and photographic evidence refuting government lies, now contains more spam than an old email account. On many sites, it's difficult to find original reporting among the right-wing diatribes and rants about chemtrails poisoning the atmosphere. Coverage of local protests often consists of little more than a few blurry photos of cops doing nothing in particular, without a single line of text explaining the context, the issues, or the goals of the protest. And forget about analysis or investigative reporting. They tend to be as rare on Indymedia as they are on Fox News.

This isn't to suggest that I've avoided Indymedia as a journalist, or that I disagree with its mission—neither are true. I've worked with various IMCs over the years during big protests, mostly as a reporter, and mostly secondarily to the various actions I was involved with. In 1999, I met early on with some of the founders of the first IMC, who wanted an outside perspective on what they were cooking up. In 2001, I covered the Zapatista caravan for the Chiapas, UK, and Seattle sites; later that year I worked in the IMC during the protests against the G8 summit in Genoa, taking phoned-in reports from the streets, confirming them, plotting movements on maps, and posting the news. In Cancún I did support work in the IMC during the 2003 WTO actions, as well as some reporting. In Miami, during the Free Trade Area of the Americas protests that same year, I reported for the short-lived paper and the website. And in 2004, in El Alto, Bolivia, I worked with locals on covering an important federal election.

On the second anniversary of the Iraq invasion, in 2005, I was in Mexico, trying to get information about antiwar protests around the United States. I looked at IMC sites based in cities where I knew there were actions, and found nothing. Eventually, I found what I was looking for—on the BBC. The experience, unfortunately, is not uncommon. Each time I try and find news among the Indymedia drivel, I ask myself the same question: What happens when—in our attempts not to hate the media but to be it—we end up hating the media we've become?

I know I'm not alone in my frustration with IMCs. "I haven't looked at Indymedia in over a year," says the editor of a nationally distributed radical magazine. "Indymedia? It's completely irrelevant," a talented documentary filmmaker tells me. "I let the IMC use my photos but I don't ever read it," says a freelance photojournalist. More and more, independent media makers (even those who occasionally publish on or are affiliated with an IMC) don't even bother looking for news on Indymedia. And for good reason: Indymedia news "coverage" is often lifted from corporate media websites, with occasional editorial remarks added. Some IMC sites limit this type of reporting to a specific section, and there it can lead to informative discussion and criticism. But most seem to rely on it to fill column space in the newswire. This isn't making media, it's cutting and pasting—relying on so-called experts and professionals to do what you are, evidently, too lazy or busy to do yourself. The few original articles are frequently riddled with unsubstantiated claims, rumors, dubious anonymous sources, bad writing, and/or plagiarism. Rarely is anything edited—and I don't mean by the collective that runs the site. Users themselves aren't editing their own work, but instead are posting 18 blurry, almost identically bad photographs, or thesis-length uninformed opinion pieces that weren't even spell checked. Verified facts are an endangered species on Indymedia, and arguments in support of fact-checking are often met with cries of "Censorship!" To make matters worse, Indymedia articles are usually posted anonymously (and therefore unaccountably), with no way to offer feedback other than the flame-ridden fray of the comments section. If the goal of Indymedia is, as its mission statement says, "the creation of radical, accurate, and passionate tellings of the truth," we are clearly falling short.

Perhaps it's useful to ask what constitutes effective communication. By any remotely sane definition, both telling and receiving are necessary. But the burden to communicate effectively belongs to the active party—the teller—not the audience. This is as true in one-on-one settings as it is in mass media. But the Indymedia mission doesn't mention audience. Instead it's all about the creation and the telling. Maybe this is, in part, where the problem lies. With the focus placed so strongly on the "tellings of the truth," the reader/watcher/listener is left to fend for herself. And if we have so little respect or concern for our audience, what on earth are we doing working in a medium based entirely in communication?

It's also a question of intent. I want my work to contribute to social change. And I sometimes end up a perfectionist, knowing that the better my work is, the greater an impact it will have.

People don't read sloppy, unedited, or disorganized stories; they don't look at bad photographs or videos. And so the potential to have an impact is greatly diminished. This isn't a philosophical question about whether trees make sounds when falling in forests. Simply put, an unread article changes nothing.

And if we change nothing, not only have we failed in our responsibility to our audience, we have failed our subject as well. If I'm writing about a social movement, I am accountable to the people who trust me with their stories. I want my article to help them, not hurt them. When I'm writing about a particular issue, I want to inform and inspire others to get involved in learning more and maybe working on that issue also. Making media is a bit like scattering seeds, in that we never know where our work will end up—if it will germinate, take root, and spread; if it will survive fire or drought; if others will notice and propagate it. We should put out the hardiest and healthiest seeds that we can, so the information stored within will have a better chance at survival.

While all IMC collectives across the global network are individual and autonomous, there are certain commonalities that hold them together. The website layout and navigation tends to be quite similar, the process of uploading material tends to work the same way, and most use the same software. There are a few that stand out in various ways—some have more intensive editing,

a few publish newspapers or have radio stations, and some are deeply linked to the communities they serve. Most people I've spoken with agree that the Portland, Oregon, site stands out a lot. Portland is known worldwide for getting technical resources and website security to other collectives in the network. In addition to their own site, they also generously host the U.S. national site. And they have other policies that set them apart as well—but in quite different ways.

In many IMC collectives, the editing vs. free speech dichotomy is argued as hotly as abortion is debated by members of congregations and Congress. It's a debate that I imagine any group with open publishing would have to face. Many sites have explicit policies about what sorts of material will remain visible on their sites. Chicago has a policy of editing or hiding posts that are "racist, sexist, homophobic, or that clearly fly in the face of our mission to serve as a space for the exchange of news, dialogue and opinion that advances economic and social justice. Posts that serve as commercials for for-profit companies will be removed." They then go on to explain the reason for this: Right-wing and fascist organizations have a history of targeting Indymedia sites, despite having plenty of their own forums in which to post. Chicago's policy is clear, and they seem to stick to it. And they are not an exception—it's quite common across the network to hide such posts rapidly. (Hidden posts do not appear in the newswire but are available for the curious through a link.)

Portland has a similar policy in writing, but it sometimes seems more a formality than a reflection of practices. In the 1980s the city was a mecca for fascists and neonazis who beat an Ethiopian immigrant to death in 1988, and were subsequently driven out of town or underground. When I lived there in 2001, they briefly reemerged, and began using the Indymedia site to post recruitment messages for Volksfront—a white-supremacist, neonazi organization—as well as announcements of an upcoming meeting and concert featuring White Aryan Resistance leader Tom Metzger. Several antifascist organizers contacted the editorial group in an effort to have the posts hidden. Our requests were denied; we were told that we were undermining free speech by requesting censorship, and were invited to post messages in response to the fascists' recruitment efforts. To us, this was inadequate. Let the ACLU protect neonazis' free speech rights—they were using a community resource to spread their hate-based propaganda, and we wanted it stopped immediately.

Though that level of fascist material has not been seen on the site to the same degree since, it is unclear if this is due to the nazis going back underground or to a policy shift at Portland Indymedia. To my knowledge, there hasn't been anything like the Volksfront postings; however, in the year prior to the original publication of this article, the Portland IMC has hosted at least seven articles by or in support of antisemitic cult leader Lyndon LaRouche, the most recent from

April of 2005. This, combined with the frequency of conspiracy theories about 9/11, mixed in with the occasional nostalgic ode to Kurt Cobain or oddball spoof on the fundamentalist-Rapturist *Left Behind* book series, seriously undermines the Portland site's usefulness.

Another Portland anomaly that detracts from its utility is the reorganization of links to other cities' Indymedia sites. Whereas most Indymedia sites list the links alphabetically by continent and country, Portland has come up with some geography- and logic-defying categories that make it absurdly difficult to find things. According to their creative cartography, St. Louis is in the "Mississippi Delta," despite the fact that the actual delta is confined to the southernmost tip of Louisiana, and the nearest Indymedia site is based over 80 miles away in New Orleans. The "Great North Woods" is not where my intuition tells me to look for New York City, and inexplicably, Tijuana is listed not with Mexico, but with the "South West" area of "Turtle Island"—described by Portland Indymedia as an indigenous term for North America. San Francisco is also in the southwest. But not Arizona. If you click on "why this cities list," you'll find an explanation of the rationale behind the restructuring process (capitalization is in the original): "The cities list has been broken up heavily to make it easier to know where a particular imc is in the world…. The basic idea was to make the categories more defining of an area and ultimately align indymedias that would be working through similar regional issues, instead of continuing the socio-political lines that have always defined the cities list." Later on, the (anonymous) authors proudly state that they spent 15 hours working on the list. Fifteen hours, apparently without consulting a map.

There are certain etiquettes established by the very nature of Indymedia. Because so much of the work is online, collectives are able to network with other groups all across the planet, wherever there are internet connections and, when necessary, translators. While this is obviously a great strength, it can also be one of the most debilitating weaknesses, as people often act differently online than when they are face-to-face. Ana Nogueira, who works with U.S. Indymedia, grew weary of this dynamic. "After four years of working on this stuff I got really frustrated and burnt out by the lack of accountability. The spontaneity of the IMC could be held back by some stranger blocking a proposal from somewhere, anonymously. I originally proposed [the creation of] the U.S. site [in order to allow the Global (indymedia.org) site to be more balanced, and less U.S.-centric] four years ago, and it was blocked and blocked. You have to be really determined to see something through; you can't be too sensitive. People can be really curt and obnoxious on email, because they don't have to see you in person."

This may be a factor in some tensions in Mexico City between the IMC collective and other radical independent media groups. The Mexico City IMC has a policy of having meetings only online, never face-to-face. And they have acted in ways that seem territorial, even competitive, with another local media collective, Informative Action in Resistance (AIRE, in its Spanish acronym), that has worked closely with Indymedia centers in Monterrey, Cancún (where, in the interest of full disclosure, we worked together), and Guadalajara during actions. AIRE has received unsigned nasty emails from Indymedia Mexico City, in one case accusing AIRE of being "pseudo-activists playing with electronic toys."

"It's no good launching attacks on each other and using the tools of the right wing when we're trying to make a new form of communication," says María Martínez of AIRE. "There are so many independent radio projects and media projects in this huge city. We want to work with everybody, but not when they attack us like this." In early 2005, AIRE sent some of its members to Brazil for the World Social Forum, where they met with some Brazil IMC folks. When word got back to Mexico City Indymedia, they were angry, apparently claiming that AIRE had no right to connect with the Indymedia network. This kind of territorial behavior can be more destructive than any of the outside forces and challenges we face. This is particularly true in the monstropolis of Mexico City, where radical organizations are already atomized due to geography and time constraints, and where sharing resources isn't only philosophically principled, but absolutely essential.

Another challenge inherent in the Indymedia form is that participation, as well as passive consumption, requires not only patience and a thick skin, but also internet access. Certain local groups have breached the digital divide, even if only for a brief spell. Seattle set a strong precedent during the week of the WTO protests by printing 2,000 copies of the daily paper *The Blind Spot* and distributing them on the streets during the actions. The paper was also available online, and was downloaded in Brussels, where 8,000 more copies were distributed. The Seattle IMC also streamed a radio broadcast that was picked up by Radio Havana and broadcast across Cuba. Additionally, they produced a nightly program that ran on public access television. Many other IMCs have followed suit during actions; what's more challenging is maintaining a presence when there isn't the momentum, surge of volunteers, and extra cash flow that an action can bring.

And cash flow is a huge issue. Many collectives, from London to Bolivia, have produced short-lived newspapers. But print is not cheap, and fundraising isn't one of the sexier parts of independent journalism. We're always short on money, and then when we do have any, it tends to come with controversy. "We have a larger budget than most," says John Tarleton of *The Indypendent*, the New York City IMC newspaper. "We've had a paid staff for the last few years, so it has been possible for us to do more. We weren't the first newspaper to take advertisements, but it was a really controversial decision.

People often have a fear that money will corrupt everything, and that's certainly something to be mindful of, but having no money is also really debilitating."

Because Indymedia is such a broad and diffuse network, decision making across the planet can be tediously slow and sometimes results in painful and frustrating situations. A few years ago, the Ford Foundation awarded Indymedia a grant of $50,000 to fund a global Indymedia conference. But there were some in the network who didn't want to accept the corporate money, and ultimately the grant had to be declined.

There's also the very real factor of laziness. It's a lot easier to block decisions than to resolve a conflict, find a compromise, let go of our precious ideologies and opinions in favor of the group's effectiveness, and move the fuck forward. It's much easier to critique new ideas than to take on a task and complete it on a deadline. Anyone who's done radical organizing or independent media has almost certainly dealt with people who attach themselves to already existing projects or works in progress, contribute nothing themselves, and then exercise a veto over anything that comes up. If our goal is to make powerful, transformative, effective media, we have to learn to neutralize these problem people—even by voting them out of the collective, if necessary. Our effectiveness and sustainability depend on resolving such conflicts and forging ahead. As Luis Gómez of the Narco News website says, "A good journalist doesn't create problems, but rather, solves them." And sometimes Indymedia just seems to lack enough good journalists.

Perhaps this has something to do with the word journalist. After all, one of the points of Indymedia is to show that anyone can be a journalist, that anyone can tell a story, and that anyone can create media. But is that really true? Sure, digital video and still cameras get cheaper and easier to use all the time. And with the widespread availability of the internet, more U.S.-Americans than ever are writing. But ease of use does not equal quality product. I don't mean that every comment on every article should be carefully crafted and edited (though I do believe every computer now has spellchecking software somewhere on its hard drive). And I don't mean that an article shouldn't be published if it doesn't have a gripping lead, an explicit nut graf, and a zinger of an ending, or if it doesn't conform to AP pyramid style. It isn't the lack of journalistic style or convention that irks me. It's the lack of journalistic principles, and the laziness. People seem to forget that writing and photography are skills that people develop over many years. They are not unattainable, they are not rocket science—but it's the worst sort of arrogance to think that your very first article, unedited, should make it to the front page. And it's laziness that keeps people perpetually posting without ever making an effort to develop their skills.

New York Indymedia is one collective that teaches people to become good journalists. "We've had lots of community reporting workshops," says Tarleton, "and people have come in off the street with little or no experience, but burning with a story they want to tell. Sometimes it takes them several months to write their first story, but they stick it out. We do a lot of skill sharing—people who want to communicate their ideas can get better at it. Anyone who sticks it out for six months or so can be writing regular news stories. The bottom line is that articles have to be well-written, accurate, fairly nonrhetorical, and convey radical ideas through quality writing and research. If half are good and half are shit, the crappy stories discredit everything else."

The Indypendent got a lot of criticism for its rigorous selection and editing process, with many people believing that the paper should publish any submission it receives. But as Tarleton says, "We're not doing the paper to boost the ego of our writers. It's for our readers—to give them the best possible information within our limited ability and resources."

Some (often anonymous) folks tend to accuse independent journalists of having "sold out" if we publish in corporate outlets, make money as journalists, take ads in our publications, or demand high quality or even rewrites of submissions. But that means media in which talent and skill are punished, mediocrity rules, and we all hold hands and congratulate each other for "telling it like it is." Is that really the kind of media we want?

This sort of self-congratulatory, self-important attitude alienates almost everyone outside of the proverbial "activist ghetto," (and plenty of us inside it, too). It manifests itself not only in the style and phrasing of reporters' posts, but also in the very nature of what gets reported on IMCs. Direct actions make up an overwhelming amount of the content, sometimes to the exclusion of almost everything else. But if most of us think of Indymedia as being useful only for mass actions—or worse, our own private way of getting updates on what our friends are doing halfway around the planet—it may never grow to be much more than that.

Some Indymedia sites have proven to be valuable community resources way beyond the activist scene, simply by being in the right place at the right time. According to Joshua Breitbart of the international site, Indymedia.org, "What we saw in Argentina in 2002 and New York after September 11 was that people decided to make Indymedia a community possession. When these unplanned conflicts came to the community, the IMC was ready and able to contain a huge increase in activity in a way that most organizations can't. What do you do when 50 people show up at your office and want something to do? In New York we gave them newspapers to distribute. What do you do when your whole government melts and you have to find your own ways of making decisions about city services and having meetings? Well, an open publishing newswire like Argentina's IMC comes in pretty handy." In such instances, Indymedia became a

community service almost as essential as trash collection, sewage treatment, and medical services. People depended on it during crises, and used it effectively as an organizing tool and information source. But we shouldn't have to wait for an act of terrorism or a government meltdown to spur us into action. We all, at least in the U.S., have access to that same resource— and yet we vastly underutilize it.

The blame for this is diffuse—I am complicit by not volunteering with IMCs over longer periods of time, by getting frustrated and walking away from disagreements rather than sticking it out and working toward resolutions, and by not publishing my work on the websites all that often. The blame also lies on all of us who have gotten sick of Indymedia and just stopped using it rather than trying to change it, or, for those of us who are less patient, starting something new. "Indymedia's biggest problem is that it is unique," says Breitbart. "People want it to solve every problem, to be all things to all people, and it just can't do everything. Some of the practices and tools that we've developed can be taken out and put into other struggles and communities where they can gain new relevance—be experimented on in new ways. We should be thinking about how to make it no longer unique, so it's not so valuable, because we have other independent media available."

I want to challenge independent media makers of all sorts, from the folks who volunteer most of their free time to keep the Indymedia sites and collectives up and running, to the people posting angry

3:00 am rants against union organizers and engaging in endless flame wars. I hope to provoke people to live up to another IMC slogan: "Make media, make trouble." I want to see our work become more accountable, better networked, more effective, and ultimately, more threatening. The best journalists are the ones who provoke, who pose a real threat to the status quo. But by tolerating low standards, forgetting our audience, and getting fetishistically bogged down in process and ideology, we succeed only in making trouble for ourselves.

Writer's note: My research was limited to IMC sites whose dominant languages are English, Spanish, Portuguese, or French. This included sites in Europe and the Americas as well as in Manila, India, Palestine, and South Africa.

IMCs that make me proud to be an occasional Indymedia reporter:

Bolivia: Many collective members are involved in the day-to-day struggles of the region and have earned the trust of social movements. They broadcast a weekly radio news program in association with community-run Radio Wayna Tambo in El Alto, and provided all-day live coverage of the 2004 national referendum on natural gas, with around 15 reporters calling in with updates and interviews from 7 cities across the country. They also host video screenings. I went to one that was attended by about 80 people, 95 percent of whom were indigenous Aymara. Before the screening, the IMC organizers poured several pounds of coca leaf on a table—much appreciated by the audience. In addition, they are working to get donations of computers from the United States, not for their own use, but in a true act of solidarity, to give to an Aymara community on the Altiplano that requested them.

▶ **http://bolivia.indymedia.org**

India: An interesting site, though not frequently updated, and with a fairly low level of participation. Certainly, internet access is a luxury on the subcontinent, and only 60 percent of the over-15 population is literate. Content is almost exclusively in English, also a luxury. So though I don't think that the site accurately represents what's happening in India and who is making it happen (a near-impossible feat for any one site to do), it still has good writing, generally constructive engagement in comments sections, and information I would be hard pressed to find elsewhere.

▶ **http://india.indymedia.org**

New Orleans: This site was heavily used in the weeks after Hurricane Katrina to find friends, housing, missing family members, and information at a time when residents who had evacuated the flooded region, especially African Americans, were not being allowed back into their city. With posts that are at times painful to read, the archives offer a glimpse into the tragic abandonment of a city. As the disaster drags on, the site continues to be a useful resource for navigating the countless planning commissions, gentrification projects, FEMA deadlines, evictions, and even further revelations of local, state, federal, and U.S. Army Corps incompetence.

▸ **http://neworleans.indymedia.org**

Urbana-Champaign: After buying a downtown post office and transforming it into a community center, organizing successfully to prevent the local police from buying tasers, and playing an instrumental role in voting out a corrupt mayor, it's exciting to imagine what the folks at this IMC might do next. Well, actually, what they did just after this first went to print was launch a low-power community FM radio station. Their website covers local and global issues, and often features people signing what seem to be their real names to their work.

▸ **http://www. ucimc.org**

Global: An excellent overview of the world's Indymedia, this site is incredibly useful, perhaps in large part because there is no open publishing—all center column stories are selected by editors. The editorial collective is accessible and responsive to stories pitched to them. With both Spanish- and English-language features teams, and with the birth of U.S. Indymedia siphoning off a lot of U.S.-dominant traffic, this site has truly gone global.

▸ **http://www.indymedia.org**

North Texas: With broad relevance to a diverse population, the site has everything a good community paper should have—news, book reviews, opinion pieces. The quality of writing is consistently high but not academic, and uses accessible language. Coverage is primarily of local events, with a smattering of regional, national, and international items.

▸ **http://www.ntimc.org**

San Francisco Bay Area: With a carefully edited website laden with news, Enemy Combatant Radio streaming, and the three-year-old bimonthly newspaper *Fault Lines,* the Indybay IMC is one of the best. The site is well organized, easy to navigate, and provides broad coverage of issues. Many collective members are involved in a slew of local struggles, and it shows.

http://www.indybay.org

NYC: Publishes *The Indypendent*, a biweekly newspaper with a circulation between 12,000 and 15,000. Its editors are highly skilled and work closely with writers. Their war coverage has been some of the best in the country, scooping several stories that even daily papers with high-salaried staffs missed. The website receives similarly attentive editing.

  ▸ **http://nyc.indymedia.org**

Ecuador: Covers a broad range of local, national, and international news, with minimal reprinting of corporate articles and very little spam or diatribe. Frequently updated and carrying excellent coverage and discussion of major issues.

  ▸ **http://ecuador.indymedia.org**

UK: With a weekly radio program on a community arts station in London, an erratically published newspaper, the *Offline*, and frequent video screenings, the UK team is on the case. Web stories range from action coverage to analysis to announcements and updates, with thorough coverage of national issues, and a broad smattering of international news. This site often features the lovely convention of an independently written article followed by links to corporate media coverage of the same topic, for folks wanting contrast, more info, or confirmation of facts and data. The UK site has also been, since its inception, the place to go for resources on longer term organizing of mass actions. The writing is excellent, even on the newswire.

  ▸ **http://www.indymedia.org.uk**

Argentina: In Buenos Aires, Indymedia set up shop for a while in a squatted building—formerly a bank and then a community center opened by the Cid Campeador neighborhood assembly. The association with the political birth of the squat has meant that participation among the unemployed, as well as the neighborhood, is high, although the physical site has shut down. Since the financial collapse in late 2001, participation on the website has come from a broad sector of the population, who have used it in their efforts to govern their own communities.

  ▸ **http://argentina.indymedia.org**

Brazil: One of the few Indymedias to do proactive investigative reporting, it's truly a political force in the country, to which municipal and state governments must occasionally respond. The center column is translated into three other languages (including, incredibly, Esperanto). They have a broad network of reporters, translators, techies, and radio stations spread across the enormous country.

  ▸ **http://brazil.indymedia.org**

Litterbug World
Overproduction, Waste, and the Limits of Recycling

Ariane Conrad
INTERVIEWS

Heather Rogers

WINTER 2004

Heather Rogers' film, *Gone Tomorrow: The Hidden Life of Garbage*, explores the "sinister success" of capitalism by looking at the life cycle of our waste. In the span of 20 minutes, the film examines the realities of planned-in obsolescence and waste-by-design in our market economy, asking deep questions from a fresh perspective. In the film (and in her book of the same name), Rogers contends that recycling is far from an actual solution, and is at best a band-aid approach—a much harder look, she argues, needs to be taken at our addiction to waste.

What inspired or motivated you to make *Gone Tomorrow*?

Heather Rogers: Two things: I wanted to know what happened to my garbage, because it seemed like it disappeared, but I knew that it didn't. I wanted to find out where it went. I also realized that "waste disposal" is a process through which the market's relations to labor and nature is made apparent. [The film] is a way of understanding that garbage is something everyone makes—everyone can relate to it. It's a way of connecting daily life and our daily interaction with waste to larger environmental crises.

In your film, you document several of the major shifts that occurred in the attitude towards garbage in the U.S.. Can you talk a little bit more about the most significant shifts?

It's not so commonly known anymore, but in the 19th century there was a huge amount of re-use going on. A lot of it came from the fact that people couldn't afford to buy manufactured goods because they were so expensive. One of the big shifts came with the Industrial Revolution, when commodities suddenly became much cheaper. The spatial component of the Industrial Revolution transformed the way people lived, so that suddenly people were leaving the countryside and concentrating in cities, to go work in the factories. They didn't have

places to save and store their waste like they had in the countryside, so it wasn't as easy to save fat, for example, or scraps of materials to re-use and repair. That, in conjunction with commodities becoming cheaper, meant that people bought more of the things they needed instead of making them themselves.

At the same time, there was a transformation in land use practices, because garden markets also grew up around cities, and geography became more important to farming. Formerly, the colonial land use and farming practices entailed using a plot of land until it was exhausted, then moving on to another plot of land. But with the growth of cities, and needing to be close to cities in order to market fruits and vegetables to the people in the cities, farmers had to suddenly start tending their soil in a different way—they started fertilizing. Wastes were sent out of the cities to the country, and produce and hay was sent from the countryside to the city. There was what Richard A. Wines, who wrote a great history of fertilizer (*Fertilizer in America: From Waste Recycling to Resource Exploitation*), refers to as an "extended recycling system" between the city and the countryside.

Then, after the Industrial Revolution, that connection between where resources come from, and where they go, and the symbiotic relationship between production, consumption, and wasting began to break down. Commodities became much more affordable, and people started consuming a lot more. The 1841 version of Catherine Beecher's *Treatise on Domestic Economy* explains how to make candles and soap; her 1869 edition of the same book tells you to just buy those things instead of making them yourself. So there was this big shift in the use and re-use of discarded materials and resources. But even though there were these transformations going on, industry still used a lot of waste like metal and rags from households. A lot of the collection work was done by men with carts who would go around to houses in the city and the countryside collecting waste from people—waste that had been sorted, like rags and different kinds of paper, board, metal, and rubber. They would take those things to the city and sell them to factories, so there was still this connection between what people discarded and what was produced. There was a direct line where household discards could be re-used in the manufacturing process.

The next big shift came with WWII. During that time, there was a massive streamlining and perfecting of the production process. Along with that came mass production and the concomitant mass consumption. The byproduct of all that was a lot of waste. One of the great inventions of the postwar period was the disposable commodity. A lot of disposable commodities like paper towels and cups

and disposable cans and bottles had been invented in the early years of the 20th century, but weren't marketed for various reasons. One reason was that producers didn't understand how profitable it was to make things that got immediately thrown away, and production wasn't as perfected as before WWII. After the war, there was real forced production, and cooperation between labor and capital—enforced by the government. And businesses had to cooperate with each other in unprecedented ways; they had to share information and they had to give in to this overarching discipline of churning out the goods for the U.S. military. When they emerged from that, they were so highly productive that, suddenly, making commodities that were meant to be thrown away made sense. It was economical, it was feasible, and there weren't controls on natural resources like there were during the war. So there was this boom in disposables—packaging was part of it—and the market share of disposable packaging has only grown since then. Also, obsolescence was a key development after WWII. It meant that durable goods began to be made to die faster than they previously had.

And that was a conscious decision on the part of industry?

Yes. Built-in obsolescence wasn't a new idea either, but there was this confluence of resources and comprehension of marketing and productive power that came together after WWII that made it all possible. Incomes were also high, and people had buying power they didn't have before the war.

And shortly thereafter, as you point out in the film, there's the establishment of one of the first industrial front groups, Keep America Beautiful (KAB).

KAB was established in 1953, and it was the first of the greenwashing corporate fronts. It started a few months after Vermont passed a law prohibiting disposable beverage containers. Ironically, the Vermont law wasn't formulated by some kind of early environmentalist movement—it was passed by a state legislature comprised of two-thirds dairy farmers. People had been tossing their empty contain ers on the side of the road. These containers were ending up in the hay that the cows were eating, and the cows were dying—so these farmers were losing their livelihood, and they passed this law. At that point, disposable containers were a new thing, and most beverages were distributed in refillable bottles. So they thought, fine, we can just stick to the refillable containers and we won't have this problem. Within months, the industry created Keep America Beautiful.

What KAB proceeded to do was to form themselves into a very public relations-savvy beautification group.

They identified a new political category of garbage called "litter," [a term which] had existed before, but not with the same meaning that KAB imbued it with. They connected with the federal government and regional governments, through politicians, local businesses, and the education system. They created this civic organization that [on the surface] was just against throwing litter on the side of the road. [Essentially], they said that the problem isn't all of this garbage that's suddenly proliferating everywhere; the problem is that individuals don't understand what to do with it! To quote a film called *Heritage of Splendor*, which KAB made in 1963 (and which Ronald Reagan narrated for them) "'Trash only becomes litter when it's been thoughtlessly discarded." Their idea is that the problem isn't what industry's doing, the extraction of natural resources at an ever-increasing rate or the destruction of the planet on a scale that had never happened before. No, the real problem is all of this garbage that individuals keep carelessly throwing around.

They've stuck to that message and it's been very effective for them, because it displaces all responsibility from the people who make garbage— the producers of disposable commodities and commodities designed to wear out faster than they need to. It shifts the responsibility away from production, and onto the individual consumer.

And didn't KAB also help popularize recycling?

They didn't embrace recycling until the late 1970s and 1980s. They only took that up when they had to, and that was because of the rise of the environmental movement. They were very sophisticated: While they were doing this kind of PR work, getting out in front of the problem, they knew that garbage was going to become a huge issue. In the early 1960s, a magazine called *Modern Packaging* had a cover story [on] "the crisis of garbage." [It predicted] that we're going to get to a point where consumers and municipalities are [questioning] all this waste.

So they worked not only on the public relations front, but also worked to undermine legislation across the country. Vermont's law was the only law of its kind ever passed in the United States. No law banning disposable packaging has ever passed again. It sounds radical now. The fact that is sounds radical now says a lot about how effective KAB has been not only on the moral front, but also on the legislative and policy front.

You mentioned this 1960s publication called *Modern Packaging*. Is that the first time packaging was spoken about as "packaging," this product that is not quite a commodity?

I don't think so. The thing about packaging that is so interesting is that it is a commodity, but it's barely perceptible as a commodity. People accept that it's a commodity that's designed to be immediately thrown away. It again speaks volumes about how successful industry has been about training us to accept disposability, which has been a very concerted project they've been engaged in for the last 100 years.

Some of the first packaging arose in the late 19th century. Some of the earliest packaging was for "Uneeda Biscuits." They were packaged in a box with wax paper that sealed in the biscuits so they wouldn't go stale. Packaging was all about easing distribution for producers, because before that, everything was sold in bulk containers. The transformation of production and distribution as well as retail sales—going from mom and pop stores to the chain supermarkets we have today—means that packaging represents the automation of the distribution system. I think producers are very conscious of how helpful packaging is in helping them centralize their businesses. In doing that, they get to downsize and streamline and create economies of scale that they couldn't create if they didn't get to consolidate—which is what a lot of the drive behind switching from the refillable to the disposable bottle and can was about. The beer and soda industries consolidated massively in the post-war period, and the number of producers shrank dramatically. And this massive consolidation in both of those industries was facilitated by the switch to disposable containers. The industry no longer has the necessity for regional bottling plants where trucks can only go so far to deliver the products because then they have to go retrieve the empties. Now they can just drive straight through, one way, and they don't have to take anything back. They can go to the next central hub, pick up more stuff, keep driving, and drop it off.

Are there any countries you know of that have made innovations in recycling that truly change this reality?

Going back to a system of refillable containers would sharply reduce packaging discards, the largest single component of the municipal waste stream. Taiwan, Ontario, the Netherlands, Denmark, Finland, Germany, and several other countries have mandated reuse laws that require producers to sell a certain percentage of their beverages in refillable bottles or face fines. In Germany, [for example] the government says that 72% of your bottles have to be refillable. The consumer leaves a deposit on the bottle at the store and, once the container is empty, returns it in exchange for the deposit. Some of today's refillable bottles are made of thick plastic while many still come in glass, either of which can be reused about twenty times. This system existed in the U.S. until the 1970s, when beverage producers phased out

refillables for disposable containers. The industry always says that they had to switch to disposable containers because customers demanded it—that [consumers] want the convenience of disposability. Actually, there have been numerous polls done over the last 30 years asking people if they want deposit laws, which means that they would then have to take their bottles and cans back to some central location to get their deposits back. The vast majority of people always say that they would prefer for there to be a deposit law. This directly contradicts what the industry always says, which is that they've given in to consumer demand for convenience.

When you see it working in these other countries, when countries like Denmark have 98% of their beverage containers refillable and they have something like a 98% participation rate, it's really hard to say this system doesn't work. The companies that are making those beverages are profitable! They haven't gone out of business, jobs haven't been lost, and the industry hasn't gone down in flames—which is another thing the beverage industry argues here in the U.S. The direct opposite has happened. They're doing well, it's good for the environment, the public likes it, and it works. It's totally realistic to reinstate the refillable bottle.

Would you care to reflect on the semantic shift that occurred: it

seems like it went from "garbage" and "trash" to "waste." With your use of the word "garbage" in your title; are you taking a stand against use of the word "waste"?

I use the word "garbage" in the title because I think it's really recognizable to people. I think that's what most people call their waste or their discards. That's why I use it; it's not a statement of my political or ideological stance on the issue of discards. A lot of people feel very strongly about choosing the right word, and I really respect where that comes from. I think that what we call the things we throw away is very important and it does relate to the way that what we throw out is constructed as dirty and not okay to touch or to consider as having value or being a resource.

In the waste industry, especially the corporate waste industry, there's been a conscious deployment of specific words to describe what gets thrown away. Often they'll call it the "waste stream"—they always try to sanitize it. They want discards to be off-limits, but also they want what they do to be perceived as environmentally innocuous. So they call all of the trash that they get from households and cities "municipal solid waste." They try and transform it into a technical problem, which blankets over the tougher questions about why are we throwing away so much stuff, and what's in there? Why are there so many resources

getting crushed into the ground, or getting burned in the incinerator? Why are we wasting so much? The semantics are a really big part of how the system works and manages public perceptions of it.

What do you think about green capitalism? Is it going to be industry vs. environmental justice, or can there be some kind of compromise, in your opinion?

Companies like Waste Management Incorporated, which is the largest trash company in the world, tout their environmental sensitivity because they use all of these [environmentally friendly] technologies—all of which, they never tell you, are required by law. They act like they're doing it voluntarily. But when you go to these facilities and you see the wealth of resources used to destroy commodities—obliterating them, annihilating them, making them disappear—it's important to ask how many resources could instead be going into making the system that we've got more sustainable.

In terms of how that happens, there's a lot of room for improvement, because the system we have is so bad right now. Obviously, it's better to recycle than to not recycle, but it's not a long-term solution. You're still producing all the waste—you're just treating it differently at the end. One thing I feel would really make a difference in environmental and human health would be to go in and look at how capitalism works—because it needs waste. I don't think that you can just make a few technical changes to parts of capitalism and expect it to work, or expect it to be an environmentally responsible system when at its core, capitalism needs unfettered access to natural resources and it needs to use them up. If you don't intervene in that cycle, you're never going to be able to deal with global warming, to stop deforestation, and the endangerment of life on the planet. That isn't going to stop unless you change the economic system that we live under, because it has this fundamental characteristic of needing to consume nature and needing to produce at an ever-increasing rate. If there isn't an intervention made on that, it will just continue.

"Green capitalists" like Paul Hawken and William McDonogh have some great ideas, like creating commodities that can be entirely disassembled, recycled and re-used. They say companies should do that voluntarily, that companies should just re-design their production systems and the raw materials they use so that they can be infinitely recycled and infinitely re-used. The thing is, that costs more at this point. If a "green company" is competing with a company outsourcing its labor to China and getting subsidies for raw materials extraction from some part of the U.S. government, as well as tax breaks on transportation, the green business is not going to be able to compete, and they're going to go out of business. It might be nice for a couple of years—it might make the owners of the green business feel good to do what they're doing, and it might make people feel good to buy those products. But at the end of the day, if they can't compete, they won't be around. The use of natural resources is incredibly profitable, and that's what will continue if there aren't regulations and controls put on production.

Do you think that the U.S. can achieve a sustainable level of consumption? That a shift can occur given how entrenched the systems of capitalism are?

I think that people like to consume because there's something really gratifying about it. In making changes like [reducing consumption,] there's a much greater chance of change coming about if we open up other channels [instead of] using the same pathway of relating to the individual consumer and their individual choices. And it's a bit problematic to say, "the state should just intervene," because the state has been intervening. They've funneled mass amounts of money to streamlining and perfecting the plastics industry, for example. The state helped create the disposable society that we have today. So it isn't enough to say the state needs to intervene—a democratized state needs to intervene, and people need to have more of a say in how much of our collective resources are being used, and how responsibly they're being used.

What are your thoughts about recycling?

That it isn't all it promised to be—today only 5% of all plastic gets recycled, only 1/3 of glass containers get reprocessed and just half of aluminum beverage cans and paper get recycled. Recycling hasn't kept pace with production, in part because the market for reprocessed materials is unpredictable—so if prices are too low, many of those dutifully separated cans and bottles will end up in the landfill or incinerator. When recycling works, there's another hurdle: All materials (except some metals) "downcycle" when they get remanufactured. Downcycling is a weakening of the substance's chemical bonds and it means that these materials can be reprocessed only a finite number of times. Plastic, glass, and paper all downcycle and eventually must be disposed of. That means recycling is not a real long-term solution.

[Of course,] recycling is better than wasting. According to the Environmental Defense Fund, the energy conserved through recycling is about five times as valuable as the average cost of disposing of trash in landfills in the U.S.. Recycling results in the extraction of vastly fewer natural resources like water, timber, minerals, and petroleum.

Significant reductions in greenhouse gas and carbon monoxide emissions are another byproduct of recycling. On the cultural level, recycling instills in the public a consciousness about discards as resources, not just dirty waste. This can lead to increased public pressure for more radical change, like mandated reuse of materials (refillable bottles, for instance) and limiting the amount of packaging manufacturers can use.

I'm curious as to whether the spectrum of options that includes recycling, producer responsibility, re-designing of products, using different materials, refillable bottles... all of these strategies, when added together: Will the equation yield zero waste?

All those things you mentioned are important changes that people are working toward. The Zero Waste movement has some great goals, in my opinion. What they aim for is to not actually throw anything away. They believe that nothing is waste, that everything continues to have value, and that everything that gets thrown away is a resource. I think that's an accurate reading of the situation. They are similar to green capitalists, [in that] they want to redesign the production system so that commodities and materials get re-used over and over again, but they actually believe there needs to be enforcement of that; it's not something that's going to happen on a voluntary basis. I think that's a more realistic approach. I think what they're doing—groups like the Grassroots Recycling Network, and the Institute for Local Self-reliance—are working on different fronts to make real change happen. They're working on public opinion and perceptions of garbage, and they're also working on the policy level.

What about population control. Does that figure into it?

I don't think that's a real issue. Like I said before, the problem the current economic system we live under has isn't being able to produce enough to supply everyone with food and the things that they need. There are enough resources and food for everyone on the planet—it's just a question of what bodies and mechanisms stand between people and the things that they need to live.

I'm curious about the links between the issue of waste and racial justice. I know there were lawsuits filed against Waste Management Technologies by African-American and Latino communities, because these communities were unfairly bearing the burden of waste sites...

Environmental racism is a very real thing, and it has been all along. In the 19th century, the poorest of the poor were forced to work in, eat from, and live in garbage. In many ways that's still true today, and it reveals the realities of a fundamentally unequal system that produces so much wealth, poverty, and environmental destruction. Inevitably, the people who have to live in the most toxic conditions are the poorest people. New York City, where I live, has the highest concentration of transfer stations (where garbage gets taken after it gets collected and before it goes to the recycling center, the landfill or the incinerator) in the South Bronx, which is one of the poorest neighborhoods in New York. They have some of the highest asthma rates in the country, and they deal with real environmental fallout on a daily basis. They deal with the diesel exhaust; they deal with the rats and the roaches that are everywhere because there's garbage everywhere. They deal with the [garbage] trucks rolling down the street where kids play. And they deal with it in a vastly disproportionate amount than the people who live on the Upper East Side. And New York City—the country's largest garbage producer, and one of the wealthiest cities in the country—ships its waste to poor, rural areas in Pennsylvania.

Internationally, you've got loads of toxic waste getting shipped overseas to countries like the Philippines, India, and China. The EPA did a study showing that it's 10 times cheaper to "recycle" a computer in China than

to "recycle" one in California. There's
an economic imperative to ship waste
to [countries] where labor is cheaper.
What that means is that those people
have to live with the toxicity of that
process. The environmental and
labor laws are more lax, and again
the poorest people end up with the
greatest amount of filth and hazardous
conditions.

* * *

In 1976 a law was passed called the
Resource Recovery and Conservation
Act. It stipulated that the EPA was to
oversee states' setting safety standards
for their landfill disposal sites, and
it took several years—a decade,
basically—for that to actually happen.
So in the mid '80s, something like
two-thirds of all landfills in the U.S.
were shut down, because they didn't
meet the new safety standards.

   Because of the landfill crisis, there
was a need to find other solutions.
The garbage industry and some of the
old-line environmental groups like
the Sierra Club endorsed incineration.
But a really impressive grassroots
resistance to incineration grew all
across the country in Brooklyn, and
Philadelphia, and Los Angeles—there
were coalitions of mostly working-
class residents who lived near where
the incinerators were going to be
built. They joined forces and taught
themselves to understand how
incinerators worked and what the
potential toxicity risks were, and

they ended up getting help from
National Resources Defense Council,
Greenpeace, Barry Commoner, and
Neil Feldman from the Institute for
Local Self-Reliance. These groups
successfully fought incineration; now
incineration is only responsible for
about 15% of waste disposal. That's an
instructive example of how grassroots
activism works in deciding policy and
deciding what happens to our waste.
A lot of environmental consciousness
was raised out of those movements.

   I also think the Zero Waste
movement has some good and realistic
solutions. They want to get rid of
landfills and incinerators. They want
to re-design the production process
so that everything is re-used, so that
toxics are removed from the process
as much as possible. This would
be enforced through government
intervention and regulation, which
means reaching back into the realm of
production and telling industry that
it can't just endlessly extract resources
and design things to be thrown away
within minutes of purchase. If you
buy a bottle of water, within minutes
of buying it you throw it away. Even
if it goes to the recycling center, it
usually doesn't get recycled; only 5%
of all plastic gets recycled today. The
Zero Waste movement has a lot of
good and realistic solutions. We can't
just leave this up to the market—we
need to intervene, because there's a
fundamental lack of democracy in the
use of our resources.

What specific things can people do if they want to go beyond recycling and adopt a sustainable relationship to their discards and their waste?

It's important for people to see the "garbage problem" as something systemic and not just the result of individual consumer choices. While we do exercise some control over the waste we make, the realm of production is the true source of trash. For every ton of household discards, over seventy tons of manufacturing wastes are produced from mining, agriculture, and petrochemical production. And all those resources go into making commodities that are often designed to wear out faster than they need to, precipitously adding to the mountains of trash. In the U.S., about 80% of manufactured goods are used once and thrown away.

To really get at the heart of the garbage crisis, there must be a serious reconsideration of the free market system. The production process must be regulated to make fewer disposables and more items with increased serviceability, so they will last longer.

In addition, people can demand that their local governments tax disposable packaging. Packaging comprises 30% of the landfills across the U.S.. If those were reduced, there would be much less waste. Struggling to reinstate the refillable bottle system would also curb disposability. While not getting at the root of the problem, choices made in the shopping aisle can also have an impact. Buying products with less packaging—from bulk bins, for example—and using canvas shopping bags are some more immediate actions people can take.

by Timothy Kreider

Five Finger Discounted
The Uses and Abuses of Shoplifting

Justine Sharrock

FALL 2004

Boosting, racking, ganking, and gaffling; whether we liberate, lift, or fence, most of us have done it: The five-finger discount is not new, nor is it rare. Everyone has a story. Bring it up at your next work party or family reunion; shoplifting is one of the few crimes that most people will admit to having engaged in at least once.

Unlike so many other crimes, shoplifting is highly accessible to most people. It doesn't require the criminal connections, know-how, equipment, or risk involved in, say, hacking, credit card fraud, tax evasion, vault cracking, or breaking and entering. The main technique of the shoplifter is to act like a shopper— something we're all trained to do.

Research shows that "shoplifting rates vary little across sex, age, ethnic background and so forth," according to Kerry Segrave, author of *Shoplifting: A Social History.* Rates of getting caught, of course, are another story. Stereotypes of criminality become self-perpetuating, as store security personnel target people they think are likely to be shoplifters, catching those who fit the profile while those who don't fit the profile walk out with their loot undetected.

Academic and criminological theories fail to offer a useful explanation of shoplifting's prevalence, instead offering up excuses that protect privilege, keeping middle- and upper-class white folks, especially women, from being defined as criminals. White people aren't supposed to steal things that they can afford—it makes no sense. The term shoplifting itself was created around the turn of the century to differentiate between poor people stealing food and the new widespread epidemic of middle-class women's theft from department stores. The stores were blamed for tempting weak, willpower-deficient women with luxury goods that were out from behind

> It only makes sense in our consumer-obsessed culture that people shoplift. More important than who we are or what we do is what we own, use, eat, wear, and drive. "There is nothing trivial about consumption in contemporary societies...

haberdasher's counters for customers to touch for the first time. Shoplifting has been cast as a way for women to act out repressed sexual desires, starting in the early 1800s with its definition as a form of hysteria and continuing through the 1960s as an explanation for the high rate of single, divorced, and widowed women who shoplifted. (Instead of recognizing that these women may have had trouble making ends meet, psychologists stressed the sexual mimicry of hiding an item in one's purse.) It has been medicalized via the diagnosis of kleptomania, and treated with Prozac. It has been situated as an addiction, addressed by groups like Shoplifters Anonymous and—after the cultural concept of teenhood emerged in the 1940s—dismissed as a phase of teenage rebellion.

These ideas have been remarkably successful at making some thefts punishable criminal offenses, and others rites of passage or even jokes. When a poor African American man takes something from a liquor store, it's called stealing (and, if he gets caught, he will likely be arrested). When a middle-class white teenage girl takes something from Hot Topic, it's called shoplifting (and, if she gets caught, she will likely be punished by her parents). Winona Ryder's 2001 shoplifting charges led her to a lucrative advertising gig and a tongue-in-cheek *Saturday Night Live* appearance. Save Winona t-shirts became a cult pop phenomenon.

Clearly, these distinctions act to protect our notions of class and criminality: Housewives are not felons; rich kids should not have permanent records.

The simplest explanation for shoplifting's prevalence is obvious, really: It's fun. It's a bit like capture the flag (the strategy of eluding of an opponent, a dash for the finish line), along with an element of hide and seek. It's also a literal and grown-up version of cops and robbers: A way of seeing what you can get away with. Scouring the aisles for blind spots, keeping an eye out for security guards and cameras, getting creative with techniques and hiding spots—anyone who has been a little kid knows the glee involved in being sneaky and mischievous. There aren't many adult avenues for that kind of fun. Many shoplifters report getting off on the rush. Leslie, a middle-aged self-described yuppie, reports, "I did it for the thrill. I like that I'm getting away with something." Valeria, a 14-year-old high-schooler, echoes the sentiment. "I came out of the store and felt like I was on a

high; at that moment I realized I could steal," she says. "And that was awesome."

U.S.-Americans have long been seduced by their outlaws: From Robin Hood to Bonnie and Clyde, people who live outside the law are highly romanticized. Shoplifting lets people flirt with criminality without commiting to a life on the lam. "Shoplifting is attractive because it's something you're not allowed to do, and you're doing it anyway," notes Tony, a twenty-something bike messenger from Oakland and a frequent shoplifter. "There's a whole mystique and romance to it. You're living beyond the law." Only a handful of my interview subjects identified themselves as criminals or thieves, even after speaking with me for hours about their stealing. One lifter I interviewed explained it forthrightly: "Since I shoplifted today, today I am a shoplifter; tomorrow, I might not be." (It's worth noting that this comment speaks loudly to both the trivialization of shoplifting and how easy it is to shoplift and still hold onto a mainstream noncriminal identity.)

While excitement may be paramount for some, for others shoplifting is more straightforwardly economic. "I was a professional shoplifter for five years. I got no joy or thrill out of it. I did it solely for financial reasons, as a way to pay the bills," explains one 49-year-old who resold the items she stole from designer clothing stores. "I shoplifted everything I ate for almost two years," reports Michael, a 35-year-old former homeless teen. "I had no money, and I was hungry." Among those who make enough—or barely enough—to get by, shoplifting can be a way to stretch the dollar: Buy the produce and steal the vitamins; buy the t-shirt and steal the barrettes. "Money is tight—I have it, but shoplifting makes it easier," explains Bennett, who works as a janitor.

It only makes sense in our consumer-obsessed culture that people shoplift. More important than who we are or what we do is what we own, use, eat, wear, and drive. "There is nothing trivial about consumption in contemporary societies.... Cultural capital can play a significant role in structuring social mobility.... [It] can help denote membership of higher-status communities and facilitate negotiation of the formal and informal boundaries to opportunity," explain several sociologists in a 1999 *Urban Affairs Review* article called "Cities and Consumption Places."

America's class system differs from that of most other capitalist cultures in the extent to which it is based on consumption more than any other status symbol. An education, a prestigious lineage, a respected occupation—none of these are important if you don't own the objects to match. An underpaid high-school teacher doesn't have the same status as a BMW-driving, suit-wearing stockbroker. The mythology of the American Dream argues that this focus on ownership rather than less tangible trappings of status translates into greater movement between classes: Anyone can get rich, even if they were born poor. Although we recognize the fallacy of that claim, it

does lead to the fact that in the U.S., the way you go about accumulating wealth is less important than how much you get. "The American Dream refers to a commitment to the goal of material success.... The importance of using the legitimate means is de-emphasized relative to the importance of attaining the desired cultural goals," write Richard Rosenfeld and Steven F. Messner in 1994's *Crime and the American Dream: An Institutional Analysis.*

While this drive to get stuff, through legitimate or illegitimate means, has a direct and obvious correlation to widespread shoplifting, the class connection can be taken a step further. More than just a means of acquisition, shoplifting allows people to immediately experience a higher class status through the very act itself. For most of us, shopping is a delicate balance of temptation, desire, and gratification—we are often seduced by offerings of what we don't have, lured by the promise of having them and reminded of what we cannot afford. However, the experience of skilled shoplifters is similar to that of the very rich: You can go into a store and know that anything on its shelves can be yours; money is no object. In much the same way that credit cards allow you to feel like you have more spending power than you actually do, shoplifting gives you full range as a consumer—a very empowering experience in a culture built on the pursuit of things. "I saw all these stores and felt disappointed that I didn't have the ability to walk in and buy something useless just because I could. I think I [shoplifted] because I felt like I was in control, in control of the stores' money, in control of what I wanted and what I couldn't have. When I dropped the necklace in my bag, in those two seconds, I owned everything," explains Valeria.

This relation to consumer capitalism is what really explains why shoplifting is so common—and so easy. Shopping is U.S.-America's national pastime. After 9/11, we were told to "shop for America" in order to express patriotism and pull our nation out of national disaster. Many of us spend our free time at malls. People go shopping on vacation and take dates to megastores. We are a nation of shoppers, and it is shoppers who become shoplifters. (Historically, when most shoppers were middle-class women, so were most shoplifters. As the activity of shopping began to be marketed more widely, shoplifters became more diverse.) Moreover, since those stealing from stores are also those providing the profits, store owners are by necessity reluctant to fully guard against or incriminate shoplifters for fear of alienating potential customers.

There is another, entirely different view of shoplifting, which not surprisingly has been overlooked by the mainstream press and most academics: That it can serve as a political tool. Along with squatting, dumpster diving, or hopping freight, shoplifting can be a way to get by while minimizing your participation in consumer capitalism. Shoplifters who view it this way stress the fact that their stealing is not gratuitous; they steal only what they need to survive. "I steal every

time I go grocery shopping," says Marina, an activist in her mid-20s. "Otherwise, I'd have to devote a lot more time to my soul-sucking money job instead of working for more important things."

Other shoplifters see their stealing as a tool of protest in and of itself. They steal from corporate chain stores and other capitalist institutions in order to disrupt the economy and protest the very ideas on which our consumer-based society is built. One shoplifter I interviewed referred to it as "a form of redistributing the wealth." This view was popularized in the 1970s by folks like Jerry Rubin and Abbie Hoffman, who called for people to shoplift as a way to free U.S.-America. Items were "liberated" from stores and people were called upon to "place the dynamite that will destroy the walls...not [just] to fuck the system, but destroy it." Hoffman noted that his *Steal This Book*

calls on the Robin Hoods of Santa Barbara Forest to steal from the robber barons who own the castles of capitalism. It implies that the reader... understands corporate feudalism as the only robbery worthy of being called "crime," for it is committed against the people as a whole.... Our moral dictionary says no heisting from each other. To steal from a brother or sister is evil. To not steal from the institutions that are the pillars of the Pig Empire is equally immoral.

That kind of call to action is still around today. Any web search of shoplifting how-to provides a wealth of information situating shoplifting as a political tool. As J. Andrew Anderson's *How to Steal Food from the Supermarket* puts it, "Unless you are shoplifting from a genuine mom-and-pop operation (which I strongly discourage), you're not hurting anyone. Steal food from supermarkets and don't feel guilty about it. Those weasels have been stealing from you since you were weaned, and believe me, they aren't missing any sleep over it."

There are also many who simply hew to a code of ethics: Much like responsible shoppers (coffee drinkers who refuse to patronize Starbucks and readers who won't set foot inside a Barnes & Noble), they believe it's important to be socially responsible thieves. "I'm not going to steal from the independent business-man; that kind of defeats the purpose," explains Tony. "If I go into Safeway and once a week steal a fifth of bourbon, the only way they're going to notice is maybe over a year or something—but small business owners, they don't get all that much money, so when you steal from them, they are going to feel the brunt of it." Though they articulate it differently from those who are overtly political, these shoplifters are often motivated by a similar anticapitalist mentality. Bill, who has been shoplifting regularly since he was a kid, explains that he was indoctrinated at a young age. "My uncle was a real pro," he says. "He'd tell me that shoplifting isn't wrong. He would say that corporate America was ripping us off. Here's our chance to rip them off."

While these shoplifters don't see their stealing as an expressly political tool, the very recognition of being a socially responsible stealer situates shoplifting within the realm of political action. With the realization that multinational corporations wield more power than governments, there has been a shift in political movements. Activists like Anita Roddick, founder of the Body Shop and advocate of socially responsible businesses, and consumer-activist groups like Global Exchange seem to imply that we are more powerful as consumers than were are as citizens. They urge people to consume responsibly, boycott companies that use sweatshop labor and unsustainable production methods and become voting stockholders (of course, the latter is financially inaccessible to most people). Much like boycotts, shoplifting has a direct impact on businesses. Statistics on shoplifting's costs vary widely, but it's clear that shoplifting costs U.S. retailers billions each year.

But is shoplifting a legitimate and effective protest against capitalism? On the "yes" side, it does create a financial drain. On the "no" side, stores just hike their prices to counter losses. Shoplifting has a minimal effect on stores—and the focus on chain stores can simply be a self-serving justification. Even some politically motivated shoplifters agree. "The trivial amounts that I could steal are not going to hurt the large corporations that much," admits Travis. However, this very same argument is made by apathetic would-be activists everywhere—my one vote can't possibly have an impact. No one hears my voice or pays attention if I attend a rally. My boycott of Taco Bell isn't going to actually change anything for tomato farmers. Yet we all know that it's the power of the numbers of individuals that make political movements.

But even if everyone were dedicated in their commitment to shoplifting from chain stores, it still wouldn't be an effective political tactic. Shoplifting has no structural impact on the stores or the institutions of capitalism. It's ineffective as protest because, to the naked eye, the shoplifter is the same as the shopper. The whole point of shoplifting is to keep the action hidden: Every aspect of the ordinary consumer experience is mimicked, minus the cash transaction. In his book *Weapons of the Weak,* anthropologist James C. Scott's analysis of the limitations of everyday forms of resistance—work slowdowns and minor sabotage—apply equally well to the political potential of shoplifting. "By virtue of their institutional invisibility, activities on anything less than a massive scale are, if they are noticed at all, rarely accorded any social significance," he writes. "Open insubordination in almost any context will provoke a more rapid and ferocious response than an insubordination that may be as pervasive but never ventures to contest the formal definitions of hierarchy and power."

For all public intents and purposes, shoplifters are supporters of the stores they're stealing from—they spend time in the stores, use the stores' items, and place

value on the stores' merchandise. Particularly with clothing chains, which depend on the visibility of their brand more than almost anything else, financial loss at one location is outweighed by the benefit of public display of their merchandise. If you see someone wearing a Gap t-shirt, she's a walking ad for the Gap whether she paid for the item or not. In contrast, boycotts, in addition to their focus on financial consequences, seek to build awareness; organizers announce their message publicly, clearly, and in a targeted way. Shoplifters, on the whole, act independently, privately, and without organization.

In addition to the problem of surreptitiousness, shoplifting also reinforces the primacy of consumption. Even if we obtain our goodies by illegitimate means, we're still consuming. And the significance of a commodity is even greater if someone is willing to take the risk to steal it. While some people argue that they only take necessities, even more report that they take things they wouldn't buy—useless crap, overpriced items, and expensive luxuries.

The very fact that shoplifting has been normalized and trivialized as a commonplace form of delinquency speaks to the fact that it poses no significant threat to capitalism. Would something truly subversive or dangerous ever become normalized in that way?

Is it possible to envision a mode of shoplifting that could be a widely used, organized and visible political anticapitalist tool? What if I shoplifted a Gap t-shirt and wrote on it, "I stole this t-shirt from the Gap. You should steal one, too"? Activist groups like Yomango use shoplifting within their larger framework of political action in a way that does have an effect. Founded in Barcelona, Yomango, Spanish slang for "I steal," is a "marketed lifestyle" that encourages "the promoting of shoplifting as a form of disobedience and direct action against multinational corporations." Yomango's actions are highly publicized and are part of a larger movement. They combine their shoplifting with art shows, dinners serving only shoplifted food, and protests outside of stores. The mass media portrays them as vandals and looters, but they maintain a platform that both educates the public and makes it clear to their targets exactly what their actions are about. Moreover, Yomango is specifically anticonsumption in addition to being proshoplifting: "Yomango is not the propagation of private property through other means. It does not propose accumulation," says one manifesto. This distinction is essential in their ability to provide a critique of consumer marketing and capitalism.

The short-lived online project, Re-code.com, which was taken down by Wal-Mart, is another example. They disseminated barcodes that could easily be attached to products in stores to change the prices charged at the register. With videos and an extensive website, Re-code.com sought not only to spark a relatively widespread stealing effort, but, more important, they vocalized their political intent.

In contexts like these, shoplifting can play a role within a greater framework of organized political protest. Without that, the five-finger discount can help individuals get by without having to give in too much—but it can't do more than that. Stealing from Wal-Mart does nothing to promote fair wages for those who stock the shelves or produce the goods on them. Stealing from Safeway does noth-

ing to protect strawberry pickers from pesticides or keep genetically modified corn out of the cornflakes. You may have the smug knowledge that you didn't pay your part, but no matter how you dress it up, shoplifting is still a way to get what you want. You are performing a covert act that has no intelligible message.

It's not that I don't condone shoplifting. I'm all for it, actually. Go out there and take what you want. Steal from the chain stores. Rip off the corporations. Get away with whatever you can. But, hey, I'm also for targeted vandalism, pranks, drinking in public, and playing hooky. That doesn't mean I think they'll get us anywhere.

The LiP Theft Ethics Quiz
What kind of thief are *you*?

1) **You're in charge of accounts payable at a large corporation where the books are so cooked that paying fake invoices from companies you "own" would be pretty easy. You:**
a. Use the scheme to skim a little here and there. It's hard to make ends meet on your modest salary.
b. Drain as much as you can get away with.
c. Amuse yourself with contemplation of such things, but do nothing.
d. Alert the higher-ups to the need for more checks and balances.

2) **Walking down the street, you find a wallet. Inside is $50 in cash along with ID, social security card, and credit cards. Your reaction is:**
a. Score! A new identity!
b. Take the $50 and credit card; go on shopping spree. The credit card company will pay, so who cares?
c. Return the wallet and cards; keep the $50 as your reward.
d. Return the wallet just as you found it. Bask in your goodness.

3) **If you were given one "get out of jail free card," which place would you most enjoy stealing from?**
a. Your work—you've despised your boss for long enough.
b. Halliburton's bank accounts—hacking has never been so much fun.
c. Wal-Mart—good clean fun!
d. The Sharper Image—that shit is dope.
e. A Lamborghini dealership—sure, they're not environmentally correct or anything, but they're sexy as hell.

4) **Sitting behind the counter at your independent bookstore job, you see someone slip the latest Michael Crichton into their pants. Do you:**
a. Call the cops.
b. Tell the manager. Your job's at stake, right?
c. Approach them and urge they put it back.
d. Smile as they walk out the door.
e. Do nothing but lament their taste in literature.

5) **It's okay to steal something if (mark as many as apply):**
a. You need it.
b. You want it.
c. You won't get caught.
d. You make your living off it.
e. You're bored.
f. You give it to someone who really needs it.
g. It's not a high-ticket item.

6) **To ease the pain of your existence at the office park job from hell you:**
a. Download software for your friends.
b. Spend your days as an online friend or other online waste of time.
c. Litter your home with pens, paper, and office supplies from your company.
d. Bring home a PC on your last day.
e. All of the above.

7) **When was the last time you stole something?**
a. Yesterday.
b. When I was a teenager.
c. Last year.
d. I stole this book.
e. I've never stolen anything!

8) You work in the IT department at a mid-sized corporation. Morale has been low lately; everyone needs some time off. You:

a. Take the network down early one Friday afternoon; you can fix it in about five minutes, but not before pretending it could take long enough so that everyone should be sent home early for the weekend.

b. Sneak out for four-hour lunches every day until you feel better.

c. Plant a virus on the main server; who knows what will happen, but it could leave everyone unable to work for weeks.

d. Think about such things but chicken out.

9) Shopping for groceries, you're faced with a problem: Flax seed oil is a whopping $15! Do you:

a. Pay the $15 and support the flax industry. Flax contains essential fatty acids that help balance mood and prevent depression, anxiety, and itchy skin.

b. Get so pissed off that you decide to steal everything in your cart.

c. Steal the flax oil—hey, you're buying lots of other groceries anyway.

d. Go flaxless.

10) While shopping at Wal-Mart for your big 4th of July picnic, you spy the latest release from the Dave Matthews Band, priced outrageously at $17.99! You're buying other stuff, but in weighing the fact that you want the Dave Matthews Band CD but don't want to pay $17.99 for it, what is the best reason NOT to steal it?

a. You might get caught; Wal-Mart will, no doubt, call the police on you.

b. It's wrong to deprive an artist of royalties.

c. It's wrong to deprive Wal-Mart of revenue; the've done so much for your community.

d. There is no good reason not to steal it.

e. As fun as quizzes are, you cannot suspend your disbelief enough to place yourself in this scenario.

11) You overhear a couple of interns at your workplace discussing a really cool idea. You:

a. Present it as your own at the next department meeting.

b. Offer to help them develop the idea.

c. Mention the conversation to your boss, pretending that you were a participant rather than an eavesdropper.

d. Hit on the smart intern that most closely matches your preferred combination of gender and sexuality.

12) About to get laid, you see you're out of condoms. You make a dash to the drugstore, where, as usual, they're totally overpriced. You realize you've forgotten your wallet. What do you do?

a. Steal them; hell, you'd steal them anyway because they're so overpriced.

b. Steal them; you need them.

c. Hey, desperate times call for desperate measures. Pandhandle the cash out front.

d. Go home alone and masturbate. Sex is fun, but come on, stealing is wrong.

13) True or false? It's wrong to:

a. Download music.

b. Skim from the till at work.

c. Walk out without paying the tab at an upscale eatery.

d. Pass off an obscure research paper as your own at school.

e. Eat out of the bulk bins at a supermarket.

14) Stealing an election is okay because:

a. You know your brother will do a great job.

b. Black people shouldn't be voting in the first place.

c. It's cheaper than buying it.

d. We don't live in a democracy anyway.

There are many different kinds of thieves in the world.
Turn to page 237 to tabulate your score and find out what kind you are.

Spectres of Malthus
Scarcity, Poverty, and Apocalypse
in Capitalist Modernity

Many people believe that human society is in crisis, even terminal crisis—through ecological disaster, food and water scarcity, the collapse of the oil economy, or some other catastrophe. But what role does ideology play in that belief? What if the *capitalist realities* of scarcity and collapse have been mistakenly interpreted as *natural inevitabilities*?

In the Spring of 2005, filmmaker and journalist David Martinez sat down to interview author and social historian Iain Boal about these and related pressing questions. A heavily abridged version of that original exchange appeared in the Sacred Cows issue of *LiP*, but what follows here is an expanded discussion about the surprisingly ill-understood origins of the long catastrophe that is capitalist modernity. Portions of this exchange will appear in a forthcoming book by Boal, entitled *The Long Theft: Episodes in the History of Enclosure*.

David Martinez
INTERVIEWS

Iain Boal
....
SUMMER 2006

David Martinez: Recently we've been hearing the phrase "peak oil" a lot— talk shows are even discussing the possible impending collapse of society due to dwindling oil supply, and obviously the invasion of Iraq brought the issue of oil into sharp public focus. But the concepts of scarcity and collapse are hardly new, and I'd like to talk with you about the sacred cows of "scarcity" and "catastrophe."

Iain Boal: Sure. With respect to oil, we should begin with the observation that the general problem for the petro-barons has always been glut, or to put it another way, how to keep oil scarce. They've done a pretty good job. The history of oil is complex, and the fluctuations in the supply of oil have an extraordinarily complicated relation to price, demand, and reserves. But in order to understand scarcity—whether of oil in particular or of commodities under capitalism in general—you have to look at the discourses of scarcity and of poverty. And that means you have to look at the historical moment of the institutionalizing of economics—defined in the textbooks as "the study of choice under scarcity"—as the dominant way of talking about the world, and the relation of these to capitalist modernity. And that story is indeed interesting.

In order to understand "scarcity" as a sacred cow, we have to go back to the Reverend Thomas Malthus. Because, no question, we are living in a Malthusian world. By that I mean that Malthus' way of framing the issue of human welfare has triumphed. And I think it's especially important for the Left to understand this. Particularly those who got drawn into politics through concern about the environment, who count themselves as "green." Scratch an environmentalist and probably you'll find a Malthusian. What do I mean by that? What is it to be Malthusian? Well, it's to subscribe to the view that the fundamental problems humanity faces have their roots in the scarcity of the resources that sustain life, because the world is finite and we are exhausting those resources and also perhaps because we are polluting them. Notice how this mirrors the basic assumption of modern economics—choice under scarcity. In his notorious essay published in 1798, Malthus argued, or rather asserted, that population growth, especially of poor bastards, would inevitably outrun food supply, unless the propertyless were restrained from breeding. He advocated that poor people be crowded together in unhealthy housing, as a way of checking the growth of population. Remember, this is the world's very first economist we're talking about here.

And Malthus was, in his own time, consciously devising a counter-revolutionary science of economics and demography: his essay was a response to a famous bestseller by the utopian anarchist William Godwin, husband of the feminist Mary Wollstonecraft and father of Mary Shelley, who later wrote *Frankenstein* as a warning against the hubris of (male) science. Godwin had written *An Enquiry Concerning Political Justice* during the euphoric period after the storming of the Bastille in 1789 and the overthrow of the French monarchy. Godwin's optimistic and atheistic rationalism was born of the revolutionary events happening in France, but as the counter-revolution set in, Thomas Malthus felt emboldened to compose his *Essay on the Principle of Population* as an explicit response to Godwin's vision of an ample life for all. Malthus invented an "iron law of nature" intended, rhetorically, to put a damper on Godwin and the perfectibilians*, and to discourage "idling" and illegitimacy and to cut away the existing welfare system, which was a safety net for the poor.

So help us understand Thomas Malthus.

Malthus was born into a well-off family in late 18th century England, and although he was ordained in the Anglican Church, he becomes the world's first paid economist, in the service of the East India Company. The company started in 1600 with a charter from Elizabeth I to monopolize trade with Asia, and by Malthus' day agents of the company ruled India, Burma, and Hong Kong for the British crown, so that no less than one-fifth of the world's population was under its authority, backed by the company's own armies, who fought under the English flag. It's no coincidence that somebody in Malthus' position, at that time and place, would be involved in devising a science of "economics," and its associated discourses of "scarcity," "laissez faire," and "poverty." The English scene that Malthus is born into was in radical transition from a world of custom and common land to one based on the absolutization of private property, in which the actual producers of food were being cut off from the land as a means of livelihood. And that's a very specific move that the capitalists and landlords in parliament at that time were making.

So here is the essential point: In 1800 the people of England—the commoners—are being literally excluded by fences enclosing the common lands that had sustained them for centuries. They are living the new scarcity that is being produced around them.

This is the same process that is now ruthlessly in train around the globe under the sign of "structural adjustment" and "conditionalities" devised by the IMF and the World Bank, being applied to the global South. But it was first described as long ago as 1515 in a powerful essay by Thomas More called *Utopia,* because he saw it happening all around him in England five hundred years ago.

---

* *Loosely speaking perfectibilians are minarchists, anarchists who believe that some minimal government is necessary to preserve liberty, and who also believe in free market capitalism.*

Expropriation of the commons was, in other words, not a one-time event at the dawn of capitalism. And Malthus was the economist rationalizing and justifying the cutting off, or another way to put it is the rendering scarce, of the means of subsistence for the laboring poor, in the name of thrift and self-control and the efficiency of private property.

So the dismal science of economics is being born at the same time people are being kicked off of the commons. It would be hard to exaggerate the role of Malthus and the way his assumptions are built not just into economics, but into a whole range of modern forms of knowledge, for example, biology, genetics, demography. These disciplines all bear the stamp of Malthus.

If you look at the impulses behind the environmental movement of the '60s and '70s, and at events like Earth Day, or back-to-the-landers and their bible, The *Whole Earth Catalog*, you will find the spectres of Malthus—scarcity, overpopulation, famine. The same goes for bumper-stickers like "Live Simply, That Others May Simply Live." Or the countercultural manifesto for vegetarians, *Diet For A Small Planet*. Francis Moore Lappe's book was enormously popular in the 1970s, and it begins with a discussion about "reaching the very limits of the earth's capacity to produce food" and how a vegetarian diet was a way out of the "the earth's natural limitations."

So how do you answer the question of carrying capacity? Are you saying that the earth's resources are infinite? That we're just going to go on and on and on?

No, not at all. I want to make this very clear: I am not in any way saying that the earth's resources should be used up willy-nilly, that societies shouldn't concern themselves with how to live on the planet in the most sane and sustainable way possible. But it's always—historically—an empirical, local, question: How much water is available? How much grazing will a pasture allow? Who's encroaching? How much firewood is X entitled to? Will we have to send Y away to work in the city?

What I'm trying to say here is that the vulgar error made by modern Malthusians is to assume that the human story hasn't in fact already been about dealing with this problem of the carrying capacity, if you want to put it that way, of particular patches of land. There's a word for it. It's called stinting. Commoners have "use-rights"—say, to pasture animals, to take fodder, to gather firewood, to harvest fruits and berries and nuts—but only if you live there, and only certain amounts, depending on the ecological, historical knowledge of the local community about what would stretch it too far. Action informed by local knowledge, typically, is not going to cause ecocide. I'm not saying ecological destruction hasn't occurred or isn't occurring, but it tends to be by non-locals and elites. Let's call it the state. The major culprit in modern times is capitalist farming in private hands.

Despite this reality, in a Malthusian world the blame is laid at the door of the world's commoners. Take as one example Garrett Hardin's quasi-famous 1968 *Science* essay, "The tragedy of the commons," this enormously influential text by a Texan zoologist, based on no sociological research whatsoever, and in profound ignorance of the actual history of commoning. Hardin asserted that all common resources (such as pasture, a favorite example) will inevitably end in ruin because of over-exploitation by selfish individuals. Hardin's fable was taken up by the gathering forces of neo-liberal reaction in the 1970s, and his essay became the "scientific" foundation of World Bank and IMF policies, viz. enclosure of commons and privatization of public property. The plausibility of Hardin's Malthusian claims doesn't survive a moment's scrutiny.

But historical facts are irrelevant. The case is an ideological one, and Hardin was holding up a mirror to modern homo economicus. The message is clear: We must never treat the earth as a "common treasury." We must be ruthless and greedy or else we will perish.

Carrying capacity is now very hard to discuss in a context of extensive agriculture under a capitalist regime which by any accounting (by anyone other than a capitalist economist) is extremely inefficient. But I refuse to cave in to Malthusian assumptions. Why is it not instead possible to imagine a reorganization of agriculture?

A lot of naturalists—natural scientists, biologists, and such—weigh in on these debates. They always seem to stand outside the realm of politics and economics. They are merely talking about Nature, of which humans are just one part. Jared Diamond is a good example.

Yes, Diamond, a tropical ornithologist turned historian of the fate of human societies. He must be discussed alongside Garrett Hardin, as well as Paul "Population Bomb" Ehrlich and the entomologist/sociobiologist E.O. Wilson—they all wrote hugely popular books. Crucially, all of these men see themselves as students of Charles Darwin, himself a brilliant naturalist. Darwin admitted that it was none other than Malthus the economist who provided the final, essential piece to Darwin's picture of the workings of Nature. He sat up one night, so the story goes, when he was reading Malthus' *Essay on Population* and he says that he realized "It's Malthus! That's how I can explain evolution!" Now evolution was not the invention of Darwin—what he brought was his conception of the *mechanism*, the *engine* that drives evolution, which leads to the formation of new species and the staggering variety of life-forms, in all their beauty and bizarreness. That's what he called "natural selection." The basic Malthus-style argument is simple: overpopulation creates competition for the resources available, and favors those offspring better adapted to exploit local conditions and resources. So this is the scenario on which economics and Darwin's account of natural history are founded—a kind of anti-Eden, with too many organisms locked in a war of all against all. Darwin was projecting Malthus onto the realm of nature.

In *Guns, Germs and Steel* Jared Diamond rehearses, without knowing it, an old 18th-century argument using the accidents of geography to explain, and in fact justify, the colonization of the planet by European powers. The only difference is that he clothes the narrative in anti-racist drag. His conclusion is a (neo)Malthusian message: Life is a struggle for survival in a world of scarcity. True enough for millions for people, but not because of any "iron law of nature." Diamond's latest book, *Collapse*, rams home the same Malthusian message in a series of historical horror stories of resource exhaustion and societal catastrophe.

I'd like to talk about why so many U.S.-Americans are attracted to catastrophism in the first place. It seems to me the underlying ideology is ultimately passive, it takes the world out of our control because it's all going to end and there's nothing we can do. But things continue on, and that's a much more difficult problem to deal with.

Again, no one is saying we aren't facing serious, extremely grave problems. What we are questioning is the millenarianism, the endism, you could call it, which is only part of a general ideology of "catastrophism." This is the idea that the human drama is played out on a finite terrestrial stage. There is an abrupt beginning and an abrupt end, the whole affair lasting in one version just six thousand years. Darwin had to abandon his Christian catastrophism and for that he depended upon the great geologist Lyell, who posited the very unbiblical idea of "deep time," and immensely slow, gradual, change. Since Darwin's time, for a hundred and fifty years or so, the predominant view in science has been gradualism.

The politics of gradualism are very important here. Conservative in many ways, and certainly non-revolutionary. A Darwinian world is a natural meritocracy, in which only the deserving survive. Perhaps you can see why secularizing Victorian gentlemen—imperialists, really—would believe that competition produces progress and the survival of the superior races of animals and, of course, men.

So for more than a hundred years the earth sciences tended to discount catastrophes, but towards the end of the 20th century, catastrophism begins coming back. Let's call it neo-catastrophism. Part of the explanation is no doubt due to the rising political power of apocalyptic Christians and evangelicals in the U.S.. But at least as important, in my view, is the catastrophe of Hiroshima and Nagasaki, and the building of a weapon that scientists began to believe could produce the end of everything. Omnicide.

I would say there's been half a century of preparation for what is now a full-blown ideological sea change, from a slow, gradual view of the world to a universe of large scale, rapid changes that shape everything.

But don't both make a certain sense? Long, slow change and rapid dramatic change?

Of course it's both! Both are true, but I'm talking about ideology here. For sure, when you're trying to understand the natural history of earth, you have to consider sudden violent events as well as wind erosion.

Asteroids hit the planet every once in a while...?

Just so. Take the major extinction event at the K/T, the Cretaceous-Tertiary, boundary. Most in the field of earth science now believe there was an

impact in the Yucatan 65 million years ago which doomed the dinosaurs, and produced a nuclear winter effect.

And produced the Gulf of Mexico?

Yes, and a tsunami which was maybe a mile and a half high. An unimaginably large event. This is not so appealing to the settled Victorian imagination of Darwin, who preferred to contemplate the action of water, and the slow scrutiny of a Malthusian god, selecting out the fitter organisms. Now, as I've said, I take it that we have to investigate the world and our condition, and our history, by examining the reality of catastrophes and extinctions together with those gradualist principles also being at work at the same time.

But one question we must ask is: Why are we so obsessed with catastrophe and "endism" right now?

I propose that it is a symptom of a state in which people in the First World, in the global North, are finally seeing some of the dire results of five centuries of capitalist exploitation. The past five hundred years have seen cataclysmic disasters like famines, plagues, etc. all over the so-called Third World. Now the denizens of the overdeveloped countries are seeing oil wars, which of course are nothing new, and mass extinctions, nothing new either. But it invites claims that civilization is about to end.

It seems like a book that helps us to understand this is Mike Davis's *Late Victorian Holocausts*. Prior to that period there had been famine, but nothing on the scale of what happened in the 19th century, in previously healthy societies. The famines in India, and in Africa, were produced by British colonialism. And the landscape there looked apocalyptic: plague, war, death...

That's a really important point. And Amartya Sen, the sociologist of famine, comes to the same conclusion from a different angle. Sen's striking claim is that you don't get famine, really, where there's "democratic" entitlement to food. When you examine starvation in 19th-century India and Ireland, yes, they have to do more with the history of colonialism. It is also helpful in thinking about contemporary "natural disasters," so-called—I'm thinking about the huge loss of life in earthquakes in the South, and the tsunami that drowned so many Achenese, or closer to home, to contrast post-Katrina New Orleans with the firestorms of Malibu, where state subsidies routinely rebuild the houses of Hollywood executives.

So what we're saying here is: It's important to notice the ideological move that naturalizes events which are the result of human decisions. It turns disasters that have as much to do with human agency and decision into natural and inevitable events.

The problem is that people confuse states with peoples, empires with humanity. Capitalism is poisoning the earth, no one is disputing that, but the ecological Malthusians see this and claim that the species as a whole is destroying the earth.

Well, I can't say it too clearly. In my critique of scarcity, I'm not saying that there isn't scarcity. But we have to understand why and how scarcity is produced, and it's crucial, I think, to do the work of unpacking the ideology behind scarcity and neo-catastrophism. For one thing, it's interesting to ask: "Why all this talk of scarcity and collapse now?" After all, catastrophes are a permanent feature of history. So when you hear someone say, "The world's food supply is going to run out in such and such a year," well, excuse me! Forty thousand children die each day from the effects of malnutrition. Or perhaps, I should say, from the causes of malnutrition. For these souls it's already too late. And there are millions of people for whom catastrophe is always looming. This isn't the future we're talking about. It's tonight, it's happening right now. So it seems a bit naive for Northern environmentalists to be proclaiming apocalypse at this point.

In other words, if we look at the history of the world under five hundred years of capitalism, we should be talking catastrophe. Of course we should. It's been one long catastrophe. But we should refuse to do so in Malthusian terms, blaming the state of affairs on overpopulation, poverty, or lack of restraint in the slums of the world. Things could be otherwise. We don't in fact live in a world of Malthusian scarcity. Far from it. Even Malthus himself acknowledged this when he spoke of "nature's mighty feast."

And yet the history of modernity is the history of enclosure, of the cutting off of people from access to land, to the common treasury and to the fruits of our own labor. Excluded by fire and sword and, now, "structural adjustment." Everywhere you look, there's nothing much natural about it, this kind of scarcity. It's a story of artifice and force. The premises of the science of economics are a disgrace, and so are all the proliferating offspring of Malthus. Our first task is to kill these sacred cows of capitalist modernity.

After All the Oil Runs Out

SHORT-RANGE, SURFACE-TO-SURFACE RAPTURING

ANIMAL POWER

SLAVERY

A RETURN TO LIGHTER-THAN-AIR TRAVEL!

by Timothy Kreider

Common Uprisings
From the Great Mexican Land Grab to the Reclaiming of Everything

The global anticapitalist movement has many beginnings, but I'd like to begin where many seem to nowadays: with the Zapatista uprising of January 1, 1994. This was the night when the Zapatista Army of National Liberation, bearing weapons both real and symbolic, took San Cristóbal and seven other cities in Chiapas, Mexico. Not coincidentally, this was also the night that the North American Free Trade Agreement (NAFTA) went into effect—the free trade agreement that Subcomandante Marcos famously dubbed "a death-knell for the indigenous people of Chiapas."

Jeff Conant

WINTER 2004

Marcos and many others foresaw the effects of NAFTA: They thought it would force Mexican corn to an artificially low price by flooding the country with cheap imported grain and put farmers at the brink of starvation, forcing them off their land. Which is exactly what it did.

From a certain perspective, the entire history of uprisings that led from San Cristóbal to Seattle, Prague, Davos, Genoa, Toronto, and back to Cancún—all uprisings against the imposition of more "free trade"—can be traced to a single act of thievery, one of the greatest landgrabs in the bloody history of Our America. That act of thievery was the wholesale amendment of Article 27 of Mexico's constitution, which, among other protections, had ensured the ancient right to collective ownership of land. Known as the Ejido law, Article 27 was the centerpiece of the agrarian reform set in motion by the Mexican revolution of Emiliano Zapata and Pancho Villa. The law designated that nearly half of the land in Mexico was neither public nor private, but outside of the marketplace altogether. The law was a direct result of Zapata's 1911 Plan de Ayala, and provided "sufficient lands and waters" to the "nuclei of population" (a strange abstraction referring to Mexico's indigenous people), stating that these lands were "inalienable" as long as they were "worked." Zapata's notion of *tierra y libertad*—"the land is for the people who work it and liberty is for the people who take it"—was a commons doctrine, or ethic of communal land management, and formed a crucial underpinning of land struggles in Mexico throughout the 20th century.

But to the architects of NAFTA, such a quaint notion had no place in the free trade order. Changes to the Ejido law were prescribed by NAFTA's proponents in 1991, and became law in 1992, granting *ejiditarios* (indigenous land stewards) the "right" to "trade" or "grant the use of" their lands, or to "associate" with outside parties. In other words, with one stroke of the pen, Mexico's century of agrarian reform—however botched, corrupt, variable, and incomplete—was done with. Overnight, the revolutionary (and precolonial) ethic of communal land ownership, which formed the very basis of Mexican indigenous culture, was wiped out to make room for Wal-Mart, Coca-Cola, Monsanto, and International Paper. The commons had been enclosed—at least on paper.

Almost immediately, as any Zapatista campesino will tell you, oil-men, hotel moguls, tourist promoters, and other land speculators began showing up on the edges of the rich Lacandon rainforest in Chiapas, their eyes alight with dollar signs. In exchange for buying up waterways, cornfields, and cattle pastures, they would sell back highways, dams, high-speed railways, manufacturing corridors, and all of the other cancerous growths of large-scale industrial development. And, as any Zapatista will tell you, they were not welcome. These investors had to be guarded and protected, both indirectly and openly, by Mexican military and federal police. When the Zapatistas banded together to expel the plunderers, thus began what has been called the first armed revolutionary movement of the 21st century.

Chiapas loses blood through many veins: through oil and gas ducts, electric lines, railways; through bank accounts, trucks, vans, boats and planes; through clandestine paths, gaps and forest trails. This land continues to pay tribute to the imperialists: petroleum, electricity, cattle, money, coffee, bananas, honey, corn, tobacco, sugar, soy, melon, sorghum, mamey, mango, tamarind, avocado, and Chiapaneco blood all flow as a result of the thousand teeth sunk into the throat of the Mexica.

—Subcomandante Marcos,
"A Storm and a Prophecy"

> Popular reactions to the theft of common property have coalesced into the dominant social movement of our time. Whether we refer to it as the antiglobalization, global justice, or anticapitalist movement matters little, but popular reaction to this theft of the commons will determine the power politics of the next several decades.

Due to the varied political, economic and cultural pressures at work in Chiapas, the war that erupted between the government and the Zapatista Army of National Liberation (EZLN) forced local agrarian crises into the open. The land grab became generalized throughout Chiapas as thousands of peasant farmers and others banded together to occupy and claim parcels. Thousands of hectares were grabbed by groups as diverse as the pro-Zapatista State Council of Indigenous Organizations and the pro-government Teacher-Peasant Solidarity Movement, which later formed the nucleus of Paz y Justicia, one of the most notorious paramilitary organizations in the state. The common notion that the struggle in Chiapas was simply a tug-of-war for land and resources between the Zapatistas, the government and the landed elites is vastly oversimplified. This was not just the Zapatistas' struggle to reclaim the commons; it was, and is, a struggle of many groups to get a piece of a commons without any framework for management. Hence the recognition by both human rights groups and the federal government that Chiapas had become "ungovernable."

Despite the generalized nature of the conflict, the Zapatistas, with a strong ideology and the best propaganda in Chiapas, dominated the political landscape and won support worldwide. Two weeks of open warfare following January 1 were brought to a close when international outcry forced the Mexican government to negotiate. For the next several years, every communiqué issued by the EZLN called for "justice, liberty, and democracy," for "peace with dignity" and for "a world in which many worlds fit." As the Zapatistas' tactics on the ground shifted from a guerilla war to a "war of position," their public statements gave voice to a global need for a political space in which to build alternatives to ownership. On paper and in cyberspace, through the writings of Subcomandante Marcos and the speeches of many indigenous leaders, they drew the blueprints for such a space.

At the same time, with their bodies, their machetes, their hunger and their tears they opened up a real space in the Lacandon jungle, the cañadas, and the altiplano of Chiapas. They occupied neighborhoods and city halls, built whole villages on former cattle ranches and established new settlements deep in the jungle. It is not coincidental that these new settlements in the heart of Zapatista territory sit in a zone of major biodiversity and natural resources. While the paper war of communiqués and books and the symbolic war of ski masks and dolls have won them many ideological victories—and sparked anticapitalist resistance worldwide—the guerilla war for territory has been more costly: massacres, torture, detentions, hunger, betrayal, and deepening poverty have been the wages of revolution on the ground in Chiapas.

Take notice that England is not a free people till the poor that have no land have a free allowance to dig and labour the commons and so live as comfortably as the landlords that live in their enclosures. And that not only this commons or health should be taken in and manured by the people, but all the commons and waste ground in England and in the whole world shall be taken in by the people in righteousness, not owning any property but taking the earth to be a common treasury.

—Gerrard Winstanley,
The Law of Freedom

The history of capitalism has been one of enclosures, and the history of anticapitalist struggle has been the story of resistance to these enclosures, or reclaiming the commons.

In his essay "The Place, the Region and the Commons," poet Gary Snyder describes many forms of common lands management across cultures and throughout history. The strain that runs through all of them is that they are based on the notion of carrying capacity: There is only so much resource use that a given area of land can bear. For example, in medieval France and England, "the commoner could only turn out to common range as many head of cattle as he could feed over the winter in his own corrals." In other words, you could only keep as many cattle in the summer as you had room to house over the winter.

Historically, the enclosure of common lands beginning in 16th-century England—the seed of the industrial revolution—is widely regarded as the defining moment of modern capitalism. Developments such as cheap textile imports from newly colonized India, industrial textile mills built with improved technology and mercantile laws that established the State's duty to protect industry (and vice versa) combined to swell Britain's merchant class. In order to produce wool for the factories, lords and merchants began to graze huge flocks of sheep on open lands that, for centuries prior, had been worked in common by peasant farmers and small pastoralists. Resistance was strong and persistent, most famously in the form of the Diggers, a small band of freethinkers and religious mystics who proclaimed the earth a common treasury for all.

From humble beginnings in the pastures of England, the enclosures have grown from simple land grabs to encompass every aspect of life. In his essay "The Information Enclosures," social historian Iain Boal writes, "Over time, enclosure was to take on many forms: the privatizing of communal land; the incarceration of production; the corralling of the dispossessed into ghettos, reservations, barracks, prisons, asylums and schools; the sequestration of the airwaves by media monopolists, and so forth." But the violence of these acts of theft has been met, everywhere and at all times, by popular resistance.

Since 1994, popular reactions to the theft of common property have coalesced into one of the dominant social movements of our time. Whether we refer to it as the antiglobalization movement, the global justice movement or the anticapitalist movement matters little; at its heart is an assertion that rights, property and values that once were held in common are being systematically stolen and destroyed. The seizure of the commons by centralized governments and robber barons has always led to the degradation of wilderness, ecosystems, and agriculture and a loss of individual freedom and social autonomy. But today it is happening at such an unprecedented magnitude that the entire biosphere is at risk. Popular reaction to this theft will determine the power politics of the next several decades.

> Part of the reason the commons thinking of the past needs revisiting is that the scale of commons issues has expanded dramatically. Several of the most important commons problems are now truly global in scale.
>
> —Protecting the Commons:
> A Framework for Resource
> Management in the Americas

The dominant strain of discourse about the commons now exists in the realm of environmentalism, among anti-GMO activists, anti-toxics campaigners and defenders of public lands. But the concept is also held dear by media activists, open source software developers, and others who find it important to maintain a social space outside of the market.

In this sense, as author David Bollier has pointed out, "The commons is less a manifesto or ideology than a flexible template for talking about diverse phenomena that are thematically related."

The Collaborative on Health and the Environment has recently published "Toxic Trespass," a report in which they look at the chemical body burdens in people, suggesting that the invasion of our bodies by synthetic chemicals is a sort of trespassing. The idea is that overuse of resources by a few—in this case, the chemical industry—is a violation of the commons of our bodies, our water, our air. Similarly, arguments against intellectual property regimes in the arena of world trade are based on an ethic of common inheritance; the global struggle against privatization of water resources is launched from a human rights perspective; the demand that GMOs be tested for risk of genetic pollution is based on the idea that genetic material is an heirloom or patrimony of humanity and indeed all living things; arguments against overconsumption in the North in order to reduce global warming are based on a measure of global carrying capacity.

Advanced capitalism, as it pushes past the fetters of even nation-states in its insatiable quest for growth, enclosed life in a much more expansive yet generally invisible way: fences are replaced by consumer culture. We are raised in an almost totally commodified world where nothing comes for free, even futile attempts

to remove oneself from the market economy. We have lost not only our communities and public spaces but control over our own lives; we have lost the ability to define ourselves outside of capitalism's grip, and thus genuine meaning itself begins to dissolve.

—Cindy Milstein, "Reclaim the Cities: From Protest to Popular Power"

Confronting the vast complexity of global enclosures demands equally complex strategies and discourses. In developing these strategies, it is important to realize that while it has a long and rich history in the annals of resistance, the notion of the commons is largely absent from North American culture, at least in the present moment.

In Mexico, the Ejido law, combined with more traditional indigenous common land agreements, provides a cultural space for the commons. There also exists in Mexico, as in much of what is often referred to as the developing world, a significant class of people whose families have been landless sharecroppers and migrant laborers for generations. A major aspect of globalization is the process that forces communities off of their land, impoverishes and criminalizes landless communities and turns them into wage laborers in the factories. This is no different from the process that occurred in 16th-century England.

In the U.S., as we know, most people do not own land. But there is no social group that we would call "landless people." We have the homeless—but not the landless. Why? Because in our self-proclaimed classless society, having a home is supposedly always possible; owning land is not. We have a small population of owners and a large and shifting population of renters, the homeless, the institutionalized, and the imprisoned. By the time the 13 colonies were fully established, merchants and aristocrats—whose fathers had themselves enforced the enclosures in Britain—had become the early landowners of U.S.-America. Despite many movements in favor of common lands—from utopian religious communities in early U.S.-America to the public lands movement of the mid-20th century—the ambitious and entrepreneurial men who made the laws of the United States were loyal to a doctrine that is essentially the opposite of the commons, and forms one of the basic elements of U.S. political culture. That doctrine is, of course, "private property."

During the recent Reclaim the Commons demonstrations in San Francisco, I joined a crowd of pagans, anarchists, and cultural radicals parading through the financial district on a Sunday afternoon before converging, in a sort of human be-in dubbed the Really Really Free Market, in Union Square, the heart of the shopping district. The purpose of the weeklong demonstration was to oppose the genetic enclosures created by the biotechnology industry, which was having its annual convention in the city. Our contingent of Sunday afternoon shit-stirrers was accompanied—escorted,

even—by a roughly equal number of San Francisco's finest motorcycle police. It was a familiar scene, and a depressing one. As we marched, we chanted, "Reclaim the commons, take them back! Seeds will grow when the empire cracks!"

The chant was creative, if not inspired. It was clever, vaguely musical, descriptive of the issue—and tactically absurd. The problem, as I felt it that day, was that very few of the bystanders in San Francisco's consumer district could have been expected to understand the key words of the chant: commons and empire. As the U.S.-American empire encloses and destroys commons in its rush for global dominance, it maintains a mantle of propaganda around both concepts that make them invisible to much of the U.S. public. What empire? What commons? What are you talking about? On a warm Sunday afternoon in the center of the city it was difficult to see the empire cracking—and more difficult still to see the commons—at all.

Maybe I'm not pagan enough, but it was as if I just couldn't see the commons for the empire, couldn't see through the glossy industrial surfaces of the city to the wild heart of nature. Not that I don't believe in a cracking empire and a commons or a wild heart of nature somewhere beyond—I do. It's just not that easy to see these visions, especially in the presence of hundreds of cops. Certainly, had the cops and everything they represent been absent, we might have been free to trample the grass in Yerba Buena Gardens, or to drum and dance in the intersections—mainstay activities of Reclaim the Streets events—or to go even further toward the liberation of public space, riding our bikes into the Museum of Modern Art, liberating food from cafés, sacking the department stores on Market Street. But even these acts of creative resistance, fun as they may be for those who participate, are a far cry from freeing some kind of commons for popular use.

The psychological gulf between demanding a political space and occupying a physical territory is vast and often unfathomable—an area rarely treaded by U.S. social movements. The Diggers had their commons to plant; the Zapatistas have their ejidos to work or ranches to occupy; the people of Soweto, South Africa, and other impoverished outlaw settlements have water and electricity grids to hook into. In the U.S., the social contract of sharing land in common was long ago replaced by the social and legal contract of private property. This is not to say there is no such land-sharing movement here: There is, for instance, the community gardens movement, where people band together in Manhattan and the South Bronx and Oakland and elsewhere to turn vacant lots into community gardens. But, overall, the story of private property is the metanarrative that protects the golf courses, strip malls, business parks, parking structures, housing developments, and other blight that define our physical spaces.

* * *

The Zapatistas were able to open a political space in the culture largely because they were also able to recoup territorial space—real estate, if you will—from which to launch their critique, and because a political space that could be called the commons already existed as an important historical concept. Even so, this liberation of space cost many lives and will cost many more. For many of the indigenous people of Chiapas, who measure time in generations rather than months or years, the sacrifice has been worth it because, as they say, "the struggle is for our grandchildren and their grandchildren."

The anticapitalist movement in the U.S. has been propelled largely by mass mobilizations and by events that challenge the private ownership of public space—without actually claiming the space for more than a moment. These events are essential to shaping a social concept of public space, and the commons concept helps us confer new meaning on collective creative acts: hence the thrill of Critical Mass bike rides, community gardens, Reclaim the Streets events, public art and street theatre, mass demonstrations and civil disobedience. By asserting the existence of creative acts free of the marketplace and consumer culture, we assert the possibility of a commons—a psychosocial space we can inhabit together peacefully, and even joyfully. Ideally, by doing this we disrupt the doctrine of private property and make way for a real land-based commons in the future.

Still, these acts of resistance are marginal and largely symbolic. Reclaiming events are a useful tactic, a kind of psychological operation in the cultural war for territory. Activists introduce the commons to our cultural vocabulary. Especially in the U.S., where not only the law of the land but a strong historically based cultural current reject the notion, the only way forward is to revive the concept of commons in ways that the majority of people can understand.

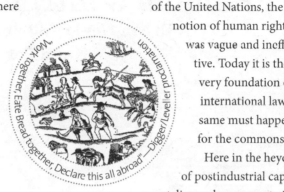

In his article "Is the Commons a Movement?," David Bollier recalls that "the environment" was a cultural invention that played a profound role in reordering social thought in the 1960s. With Rachel Carson's *Silent Spring,* the Public Lands Conservation Movement fostered by people like John Muir and Aldo Leopold, the watershed reasoning of Gary Snyder and other deep ecologists and the growth of advocacy groups like Greenpeace and direct action groups like Earth First!, "the environment" became an organizing concept that unified problems as diverse as pesticide drift, topsoil erosion, genetic mutations, big dams, acid rain, and species extinction. The first Earth Day, in 1970, coincided with the establishment of the Environmental Protection Agency. Forty years later, nearly every country and the United Nations have policy sectors devoted entirely to protecting—or, at least, managing—the environment.

A similar progression exists in the concept of human rights. Until the Universal Declaration of Human Rights, in 1948, and its adoption as a founding principle of the United Nations, the notion of human rights was vague and ineffective. Today it is the very foundation of international law. The same must happen for the commons.

Here in the heyday of postindustrial capitalism, when property is the basis of nearly all exchange, the concept that property is theft has been tossed into the already overflowing dustbin of history. The tactic of occupying land used so widely in rural Chiapas has no strategic equivalent in the urban information-age First World. To bring to life a positive vision for the anticapitalist movement, to forge legal mechanisms to fight the excesses of the market and to give moral authority to popular resistance movements, the commons must be not only reclaimed, but reinvented. But first, it must be named. Neither reclaiming the streets, nor declaring GMO-free zones, nor squatting apartment blocks, nor passing laws prohibiting contamination by CFCs or mercury or dioxin, nor practicing bioregional awareness are by themselves revolutionary. All of them together, within a framework of collectively reinventing the commons, just might be.

Remote Control Hip Hop
Urban Neglect, Planned Shrinkage, and Polycultural Revolt

In 1993, Jeff Chang co-founded SoleSides (later Quannum Projects), a protean independent label out of Davis, California, whose brainiac impact hit hard, twisting heads in the underground and beyond while helping launch the careers of Blackalicious, DJ Shadow, Lyrics Born, and Lateef the Truth Speaker. He was a founding editor of *ColorLines*, the nation's leading magazine on race, culture, and organizing, and his writing has appeared in the *Village Voice*, *Vibe*, *Spin*, *The Nation*, *Mother Jones*, the *Washington Post*, and more. He was also an organizer of the National Hip Hop Political Convention in 2004.

Chang's book, *Can't Stop Won't Stop: A History of the Hip Hop Generation* (St. Martin's Press), is a near-encyclopedic and always lyrical exploration of how a generation marginalized by deindustrialization, globalization, and planned shrinkage turned their abandonment into a vibrant multiracial movement that dramatically transformed America's musical and cultural landscape.

Brian Awehali
INTERVIEWS

Jeff Chang

SUMMER 2005

You begin *Can't Stop Won't Stop* in the '70s, in the South Bronx and Jamaica, talking about the socio-economic factors that gave birth to hip hop. I wonder if you could talk about a few of those factors, and the musical and cultural threads that really set the stage.

Well, I was trying to basically take a broad view of many themes that have shaped our generation: the politics of abandonment and the politics of containment. That's not to say those didn't exist for other generations—but these are themes that you can see if you look closely at what has happened over the last three or four decades of U.S.-American life. The politics of abandonment is the shift from the whole [John Kenneth] Galbraith idea of a society where a rising tide lifts all boats, [that] there's a lot of room to be able to make social change and improvement to a government. There's an optimism, and a faith—a basic sense that people can move toward a better life if they are given an opportunity. Those are the motivating ideas after World War II. They undergird the GI Bill, they undergird the Great Society, they even undergird the growth of public investment in highways and all this other stuff: this idea that folks can create, literally, a new frontier, and that there's progress to be made. After the civil rights movement, there's a powerful shift and that faith begins to be shredded by right-wing

ideologues. That in turn results in increasingly harsh and punitive public policy that's about self-preservation, everyone for themselves.

The politics of abandonment is the values of vulture capitalism put into government. What you have in the Bronx is the underside of this: benign neglect, planned shrinkage—these are the terms government uses to justify cutting back on welfare and social services. So revolution's in the air.

And the underside of suburban growth is white flight and the devastation of the cities. So abandonment becomes a major theme of urban areas beginning in the late '60s and running all the way through to now.

At some point during the '80s, this transforms into a politics of containment, where you've literally alienated a generation and now you've got to figure out a way to keep them from interfering with the engines of capitalist progress.

Containment comes from the intensification of punitive laws directed largely at youths, particularly youths of color. So everything from your anti-breakdancing ordinances and the "war on graffiti" from the mid '70s to the mid '80s all the way through to the anti-loitering ordinances and the huge growth in the prison industrial complex at the end of the '90s is part and parcel of this politics of containment.

In this epicenter of benign neglect, the South Bronx, one crucial moment

you talk about early on is the truce between the gangs there and the shift from a largely defensive group posture, where you went out as a member of your gang, to a more individualistic expression, where style—tagging, b-boy battles, the braggadocio MC style—became the battleground. Do you think the emphasis on individuality as a preeminent value in hip hop had a lot to do with the later commodification and corporate hijacking of hip hop you describe?

Yeah, possibly. It's interesting, because that notion of the individual and individual style can only take place within the context of the community and the culture of hip hop. So if you went out dressed in Adidas and all black, with a black bowler hat on and stuff like that, and you were walking through Beverly Hills in 1984, that wouldn't necessarily signify anything other than you were on the wrong side of town, you know what I'm saying? That wouldn't necessarily signify, "Wow, this guy is doper than me," you know?

So it's important not to divorce it from the context. But what changes between the 1980s and 1990s, especially after the LA riots, is this sense that style is going to be driven increasingly by urban youths of color. The baby boomers are getting older, they're no longer interested in brands—this is Naomi Klein's argument—they're increasingly interested in generic, low-cost stuff, and so as a result large corporations are beginning to lose their market share. At the same time, the demographics are shifting drastically to the point where folks are quickly beginning to see many schools becoming increasingly populated by kids of color—first in the cities, then moving out to the suburbs as the suburbs grow and expand. As all this is beginning to take place, there's a huge shift from thinking of culture as a broad, mass-marketed type of thing to a number of different niches. Race becomes more of a factor in the way corporations begin to see their product and the placing of their product.

Parallel to that comes the rise of an interest in hip hop. Hip hop moves quickly between 1993 and 1999 to the center of popular culture, driving everything from the sales of shoes to Sprite.

And in that sense—getting back to your question about individualism vs. collectivism—in that sense, it's an attempt to really colonize hip hop and colonize these formerly outcast communities. But in the process of doing that, you give up a lot of power.

How so?

As a corporation you give up a lot of power. It used to be the type of thing where these corporations would say, "Ok, this year it's going to be pet rocks." And every kid has a pet rock.

"And next year, it's going to be break-dancing," and every kid's going to be breakdancing. "The year after that, everyone's going to be roller skating," or whatever the next thing's going to be, right? And you realize you have to give up power to these so-called underground scenes, where style is driven by smaller and smaller, more decentralized groups of people. So in that sense, once that occurs, during the late '90s, those folks become increasingly influential in this particular kind of industry. And at the same time, corporations are looking for those exemplars able to drive synergies, so to speak.

Someone like a P. Diddy comes along, or a Russell Simmons comes along, or a Jay-Z comes along, and these folks are as interested in the *content* of the culture as they are in moving the *context* of the culture in their particular direction. They're interested in playing into what industries are now beginning to call "aspirational lifestyles."

And suddenly this idea of urban is no longer just a thing you hear with regard to radio or with regard to fashion, or shoes. It's now a catch-all for an aspirational lifestyle that includes everything from what you wear to what you drink, to what you drive around in, and suddenly your whole being—the way you've lived, for years and years—is now something you can make a lot of money off of. Well, heck, I'm going to try and figure out how I can make as much money as I possibly can on it.

And so these people get raised up as the individualists who have made it, who are fulfilling the American Dream. And that's fully incorporated into good old fashioned American capitalism.

At the end of the 1980s, and at the beginning of the 1990s, corporations began to realize that these were the folks that were going to save the logo, were going to save the brand, and so now you've got hip hop as a brand generator, or a brand solidifier, a brand buttresser—

But why do you think hip hop exploded at that time?

Mostly, I think it was *Yo, MTV Raps!* Once it was available on TV, by remote control, you know, it instantly *was*. Tommy Boy Records became one of the leaders filling this niche early on, when they realized they're not in the music business anymore, they're in the lifestyle business.

To put it back in the whole historical context, there's that shift that begins to occur once the images are readily available and consumable and are literally at remote control level. Now there isn't the need for you to go to the inner city to get those records anymore, to have to really understand what folks are talking about in order to feel like you're really part of that scene, to have to hunt down the rarest, hardest core graffiti magazines, or music magazines, to find out what the hottest things are. Now you get it via cable television.

That's the structural thing that's going on. The psychological thing that's coming on is a lot deeper and is something a lot of people have written about, from [William] Upski [Wimsatt] with *Bomb the Suburbs*, to Kitara Kitana coming out with a book called *Why White Kids Love Hip Hop*, and Adam Mansbach, who's written this book, *Angry Black White Boy*, talking about the psychological elements of race and how hip hop may or may not be changing longstanding attitudes about race in this country.

· * * ·

The thing is, when you came into hip hop at the time I did, it was not about remote control hip hop. I got hip hop through cable TV, true, [but it was] through U.S.A Networks playing *Wild Style* late at night, never announcing when it was gonna come on—waiting all night for it to come on, and then being, like, "Oh shit, did you see that last weekend?" on Monday at school with a handful of other kids. And for me, it was the kind of thing where I consciously moved to a point where I wasn't consuming the stuff anymore, I wanted to participate in it.

Toward the end of the book you make the claim that the hip hop generation is more politically active than the civil rights generation, and you cite a survey of UCLA freshmen saying that three times more people claimed to have participated in a mass organized protest in 2001 than did in 1966.

But do you think it's fair to equate political activism with something as specific as college freshmen attending demonstrations? It seems to me in the last few years we've seen a lot of demonstrations achieve almost nothing in terms of altering policy or challenging power.

That's an interesting question. Okay, so the UCLA survey stat is a number I can grasp at to quantify what I think I'm seeing around the country. I think that young people today are a lot more politically aware in some senses than the baby boomer generation, in large part because a lot of their teachers are folks that came up in these movements. And so that particular number didn't surprise me, that you would have three times as many people out there, in the hip hop generation—okay, we should be a bit more clear—three times as many college freshmen having participated in some sort of a political demonstration as their elders in the baby boomer generation. It didn't surprise me at all.

Is that a good sampling for the larger picture of what's going on? Maybe, maybe not. I think it is, in the sense that it speaks to being committed. You're not going to go and attend a demonstration if you don't deeply believe in something, in a particular kind of cause. And again, it might seem counterintuitive because voting numbers are down—or they were until this past year—and it seems as if there's less evidence of youth movements having positive effects.

The battleground of politics has shifted from the national level to the local level. Because of the right-wing revolution we've had over the last three or four decades, a lot of budget-making powers, a lot of government initiatives, are relegated to municipalities and state politics. You just do not have any kind of media presence in the state capitals or in the media around the country, and you certainly don't have them in the neighborhoods, if you ever did. So if there's a political demonstration or action, it's not necessarily being reflected back on that kind of a level. When you have kids getting sprayed by firehoses on Walter Cronkite's news on CBS, there's a sense that that's a national cause. You're not going to see that kind of thing on the national TV anymore, if anybody even watches the national network news anymore.

What would you say are the top political priorities of the hip hop generation as you conceive of it?

Well, on the agenda set at the National Hip Hop Political Convention, education was the number-one issue. Environmental justice was up there.

Healthcare issues and human rights, which included racial profiling and stuff like that, criminal justice issues of course, were up there. So those are the five issues that folks came up with, but across the board it was all about education, frustration with the educational system, and how it's been increasingly segregating folks from kindergarten all the way on up. Most public universities have steadily been closing off access over the last decade.

Public education creates an air of entitlement, cross-racial alliances, and kind of an equal playing field, so they've gotta get rid of it.

Absolutely. Just take higher education as a microcosm. You have basically 15 years of huge tuition increases. And access has been steadily cut back. Here again is a perfect example of the politics of abandonment, going from free education, and open education and strong affirmative action, to no affirmative action and tuition [increases] for public universities at the same time that all this money is going into prison growth. So people make that comparison a lot, and it's actually really relevant, because in 2000 that's when spending on prisons exceeded spending on higher education.

So the postwar era of openness in which the GI Bill was put into place is over. It's been wiped out. People haven't even had the chance to mourn it, but it pretty much ended in 1996. That's when the door slammed shut on this era of openness.

You close the book describing the Belmont Learning Center in LA, in a largely Latino and Philipino neighborhood west of downtown. After it was built they discovered it was built on soil so toxic they were worried about potentially explosive methane leaks. Parents and the community were outraged enough to actually stop the school. It sat empty.

You describe a protest march that happened after the school was sitting empty, and then make an explicit comparison between that point and the political realities of protests against the Democratic National Convention in Chicago in 1968. The culmination of the march in Belmont is when protestors arrive at the state building, stop the march, stop the music, and raise defiant fists in protest.

You're giving away the ending!

Sorry.

It's okay.

What do you think the Belmont protest achieved, and why did you choose that anecdote to close the book?

Well, I was using it to talk about how hip hop is beginning to try to transform what little cultural power it has been able to achieve and leveraging it into political power. And the book ends at a midpoint in some respects. You know, the 2000 election was when young folks really began to see themselves as a national type of movement.

And it's because they were able to gather on the streets there. It wasn't just local folks who were marching. It was folks from all over the country marching, in Los Angeles and at the RNC as well. These folks have seen what was going on with the antiglobalization protests, at A16, and the World Trade Organization in Seattle before that. These are folks that ended up in Miami later on. They're beginning to see themselves as something national, possibly even global, in scope.

This was the first year folks were really trying to structure that, at things like the National Hip Hop Political Convention, and the League of Young Voters and so on. So the book is at a midpoint in that respect. It's not a complete story, it's not a finished story.

But your question of what did the actual protest achieve—it's a good question…. What the story was meaning to do was to illustrate folks beginning to think of themselves in this larger type of way, that this identity that you've adopted as somebody who's of the hip hop generation, somebody who's a rapper or a DJ or something like that, or just down with hip hop, can now see politics appended to that particular kind of identity. And that's what the protest reflects.

In the book you talk about Chuck D [of Public Enemy] and Harry Allen launching something significant in *Black Radio Exclusive* in 1988. It seems like they were trying to do this very same thing back in '88, expressly trying to politicize hip hop. I wonder if you could talk a little bit about what they were doing and what the significance of that was?

Well, this is where the idea of hip hop activism originates. This is where, Harry says, he was using the term hip hop activism to talk about the ways hip hop could activate a mind to work towards racial justice and positive social change. They saw themselves as launching a Trojan horse guerrilla attack through the media. So the idea was, "Whatever forms we got, we're going to utilize to our advantage," whether it be journalism in the case of Harry, music in the case of Public Enemy, video, print media, radio—all these different venues are sort of going to become, now, channels. They're not going to be channel zero anymore, they're going to be moved toward channels to educate and develop black leadership and black activism.

And so that's a really interesting type of thing, and it's audacious in a

lot of ways, you know. Even if you go back to the Black Panthers or the cultural nationalists, the U.S. organization and stuff of the 1960s, all of these folks looked at culture as something that was subordinate to politics, you know what I mean? So in many senses the cultural movements they produced were not necessarily about trying to put your tentacles out to the mainstream media. It wasn't even available at that point.

So in that sense, they're audacious. They're like, "Okay, we're gonna get to a point where we're just gonna take over this shit." And in some respects there aren't too many ways to imagine what it was like before this. To be able to think of yourself as not just trying to get a representation of your self out there, but to be radical about it—that was an audacious way to understand popular culture.

So what Public Enemy did was, in many ways, to begin to theorize and then to implement, literally, what we're seeing now with hip hop activism, trying to leverage the media in a million different ways to get our message out there. Now, translating that into politics was where Public Enemy ran into issues and troubles. And we still haven't necessarily been able to figure that out, but I'm optimistic, I'm thinking that it's moving in a positive direction, that it's actually getting more sophisticated as we move on through this.

The Evolution
of Revolution
Word with emcee and activist Boots Riley

Neela Banerjee
INTERVIEWS

Boots Riley

SUMMER 2006

"**P**olitical party, Communist party, revolutionary party, zapatista, whatever you want to call it. It's also party music," Boots Riley told an interviewer on September 10, 2001, explaining the title of hip hop group The Coup's last album. The day after that interview, the political humor of the *Party Music*'s original cover (in which Boots and DJ Pam the Funkstress stand in front of an exploding World Trade Center, mock detonators in hand) took on a much, much heavier meaning. As you might expect, the cover was pulled, replaced with a more mundane image of a cocktail glass (filled with gasoline).

On The Coup's latest, *Pick a Bigger Weapon*, the political intent is just as serious, and the sense of humor just as outrageous. The idea that changing a bad system is better than electing the puppet of one party or another within that bad system is still front and center, but a lot of the understanding beneath has evolved.

LiP: How has your work changed as your own political understanding has developed?

Boots Riley: A lot of times when people get into something new, whether it's collecting stamps, or getting caught on to a different world view or a political way of thinking, or a new religion, they have a way of expressing those things that's more zealous than it will be later on. They'll make some artwork that's what I would call "straight off the pamphlet," which is guided more by the general slogans that represent the ideas than the actual ideas themselves. It's not that people that are new [to a movement] don't really believe in it, it's just they're getting used to what it means to communicate with people. As I've gone along, I've become more clear on my ideas, and I've become a lot more comfortable with myself. So I'm able to talk about more aspects of my personal life, whereas a long time ago I would have said a love song or a song that's just about personal relationship things was a song that I didn't need to make because there were enough of those.

But, you know, there are songs on this album like "Laugh, Love, Fuck," and "I Just Want to Lay Around All Day in Bed with You," and while those *are* personal songs, they're also coming with a class analysis. So "I Just Want to Lay Around All Day in Bed

You could elect me President tomorrow, and even if I don't get assassinated, I would not be able to stop the wheels of the machinery. Elected officials are puppets, and a puppet can, at most, go limp. Puppets can't affect their puppeteers.

with You" is about exploitation and what it really means. Is a conversation about exploitation confined to dollars per hour, or is it something deeper? Is it the fact that our existence is not able to be quantified in much else *but* the time we're awake on this earth? And if so, what are we doing with that time? We find that we're selling that time in order to exist, we're selling that time in order to be able to survive.

A lot of people may say, "Well, you would have to spend a certain amount of time producing and finding food in any society," but in reality, we're overproducing and spending more energy making more things than we personally need, and the rest of the things and the energy and work we put out there doesn't go to other people in our community—it builds up wealth, and that wealth goes to the top 1%. So we're spending our lives working for this 1%, and we miss out on things like being able to sit around and ponder the meaning of life, or being able to, you know, lay around in bed and just enjoy the fact that we're here.

Who do you see as The Coup's core audience? Has it shifted during the 14 years since you started?

For hip hop in general, the core audience has shifted, and grown. Whether it's The Coup, Lil John, Jay-Z, Master P or whatever, the biggest audience for all of those is white kids ranging, depending on the artist, anywhere in age from 11 to 30 years old. And the simple fact of the matter is that we're in the United States, and most of the people who buy FUBU are white kids. Most of the people who buy Nike are white kids. Most of the people who buy Cadillacs are white. All of these things that are symbols of blackness and symbols of people of color, in reality—if it's being sold successfully, it's being sold to white people, for the most part.

The difference now is that there's been a concerted effort to keep black people away from hip hop. There's been almost a gentrification of hip hop in the sense that, in the mid-1990s, you had many towns—Oakland, San Francisco, Berkeley, and then all throughout the Midwest—that had official bans on hip hop put forth by the city council and the local police. Documented bans. Some places didn't have documented bans, but the police regulated things through who they allowed to have party permits. In the mid-1990s, many times we would be number two on BET or something like that, and be very popular in the world, but most of the shows we got booked for would get cancelled before we got on the plane.

Then, all the sudden in Berkeley we'd see lines of white kids lining up, and be like, "What's going on over there?" And it was a hip hop show. There was still the ban, the official ban in Oakland and Berkeley, and still if you threw a party where flyers were passed out in East Oakland [*the blacker, and poorer, "side" of Oakland –ed.*], the police would show up before people got in there and shut it down or start telling everybody they had to go home or things like that. But if it was a promoter that was "smart" enough not to pass out flyers in the black community, their event would go on.

What music did you listen to when you were growing up? And what

have you been listening to in the four years since your last album?

As a kid my parents listened to a lot of Stevie Wonder and Ohio Players. When I started coming into my own as a teenager I was really hooked on Prince. And I think that's still apparent in my music—that my first inspiration to get involved in music was, "I want to play guitar and do something like Prince." And that got sidetracked with wanting to be part of a movement, which was kind of part of the same thing, because a lot of times people want to be famous and be noticed because you feel insignificant and you want to be part of "the world," and so you think being part of the world is like if everybody noticed you, but what better way to be part of the world than actually being able to change it? Because then, you know, that change lives forever.

Some influences: rappin', definitely Ice Cube, KRS-One, Whodini, and, as I've gone on, there's contemporary influences, like E-40, like Lauryn Hill. One album I kept listening to over and over was Me'shell NdegeOcello's *Bitter*, which is a very sad album. She's really saying some fucked-up things about herself in that album, and it's refreshing to hear somebody be able to do that, and to say, "okay, this is just the truth, this is the way it is."

Shifting gears a bit, a lot of dialogue and political analysis in the U.S.

is focused on personalities, for example, the idea that things would be better if Bush were out. Judging from your lyrics, you don't really seem to buy into this idea. Why not?

Well, I know that things weren't good while Clinton was in. I know that it's not a contest of personalities. It's not about one evil person or even about one evil corporation—or two evil corporations. It's about a system that allows exploitation of people, and a government that facilitates that exploitation. And so no matter who you are—you could elect me president tomorrow, and even if I don't get assassinated, I would not be able to stop the wheels of the machinery. Elected officials are puppets, so you can only elect a puppet. And a puppet can, at the most, go limp. Puppets can't affect their puppeteers. And Al Gore, if he had won, well, his family owns [a substantial number of shares in] Occidental Oil, and he would've gone to war, too. He might have done it differently, and we would have had

less of an antiwar protest, because there are many people who would have been fooled by that.

I know that everybody isn't exactly the same. Jeb Bush might be a little different from George Bush. And John Kerry might be a little bit different from George Bush, too—a little *more* different. But is that difference enough? No, it's not enough for me.

As long as we don't look at how things work in the system and understand that these basic things won't change until we work against the system, then we won't get what we want. And I'm not saying that the only thing to fight for is revolution and nothing before that. I think there are a lot of things that are worth fighting for before that—higher wages, better housing conditions, medical care for everyone, things that are not necessarily revolution, but can be revolutionary in the sense of building a movement that wins those things.

Ending the war—building a movement that could end the war—would be a revolutionary act. Unfortunately, again, we got duped, and we had an antiwar movement that was growing really big, but then foundations, and leaders of organizations, changed their focus from ending the war to electing Kerry. We came out of there with a lot less of an antiwar movement, trying to elect someone who wasn't going to end the war in the first place.

So my point is this: You can make any politician do what you want if you have a big movement going on. But you can have the most progressive politician and no movement going on, and nothing will change. Affirmative action came during a time when, you know, people like Nixon were in office, and it wasn't because people got together and voted, and things like that. It was because [those in power] were scared of people doing direct action and stopping industry from moving.

The massive protests against the U.S. attack on Iraq, supposedly the largest in human history, failed to stop the war. What do you think they achieved?

They inspired people who wouldn't necessarily come to the demonstrations to say, "Hey, I'm against this war." [...] These protests let it be known. They're kind of like an unofficial vote that says, "Wow, there *are* people out there who *are* against this war," and even people who aren't involved in demonstrations know that if there's a demonstration, it only represents a small percentage of people who have the same sentiment.

With any movement, you have the danger, though, of people feeling like there's nothing we can do. "There are all these problems, and we don't have the power to change it." And that's something that any movement has to deal with, and that's why we have to deal with things on all fronts. The big things and the small things, we need to also fight around issues that we *can* claim victories over. To show that, yes, power in numbers works. That idea works. And so when we're involved in these longer fights, these harder fights, people are inspired by ideas that they've seen in action.

What does revolution look like to you; how might it unfold?

The revolution is a process that's ongoing. It has infant steps and then long, adult strides. And then it doesn't stop. But I think that there are clear points at which significant change happens. At different times I've called myself communist, socialist, you know, whatever. You can call yourself a communist, socialist, anarchist, whatever, but I'm down with you if what you're fighting for is for the people to have democratic control over the profits they create.

Now, how would revolution happen? I think there *will* have to be these smaller struggles around everyday material things. We're not just going to go around and say, "Shouldn't we have a different society? You agree? Okay, cool, let's have it." It's not going to happen like that.

People aren't going to be down, because right now, in many communities, and especially in the black community, people say, "Boots Riley's a communist? Oh, okay, so what? Um, I need to go to work now, so I can pay

some bills." They might say, "I'm down with whatever's against the system, I'm down with it," but they look at that from afar.

People are interested in the struggle that they're involved in. So all these smaller struggles have to be collectivized into larger struggles. We need to struggle around these so-called smaller issues, get some victories, build up for bigger things, and then, at some point, people will take over the facilities that are around them, they'll take over the restaurants, they'll take over the retail outlets, they'll take over the factories, and say, "These are ours now." It wouldn't even have to be taking it over, it'll just be, "We work here, this is ours. We're not paying the boss anymore."

But there's a lot of building up that has to be done for that, networks, parties, and organizations that have to work together, and that's a long way down the road. But when that happens, at that point, that's when the fighting will really start. It could *not* be a fight, if everybody just agreed, but there's going to be military fighting, and at some point there will be a victory by the people, the people will claim some sort of power over certain areas, and we'll have to keep working from there. We'll create a society that works, but it won't be perfect. And we'll have to keep updating, you know? Version 2.0, version 3.0.

Sweatshop-Produced Rainbow Flags and Participatory Patriarchy
Why the Gay Rights Movement is a Sham

Mattilda
AKA

Matt
Bernstein
Sycamore
....
SUMMER 2005

As legends go, San Francisco is the place for sexual debauchery, gender transgression, and political deviance (not to mention sexual deviance, gender debauchery, and political transgression). The reality is that while San Francisco still shelters outsider queer cultures unimaginable in most other cities, these cultures of resistance have been ravaged by AIDS, drug addiction, and gentrification. Direct on-the-street violence by rampaging straights remains rare in comparison to other queer destination cities like New York, Chicago, or New Orleans, but a newer threat has emerged.

> Gay assimilationists have created the ultimate genetically modified organism, combining virulent strains of nationalism, patriotism, consumerism, and patriarchy and delivering them in one deadly product: state-sanctioned matrimony.

San Francisco, more than any other U.S. city, is the place where a privileged gay (and lesbian) elite has actually succeeded at its goal of becoming part of the power structure. Unfortunately (but not surprisingly), members of the gaysbian elite use their newfound influence to oppress less privileged queers in order to secure their status within the status quo. This pattern occurs nationwide, but San Francisco is the place where the violence of this assimilation is most palpable.

I first moved to San Francisco in 1992, just before my 19th birthday, and was completely terrified by the conformity, hypermasculinity, and blind consumerism of the legendary gay Castro district. I quickly figured out that this could never be my "community," and always assumed that it wasn't anyone else's, either. Then one day, just recently, I was walking through the Castro with a friend of mine, whose social group includes a number of gay white men in their 50s, and everywhere guys were smiling at him and reaching out with great big hugs. I realized, then, that the Castro was somebody's community, and this was, for a moment, a revelation.

What is sad about the Castro (and similar gay neighborhoods across the country and around the world), and indicative of what gay people do with even a little bit of power, is that these same smiling gay men have failed to build community for queers (or anyone) outside their social groups. Many gay men (even in the Castro) still remain on the fringes, either by choice or lack of opportunity. But as the most "successful" gays (and their allies) have moved from outsider status to insider clout, they have consistently fought misogynist, racist, classist, ageist battles to ensure that their neighborhoods remain communities only for the rich, male, and white (or at least those who assimilate into white middle-class norms). They've succeeded in clamping down on the anger, defiance, flamboyance, and subversion once thriving in queer subcultures, in order to promote a vapid, consume-or-die, only-whites-need-apply version of gay identity. Homo now stands more for homogenous than any type of sexuality aside from buy buy buy.

In 1992, there were still a few slightly interesting things about the Castro: a gay bookstore with current queer zines, and freaks and drag queens on staff; a used bookstore with a large selection of gay books; a cafe with live cabaret shows; a 24-hour donut shop with a rotating cast of tweakers; a tiny chocolate shop filled with delicate creations; a dyke bar; and a cruising park where faggots actually fucked. These meager (and mostly fag-specific) resources have disappeared, as rents have skyrocketed and corporate chains have replaced local businesses. A glittering Diesel clothing store now dominates Harvey Milk Plaza, the symbolic heart of the Castro, and the historic Castro Theater shows *Eating Out*, a movie about a straight guy pretending to be gay in order to get the girl with the gay friends. (The tagline reads, "The fastest way to a girl's heart is through her best friend.")

Gay bar owners routinely call for the arrest of homeless people, many of them queer youth, for getting in the way of happy hour. Zephyr Realty, a gay-owned real estate company, advises its clients on how best to evict long-term tenants, many of them seniors, people with HIV/AIDS, and disabled people. Gay political consultants mastermind the election of anti-poor, pro-development candidates over and over and over.

In 1998, wealthy gay Castro residents (don't forget lesbians and straight people!) fought against a queer youth shelter because they feared it would get in the way of "community property values." They warned that a queer youth shelter would bring prostitution and drug-dealing to the neighborhood. For a moment, let's leave aside the absurdity of a wealthy gay neighborhood, obviously already a prime destination for prostitutes of a certain gender and drug-dealing of only the best substances, worrying about the wrong kind of prostitutes (the ones in the street) and the wrong kind of drug dealers (the ones who don't drive Mercedes) arriving in their whitewashed gayborhood.

One sign of the power of San Francisco's gay elite is that any successful mayoral candidate must pander to the "gay vote." It was no surprise when, in February 2003, Gavin Newsom (a straight, ruling class city council member representing San Francisco's wealthiest district) hosted a lavish, $120-a-plate fundraiser at the new $18 million LGBT Center. At that point, Newsom was most famous for a ballot measure called "Care Not Cash," which took away homeless people's general assistance checks and replaced them with "care." Gay Shame, a radical queer activist group, gathered to protest Newsom's agenda of criminalizing homeless people in order to get ahead at the polls, as well as to call attention to the hypocrisy of the center for welcoming Newsom's dirty money instead of taking a stand against his blatantly racist and classist politics. Whose center was this, we asked? Was it a center for marginalized queers—queers of color, homeless queers, trans queers, disabled queers, radical queers—or a center for straight politicians to hold dinner parties?

Our questions were answered when police officers, called by the center, began to bash us as soon as they escorted Newsom inside. One officer bloodied a Gay Shame demonstrator's face with his baton, shattering one of her teeth. Several of us were thrown face-first into oncoming traffic; and one protester was put into a chokehold until he passed out. As four of us were dragged off in handcuffs for protesting outside "our" center, center staff stood and watched, and did nothing to intervene. Neither Newsom nor the center has ever made a statement condemning the police violence of February 2003. In fact, one year later, newly-elected Mayor Gavin Newsom rewarded those same powerful gays who stood on the center balcony and watched queers get bashed. Newsom grabbed national headlines and solidified his San Francisco support base by "legalizing" gay marriage, after which throngs of gay people from across the country descended upon city hall at all hours of the day and night, camping out, sharing snacks and wine, and toasting Gavin Newsom as the vanguard leader of gay civil rights.

I Think We're Alone Now: Citizenship, Gay Marriage, and the Christian Right

In the fall of 2004, Marriage Equality, a brand new brand of "nonprofit," held two amazing benefits in Washington, DC and New York City. Called "Wedrock," these star-studded events featured numerous celebrities and major-label activist rockers. Just to get people all excited about marriage equality, the promotional email for the events concluded by stating, "Get angry, protect your citizenship."

If gay marriage is about protecting citizenship, whose citizenship is being protected? Most people in this country—especially those not born rich, white, straight, and male—are not [enjoying the rights supposedly granted to] full citizens. The not-so-subtle demand to "protect your citizenship" evokes images of George W. Bush's screeds against "enemies of freedom." Gay assimilationists want to make sure they're on the winning side in the citizenship wars, and see no need to confront the legacies of systemic and systematic U.S. oppression that prevent most people living in this country (and everywhere else) from exercising their supposed rights. This willful participation in U.S. imperialism is part of the larger goal of assimilation, as the holy trinity of marriage, military service, and adoption has become the central preoccupation of a gay movement centered more on obtaining straight privilege than challenging power.

Gay assimilationists have created the ultimate genetically modified organism, combining virulent strains of nationalism, patriotism, consumerism, and patriarchy and delivering them in one deadly product: state-sanctioned matrimony. Gay marriage proponents are anxious to discard those tacky hues of lavender and pink, in favor of the good ol' stars and stripes, literally draping themselves in Old Glory at every pro-marriage demonstration as the U.S. occupies Iraq, overthrows the only democratically elected government in the history of Haiti, funds the Israeli war on the Palestinians, and makes the whole world safe... for multinational corporations to plunder indigenous resources.

A gay elite has hijacked queer struggle and positioned their desires as everyone's needs—the dominant signs of straight conformity have become the ultimate signs of gay success. Sure, for white gays with beach condos, country club memberships, and nice stock portfolios with a couple hedge funds that need trimming every now and then (think of Rosie O'Donnell or David Geffen), marriage might just be the last thing standing in the way of full "citizenship," but what about for everyone else?

Even when the "gay rights" agenda does include real issues, it does it in a way that consistently prioritizes the most privileged while fucking over everyone else. I'm using the term "gay rights," instead of the more popular term of the moment, "LGBT rights,"

because "LGBT" usually means gay, with lesbian in parentheses, throw out the bisexuals, and put trans on for a little windowdressing.

A gay rights agenda fights for an end to discrimination in housing and employment, but not for the provision of housing or jobs; domestic partner health coverage, but not universal health coverage. Or, more recently, hospital visitation and inheritance rights for married couples, but not for anyone else. Even with the most obviously "gay" issue, that of anti-queer violence, a gay rights agenda fights for tougher hate crimes legislation instead of fighting the racism, classism, transphobia (and homophobia) intrinsic to the criminal "justice" system.

The violence of assimilation lies in the ways the borders are policed. For at least several decades, there has been a tension within queer politics and cultures between assimilationists and liberationists, conservatives and radicals. Never before, however, has the assimilationist/conservative side held such a stranglehold over popular representations of what it means to be queer. Gay marriage proponents are anxious to discard generations of queer efforts to create new ways of loving, lusting for, and caring for one another, in favor of a 1950s model of white picket fence, "we're just like you" normalcy.

The ultimate irony of gay liberation is that it has made it possible for straight people to create more fluid gender, sexual, and social identities, while mainstream gay people salivate over state-sanctioned Tiffany wedding bands and participatory patriarchy.

Many straight people know that marriage is outdated, tacky, and oppressive—and any queer who grew up in or around marriage should remember this well. Marriage still exists as a central site of anti-woman, anti-child, and anti-queer violence, and remains a key institution through which the wealth and property of upper class and/or white families are preserved. If gay marriage proponents wanted real progress, they'd be fighting for the abolition of marriage, and for universal access to the services that marriage can sometimes help procure: housing, healthcare, citizenship, tax breaks, and inheritance rights.

Instead, gay marriage proponents claim that access to marriage will solve fundamental problems of inequality. This is not surprising, given that the gay marriage movement is run by groups like the Human Rights Campaign and the Log Cabin Republicans, who have more in common with the National Rifle Association than any sort of left agenda, queer or otherwise.

These are the same gays who routinely instigate police violence against people of color, homeless people, transgender people, sex workers, and other marginalized queers, in their never-ending quest to "clean up" the neighborhoods they've gentrified. Their agenda is cultural erasure, and they want the full Monty.

For a long time, queers have married straight friends for citizenship or healthcare—but this has never been enshrined as progress. The majority of queers—single or coupled (but not desiring marriage), monogamous or polyamorous, jobless or marginally employed—remain excluded from the much-touted benefits of legalized gay marriage. Furthermore, in order to access any marriage benefits, those not entirely "male" or "female" would need to accept gender tyranny. As gay marriage continues to dominate the mainstream gay agenda, resources are directed away from HIV prevention, AIDS services, drug treatment, domestic violence services, and other programs desperately needed by less privileged queers—instead, millions of dollars are being poured into the marriage coffin. The fight between pro-marriage and anti-marriage queers is not a disagreement between two segments of a supposed community, but a fight over the fundamental goals of queer struggle.

Gay marriage proponents are anxious to further the media myth that there are only two sides to the gay marriage/ assimilation debate: foaming-at-the-mouth Christian fundamentalists who think gay marriage marks the death of Western civilization, and rabid gay assimilationists who act as if gay marriage is the best thing since *Queer Eye for the Straight Girl*.

It is no coincidence that queers who oppose gay marriage are shut out of the picture, since it's much easier for a gay marriage proponent to win an argument with a crazed homophobe than with an anti-marriage queer. And every time some well-meaning straight leftist thinks they're being open-minded by taking the gay marriage side, they need to go back to Feminism 101.

Of course, Christian fundamentalists make no distinction between diesel dykes and Diesel jeans, or, to be more direct—they think all queers are gonna burn in hell, Tiffany or no Tiffany. Every time gay marriage proponents patiently explain to fundamentalists, "One, two—we're just like you! Three, four—we bash queers more!" the Christian right gains authority. But this false polarization serves gay assimilationists as well, by silencing queers who threaten the power that lies behind their sweatshop-produced nylon rainbow flags.

When gay assimilationists cheerfully affirm, over and over again, to lunatics who want them dead, that of course gay identity is not a choice (because who would choose it?), they unwittingly expose the tyranny of simplistic identity politics. Not only have the dominant signs of straight conformity become the central goals of the gay assimilationist movement, but assimilationists see a threat to Christian fundamentalist security as a threat to their version of progress. Forget about choosing our gender, sexual, or social identities, forget about building community or family outside of traditional norms, forget about dismantling

dominant systems of oppression—let's just convince the Christian right to accept us on their own terms.

Movement Rights, Civil Community

On January 13, 2005, 22 national LGBT rights organizations issued a joint statement with the leaden title, "Civil Rights. Community. Movement." Unsurprisingly, this document is filled with empty rhetoric such as, "We, literally, are everywhere," and "Stand up. Spread the word. Share your story." It even quotes gay rights pioneer President George W. Bush from an interview in *People*, where he agrees, in spite of his support for a constitutional amendment banning gay marriage, that a couple joined by a civil union is as much of a family as he and Barbara.

"Civil Rights. Community. Movement," opens by defining civil rights as "the rights belonging to an individual *by virtue of citizenship* [italics added]." Here we can already glimpse the exclusionary agenda of the gay rights movement. Instead of calling for universal access to benefits generally procured through citizenship (such as the right to remain in this country), this document seeks to secure a gay place at the red-white-and-blue table of normalcy, on the fashionable side of the barbed wire.

This opening paragraph also attributes the successes of civil rights movements to "the complex interweaving of legal victories, political progress, and advances in public opinion." Even a mainstream liberal would agree that many "civil rights" victories came about in large part through mass protests and extensive civil (and uncivil) disobedience campaigns. But the LGBT movement prefers empty terms like "political progress" and "advances in public opinion" to any recognition of direct action struggles. You don't want to frighten the funders!

The document continues by talking about challenging the family values rhetoric of "a small but powerful group of anti-gay extremists" by "[opening] America's eyes to the true family values that LGBT couples, parents, and families are living and demonstrating every day." This is where "LGBT rights" becomes most sinister. In allegedly attempting to challenge the "radical right," this document still insists on defining "family values" along heteronormative lines, rolling back decades of queer struggle to create chosen families that do more than just mimic the twisted ones assigned to us at birth.

When the report notes that, "Binational LGBT couples and families can be cruelly torn apart by deportation and immigration laws that treat them as legal strangers," we are led to believe that marriage is the only solution to this citizenship dilemma. No mention is made of non-coupled queers who are deported while seeking asylum, systemic racial profiling in citizenship decisions, or routine murders of undocumented immigrants on U.S. borders.

Instead, the document states, "We must fight for family laws that give our children strong legal ties to their parents." One must infer that this pertains to the cases of lesbian and gay parents who lose custody of their children due to homophobic courts, though this is, astoundingly, not mentioned.

While a shortsighted focus on parental control should be no surprise when coming from a so-called movement centered around marriage, it is particularly striking given the extremely high rates of suicide, drug addiction and homelessness among queer youth, especially those escaping scary families of origin. What about family laws that allow children to get away from abusive parents? What about providing support systems for queer youth?

The organizations behind "Civil Rights. Community. Movement," prefer to talk about the "true family values" of straight-acting gays than to resist the tyranny of assimilationist norms. Apparently, "true family values" call for more inclusive hate crimes legislation, but no challenge to the prison-industrial complex. "True family values" call for overturning the military's anti-LGBT ban instead of confronting U.S. imperialism. "True family values" require all of us to "invest" in the movement, to "invest in our future." That's right—send in your check NOW, before you get priced out.

Gender Pirate, Gender Ninja

Nadyalec Hijazi

AND

Ted Infinity

SPRING 2006

"**Y**our silence will not protect you, unless you are a ninja."

Anaïs repeated the words in his head like a chant as he marched around the subway station. Like the rest of the protesters he was a ninja, and like the rest of them he was carrying a blank sign. As traditional wisdom states, the strength of a ninja is inversely proportional to numbers: A single ninja is an unstoppable, invisible wind of destruction; a dozen ninjas, no matter how well-trained, will get their asses handed to them by a single down-on-his-luck detective with a judo class under his belt.

Under the glow of the disco ball, anything is possible.

This did not lend itself to collective action, and yet here they were, all dressed in masked black body suits, marching, demanding invisibility.

A skinny Caucasian in thick-framed glasses and a Decepticons T-shirt approached Anaïs. "Hey, this is great! I love how ironic you are! Are you guys on Tribe?"

From nowhere, a poisoned dart flew through the air, into the young man's neck. He crumpled to the ground, muttering, "I...just wanted...to...blog you."

Ninjas are masters of disguise. They could be anyone. Your boss. The nice old lady at the library. The person sitting next to you at a literary event. Your cat. Anyone.

Anaïs found that being a master of disguise was his favorite part of being a ninja. He really liked dressing up. Frilly lace skirts and power suits, McDonald's uniforms and nun's wimples. He'd toss down an eggshell grenade, and before the smoke cleared, he could change from a blonde bombshell wearing enough red to remove all free will from hapless onlookers, to a Tom of Finland sailor boy bulging in all the right places. He was a gender ninja.

* * *

Anaïs thought everything was going well, until he saw a pirate swaggering down the sidewalk.

He *hated* pirates.

You could tell he was a pirate because of all the intellectual property hanging off of him. Everything about him was an illegal copy; he wouldn't be caught dead using unpirated software, DVDs, music, or genetically modified organisms. He had his name legally changed to the lines of code needed to crack a DVD, and insisted that everyone call him by his full name, but most people just called him the gender pirate.

The pirate laughed when he heard that people like him were destroying capitalism, the economy, and Western civilization itself. He made a point of leaving the FBI warnings on his DVDs, just to mock the state. The only real theft was what the multinational corporations did: patenting organisms from rainforests with no payment to the indigenous inhabitants; patenting styles invented by runaway teenagers and then suing them for copyright violation; charging restaurants that let people sing "Happy Birthday," and sneaking into tranny nightclubs and patenting the genetic code for all the hip new genders.

* * *

What was the difference between piracy and cultural appropriation? If you asked the gender pirate that question, you'd get a poke in the eye and a kick between the legs. If you were unfortunate enough to stay conscious while you were down you'd get a long lecture on the subject. Or even some spoken word.

The gender pirate had just copied some genetic codes, and he was headed to a good hijackable wireless hotspot so he could upload the whole thing. He'd got as far as the subway station when he saw something that made him see red.

A ninja. He *hated* ninjas.

* * *

The rest of the ninjas threw down smoke bombs and slipped off into unseen street corners when they saw the gender pirate, but Anaïs Ninja was too angry. She attacked him immediately. She dove toward the pirate and launched one of the most secret and deadly maneuvers she had been taught: the terrible and fearsome *Lightning Fist of Seven Drunken Fairies Who Are Totally Straight When Sober.*

The pirate copied the maneuver—a patented ninja technique—and blocked it immediately! Anaïs kept attacking, but to no avail. Every secret technique she used on the pirate, he immediately copied and posted onto the internet.

Anaïs ran down the escalator of the subway station, changing clothes as she fled. By the time Anaïs reached the ground below, he was a metrosexual vanilla man in his mid-twenties. But the pirate was still following him.

Anaïs leapt over the turnstile, distracting the attendant with four throwing stars and a razor-sharp strap-on. He darted to a six-car southbound train, quickly switching genders. When the doors closed, Anaïs was a FTMTF post-op pre-transition soft butch bi-curious lesbian service top switch. The gender pirate kept following, undaunted by the changes, but the train sped away just in time.

"Every time you steal a new gender, you're making it worse for yourself!"

shouted the pirate as the train sped off, "I can smell your crypto-heteronormative principles from miles away!" Anaïs Ninja breathed easy for a while as the train sped away.

No one around her knew she was a gender ninja. She switched trains and genders three times just to make sure she wasn't being followed, then headed toward the top secret ninja safe house: a disco bowling alley.

* * *

The gender pirate was there, waiting for Anaïs. He slipped quickly past the pirate and into the dim strobe-lit safety of the bowling alley. The disco was blaring from speakers everywhere. Anaïs was invisible. Inaudible. Disco bowling is pretty good for birthday parties, corporate events, and second dates with someone you may want to sleep with but definitely don't want to look at or talk to. It's absolutely perfect, though, for ninja ambushes. The pirate was relentless in his pursuit. Anaïs grabbed a glittery sixteen-pound ball and attacked him from the shadows.

They stood face to face.

And then it happened.

The music changed. The strobes solidified into a luscious red light. Suddenly the pirate's filthy spiky hair looked soft and pettable, and the ninja's generic yuppie scum ken-boy thing took on some redeeming value. The scowling awkward teenagers surrounding them began ball dancing in

> When the doors closed, Anaïs was a FTMTF post-op pre-transition soft butch bi-curious lesbian service top switch. The gender pirate kept following, undaunted by the changes...

a perfect circle, gazing at each other dreamily. Nobody in the building had anything snarky to say. Marvin Gaye was singing, "Let's get it on."

Seductively, Anaïs swiveled and elegantly tossed the bowling ball down the lane for a perfect strike. He looked over his shoulder coyly at the pirate.

"We are all such sensitive people, with *soooo* much love to give," sang Marvin.

The pirate grabbed Anaïs by the hips and kissed him on the lips, holding him as he swooned.

"And givin' yourself to me can never be wrong." They stared soulfully into each other's eyes, swaying hypnotically, hips rocking together.

Then the Gay Pimp song "Soccer Practice" came on. Anaïs's smile became a sneer. "Hey dude, I was thinking we could go do something dirty."

The pirate looked confused when Anaïs slapped his ass and ground her crotch into him. Anaïs started bucking and thrusting her hips.

"There is nothing wrong with helping a buddy out," sang Johnny McGovern. Anaïs grabbed the pirate's spiked dog collar and dragged him onto the waxy wood floor of one of the bowling lanes. The pirate started to ask what was going on, only to find Anaïs's strap-on shoved into his open mouth.

"You're not talking about joining the army or soccer practice at all, are you? " asked Johnny.

* * *

The music and Anaïs's gender changed again. Without even realizing it, the pirate was hijacking the music system of the bowling alley. The speakers and the mood couldn't stay still past a single song. Pirate radio at its finest.

After Anaïs settled on a gender-neutral punk skatergoth, ze smiled down at the pirate, hips bucking and thrusting into the pirate's throat as he tried not to choke to death on the gargantuan tool while simultaneously fumbling in all of his pockets trying to turn off shuffle.

"And the night when the wolves cry out, listen close and you can hear me shout," crooned Joey Ramone. Anaïs howled. The pirate found the switch. The music, and Anaïs, stabilized.

"You make me feel so brand-new," sang Al Green. Anaïs, looking down at the pirate's distended mouth, was surprised to find it was true. Ze felt terribly romantic.

Anaïs pulled the pirate back onto his feet, grasped his ass firmly in both hands, pulled him close, and thrust hir tongue down the pirate's throat.

The pirate was surprised to find himself pressing his ass back against Anaïs's hands and moaning.

The ninja executed a series of ancient erotic moves so powerful that the pirate found himself incapable of uploading them to the internet:

Monkey Grasps the Bamboo Tree! Thousand Lotus Petals Unfold! Ape Fights the Crane! Carp Swims Against the River! Jade Princess Sword! Cherry Blossoms Do Something Sexy! Tiger Gobbles the Dragon!

The pirate was naked on his hands and knees, panting too heavily to ask Anaïs about hir ethnic background and cultural connection to these erotic moves.

The ninja pulled a condom out of a secret compartment and handed it to the pirate who started to unroll it onto hir cock with his teeth...

* * *

Ah, but you, my dear reader, are doubtless none too interested in the excesses and frivolities of a pandering play-by-play. The dramatis personae have been established, and the particulars are surely best left to your vivid and vibrant imagination, dear reader. Let us then do ourselves the courtesy of a dignified summary: Butt sex ensued.

Bad Vibes
Poison Pleasure Products for Profit?

When Jennifer Pritchett, Jesse Jacobsen, and Jessica Giordani opened up their Minneapolis-based sex toy store, The Smitten Kitten, in 2003, they wanted to open a fun, sex-positive feminist business while saving fellow Minneapolites the inconvenience of having to drive eight hours to Chicago just to buy a leather harness or sparkly purple butt plug. However, their entry into the sex toy business brought them face-to-face with some unpleasant health- and ethics-related realities of the industry. Most major sex toy vendors, they discovered, were selling highly toxic products to customers.

Horrified by the idea of selling products containing hormone-disruptors and known cancer-causing chemicals to their customers, the, ahem, Kittens decided to form the Coalition Against Toxic Toys (CATT). LiP editors Brian Awehali and Lisa Jervis called up Smitten Kitten and CATT co-founder Jessica Giordani to talk about ethical business, the reasons for their new campaign, the specific challenges of advocating for safer sex toys, and why not to say "butt plug" to the government expert on phthalates.

Brian Awehali

AND

Lisa Jervis

INTERVIEW

Jessica Giordani

....

SUMMER 2006

Brian: Let's start with jelly rubber toys. What are they, and why are they a problem?

Jessica: Well, "jelly" is this kind of nebulous non-scientific term that doesn't refer to anything specific. It's a term commonly used to describe lots of different kinds of rubber materials most sex toys are manufactured out of, but doesn't specifically define any one thing. Most commonly, jelly toys are made of PVC.

Lisa: Which also can be found in vinyl siding, and is used in a lot of other places, right?

Absolutely. PVC is ubiquitous in our environment. It's in lots of different consumer products—everything from the vinyl siding on your house to packaging for food; it's the main material in lots of different sex toys, and it's a hard plastic. In order to make it soft, so it can be processed into something like a jelly dildo or a vibrator, it's mixed with chemicals that act as plasticizers. And commonly, you'll find phthalates [a potential carcinogen and hormone disruptor] are the plasticizers that are used.

Jelly toys are porous, too, so there's no way to clean them.

B: Meaning stuff leaches into them, they absorb things, and there's absolutely no way to purify them or get rid of that?

Yep. Your jelly toys are kind of like the sponge in your kitchen sink. They're not hygienic. If you have a jelly dildo or vibrator, it'll collect bacteria and viruses—and if you see it get cloudy as it gets older, that's mildew growing in those pores. So there are a number of ways to give yourself infections.

B & L: (chuckling and snorting)

L: Mildew and mold.... Yeah, I really want a dildo full of mildew and mold.... that sounds lovely...

Oh yeah. You know, when we first opened [the store], UPS showed up, and brought in box after box after box, and some of the boxes had stains on them, but we didn't really pay much attention. But when we opened up the packages, a lot of the packaging looked like it was destroyed. It was greasy and oily and the toys looked like they had started to melt, and it stunk horribly.

L: And this was a complete surprise?

Oh, it was shocking! We didn't know what we had on our hands at all. We called our distributor and told him, "Hey, we don't know if these toys melted or not, but we've got a big problem." And he explained that things like this happened, that it was nothing to worry about, they'd get us some new stuff.

And we thought, well, that doesn't sound right, but we didn't know! So we made some phone calls, and learned that phthalates are linked to a number of different cancers. Phthalates disrupt hormones, so basically they block testosterone and can cause birth defects in male fetuses, among other things.

L: And when you found all of this out, this is what led you and the other Kittens to form the Coalition Against Toxic Toys (CATT)?

We were worried for quite a while but kept doing research, and started to find [studies like] "Skin Deep" and "Not Too Pretty," which [have] to do with phthalates in cosmetics and other skin care products. Women have huge exposure rates.

L: How about the food industry, and specifically food packaging?

Food packaging tends to be a bit safer, because the FDA regulates what a food-quality vinyl is. The easiest way to tell if you've got vinyl packaging for your food is to look at the recycling code. The little arrow triangle symbol at the bottom of your packages—if it has a number three, it's PVC.

L: Good to know. What's your take on what people's responsibility is, both for choosing what to sell, and what information to provide?

I think retailers should be as informed as they can possibly be about these issues. You need to know what you're selling

your customers. That's part of the reason we're starting CATT. People don't have access to information, so right now, for lots of retailers, they don't have any more choice in what they sell to people than consumers have in choosing what they buy.

In the bigger stores, and more progressive or feminist-identified sex toy stores, there *is* this kind of information. [Toys in] Babeland, in particular, has links on their web site. And that's almost more disconcerting to me— they have the information, they know that vinyl is hazardous, and they know that phthalates are problematic, but they choose to offer it to ther customers anyway.

B: They seem to say that you should always use a condom and never have direct contact with these products, right?

Right. When you put a condom on your porous vinyl toy, your jelly toy, that protects you from the porosity of it. The problem with phthalates is that, if you can smell them, you're ingesting them into your body through your lungs, and into your bloodstream. You don't even have to touch a jelly dildo; if it's out of the packaging and you can smell it, you're being exposed to those chemicals.

I suppose the real question is, is it ethical, is it right, is it our responsibility to give people the option to buy things that are toxic to them? A lot of stores will say that they do it in the name of being economically friendly, but how ethical is it to sell poor people things that are toxic to them? I don't think that it is.

B: Citizens groups like CATT are often started by companies for commercial purposes, and sometimes very transparently to stimulate demand for products. Isn't CATT a little bit like that, given that The Smitten Kitten has a financial stake in selling, and being identified with selling, safe toys?

Good question. We talked a lot about that when we started planning CATT, but we came to view it as a consumer education issue first. When you go into a grocery store and there's information there about the risk of pesticides and why organic produce is a healthy option for you, that's not a conflict of interest. This information will give other retailers the option about what they want to carry in their stores.

B: Is CATT going to be focusing just on sex toys, as the name would seem to indicate, or are you going to be trying to form alliances with other groups?

We've made connections with an independent laboratory that's got lots of certifications and is recognized by the government as a reliable place to get your testing done, and right now we're in the process of having them de-formulate toys, starting out with best sellers at other stores to try and figure out what is in these jelly materials. We'll be publishing that information on the site. We'll have CATT focus specifically on products in the sex industry, but we're excited at the possibility of forming alliances with other groups that are working on the same types of issues in other industries.

L: Do you think the stigma around the sex industry and having products that are used for sexual pleasure might hinder the alliance building?

We've found that there are a number of different people who either aren't ready to work with us yet or can't even conceptualize what we're doing; as soon as you start talking about sex, they shut off and they don't want to hear about it. There is an office in the government which tries to figure it all out—there's a man named Ken there, and Ken is in charge of phthalates and a number of other issues in consumer products.

L: Ken, from the phthalates department!

We called Ken when we started doing this research and tried to talk him about it, and Ken would talk to us about phthalates in baby toys, he was happy to talk to us about pacifiers, but as soon as you said "butt plugs" to Ken, he shut off.

Lunchbox Hegemony
Kids and the Marketplace, Then and Now

I
f you want to catch a glimpse of the
gears of capitalism grinding away in
America today, you don't need to go
to a factory, business office, or economic
summit.

Instead, observe a child and parent
in a store. That high-pitched whining
you'll hear coming from the cereal aisle
is more than just the pleadings of a single
kid bent on getting a box of Fruit Loops
into the shopping cart. It is the sound of
thousands of hours of market research,
of an immense coordination of
people, ideas and resources, of
decades of social and economic
change all rolled into a single,
"Mommy (or Daddy), pleeease!"

**Dan
Cook**

FALL 2001

"If it's within [kids'] reach, they will touch it, and if they touch it, there's at least a chance that Mom or Dad will relent and buy it," writes retail anthropologist, Paco Underhill. The ideal placement of popular books and videos, he continues, should be on the lower shelves "so the little ones can grab Barney or Teletubbies unimpeded by Mom or Dad, who possibly take a dim view of hypercommercialized critters."

Any child market specialist worth their consulting fee knows that the parental "dim view" of a product most often gives way to relentless pestering by a kid on a quest to procure the booty of popular culture. Officially, marketers refer to the annoyance as children's "influence" on purchases, unofficially it is the "nag factor." The distinction is important because businesses are discouraged from explicitly inciting children to nag their parents into buying something, according to advertising guidelines from the Better Business Bureau.

Do Kids Use Products, or Vice Versa?

Tne strain of academic thought asserts that media and consumer products are just cultural materials, and children are free to make use of them as they will, imparting their own meanings to cartoons, toys, games, etc.

There's little doubt that children creatively interpret their surroundings, including consumer goods. They color outside the lines, make up rules

to games, invent their own stories and make imaginary cars fly. But granting children magical transformative powers of the imagination only further romanticizes an already oversentimentalized view of childhood. Children are human. Imaginations can be colonized. As any marketer will tell you, exposure to target market is nine-tenths of the brand battle.

It's Not Just the Corporations

How has this kid consumer world come to be? Easy explanations abound, from spoiled children to over-indulgent or unengaged parents. Easiest of all is to accuse corporations of turning kids into blank-faced, videogame-playing, violence-saturated, sugar-mongering, overweight, docile citizens of the future. Everyone—from Joe Lieberman and Ralph Nader to concerned mothers and the religious right—have found an ideologically comfortable vantage point from which to voice their opposition to the corporate incursion into childhood.

Soulless advertisers and rapacious marketers alone, however, cannot account for the explosion of the kids' 4–12 market, which has tripled since 1990, now raking in around $30 billion annually.

Marketers and advertisers tell themselves—and will tell you if you ask—that they are giving kids what they "want," or providing educational devices or opportunities for "self-expression."

And on some level, they're right. What is most troubling is that children's culture has become virtually indistinguishable from consumer culture over the course of the last century. The cultural marketplace is now a key arena for the formation of the sense of self and of peer relationships, so much so that parents often are stuck between giving into a kid's purchase demands or risking their child becoming an outcast on the playground.

The relationship is reciprocal. Childhood and consumer capitalism inform and co-create each other. It is not just that the children's market is the Happy Meal version of a grown-up one. It stands apart from others because childhood is a generative cultural site unlike any other.

Childhood makes capitalism hum over the long haul. Kids' consumer culture takes a most intimate thing—the realization and expression of self—and fuses it with a most distant system—the production of goods, services, and media in an impersonal market.

Cumulatively, this fusion has been forged cohort by cohort and generation by generation, making each of us a conspirator in its reproduction. The process is so insidious that by the time a child gains the language and capacity to grasp what is occurring, his or her attention patterns, preferences, memories, and aspirations cannot be neatly separated from the images and poetics of corporate strategy.

The History We Are

Adults are the living legacies of commodified childhoods. Our memories, our sense of personal history are to some extent tied to the commercial culture of our youth: an old lunchbox with television characters on it, a doll, a comic book, a brand of cereal, a sports hero perhaps, certainly music of one sort or another.

These may seem like benign artifacts of a fading past, fated to become pieces of nostalgia at junk shops and yard sales. They might seem benign when viewed against the backdrop of today's hyper-aggressive children's marketing strategies which target children who eat branded foods and play in branded spaces, who are exposed to television in school courtesy of Channel One and who, to take one infamous example, learn geometry by measuring the circumference of Oreo cookies.

The "hegemonic power" of that *Starsky and Hutch* lunch box of yesteryear seems almost laughable by comparison.

But the joke unfortunately is on us, in part, because the *Teletubbies* and *Pokemon* of the 1990s would not have been possible without the *Starsky and Hutch* of the 1970s, and those crime-fighting hunks would not have been possible in some measure without the *Mouseketeers* of the 1950s, whose apple-pie smiles would not have been possible without the Lone Ranger of the radio days of the 1930s. If we are to intervene in the rampant commodification of childhood, we need to balance the impulse to place exclusive blame on corporations for polluting children's minds and bodies with a larger, historical perspective.

Creating the Child's Point of View

At the beginning of the twentieth century, working-class children still toiled in the factories or worked the streets of the rising industrial city as bootblacks, newsies, and helpers. They (mostly boys) spent their money on food and candy, in the new nickelodeon theaters, pool halls, and restaurants. Aside from these amusements, there was no children's consumer market to speak of.

Enter the "bourgeois child" at the end of the nineteenth century, whose value was no longer economic, but sentimental. Liberated from direct, industrial labor and placed into school, this child was trained in the technical skills and social posture appropriate for a new bureaucratic order. His (again, usually his) childhood was to be full of fancy, not preoccupied with factory or farm work; his first school, a "children's garden," as close to Eden as possible.

The image of the bourgeois child would spread beyond the confines of a rising urban, white, middle class to become the model for virtually all childhoods in industrialized nations by the millennium.

During the second decade of the twentieth century, department stores began to recognize and welcome the bourgeois child, providing separate, modest toy departments with play spaces where mothers could "check" their children while they shopped. Prior to about 1915, there were also no separate infant's and children's clothing departments in department stores—clothes tended to be stocked by item, not size. One could find children's

socks in hosiery, children's shirts in the men's or women's department, etc.

A Chicago manufacturer of baby garments, George Earnshaw, hit upon something when he began to convince department store management to devote separate space to children's clothing and furnishings. Mothers and expectant mothers were to be served by this new arrangement, which would have "everything they needed" in one place.

Much ink was spilled in the trade and consumer journals throughout the 1920s, 1930s and 1940s in the attempt to discern the tastes, priorities and foibles of "Mrs. Consumer," a caricature which continues today as something of an icon of consumer society. (How else would we know that "Choosy mothers choose Jif"?) The first children's retail spaces were built, located, staffed, and stocked with the consuming mother, not the child, in mind.

By the 1930s, however, individualized clothing and toy departments in department stores gave way to entire "floors for youth" complete with child-size fixtures, mirrors, and eye-level views of the merchandise. Merchants hoped to provide children with a sense of proprietorship over the shop or area by visually, acoustically, and commercially demonstrating that it was a space designed with them in mind.

The basic arrangement was to display older children's clothing and related furnishings at the entrance to a floor or department. As kids moved through the department, they encountered progressively younger styles until reaching the baby shop in the back. A designer of one such floor explained:

> Older children . . . are often reluctant to shop on a floor where "all those babies" are shopping. The younger children are delighted to see the older children shopping as they go through these departments, for all children want to be older than they are. The little boy and little girl seeing the big boys and big girls buying will long for the day when he (sic) too can come to these departments and buy . . . In this way a valuable shopping habit is created. (*Bulletin of the National Retail Dry Goods Association*, Oct. 1939.)

Note here how the child's viewpoint, agency, and emergent autonomy are transformed into exchangeable, marketable values. What's new is the way that the child's perspective is invoked as legitimate authority within the context of commercial enterprise.

This was the beginning of a fundamental shift in the social status of children from seen-and-not-heard, wait-till-you-grow-up dependency to having retail spaces, shelving in stores, and media messages tailored to their viewpoint, making it the basis of economic action. Today, we expect to see video monitors flashing images of Britney Spears, oversized replicas of teddy bears, and primary-colored display fixtures every time we walk into a Kids 'R' Us.

And Now a Word from our Sponsored Kids

Over a number of generations, children and younger adults became key arbiters of kid-taste in the U.S.

Children moved to the front-and-center of popular culture with the early successes of Shirley Temple and others like Mickey Rooney in the 1930s. Their images provided a foundation for the publicly shared persona of the bourgeois child as one who moves in a world virtually independent from adult concerns and preoccupations—one that makes sense only in reference to its own child-logic. Think of the Peanuts characters whose world is totally devoid of adults of any consequence: all framing is child's-eye level, only the legs of adults are shown, and when adults speak their voices are non-linguistic trombone-like notes.

Meanwhile, back in the marketplace, children were also acquiring status as spokespersons for goods throughout the twentieth century—from fictional icons like Buster Brown (1910s) and the Campbell's Soup Kids (1920s), to actors like Cowboy Bobby Benson (1930s), to voice-overs for commercials during the Saturday morning "children's" television time (1960s). By the 1960s, the child spokesperson had become such a fixture that market researchers felt comfortable enough to query children directly for their product preferences, giving them a "voice" in the market sphere.

Children—or to be precise, media-massaged images of children—now routinely and aggressively hawk almost any kind of product, from car tires to vacations to refrigerators to grape juice, as advertisers make use of both "cute appeal" and safety fears.

Kids frequently serve as peer arbiters in newspapers, magazines, and websites, reviewing movies, videogames, toys, and television shows—as it is assumed, often correctly, that they have more intimate knowledge about the detail and appeal of these things than adults do. This is a world under continuous construction and it is theirs: oriented around their "desires," retrofitted to their physical size and tweaked in just the right way to produce that all-important feeling of inadequacy if this or that product is not in their possession.

Factoring in the Nag

Kids not only want things, but have acquired the socially sanctioned right to want—a right which parents are loathe to violate. Layered onto direct child enticement and the supposed autonomy of the child-consumer are the day-to-day circumstances of overworked parents: a daily barrage of requests, tricky financial negotiations, and that nagging, unspoken desire to build the life/style they have learned to want during their childhoods.

Sometimes the balancing act is overwhelming. "Moms have loosened nutritional controls," enthuses Denise Fedewa, VP-planning director at Leo Burnett, Chicago. "They now believe there are so many battles to fight, is

fighting over food really worth it?"

Unsurprisingly, mainstream media provides few correctives. The August 6th, 2001 *Time* cover story on kids' influence on parents gushes over the excesses of the upper-middle-class in typical fashion, sucessfully detracting from the larger, more generalized problem of struggling parents.

Slipping the Parent Trap

If kid marketing tactics were merely blatant, their power would not be so great. Places like zoos and museums are promoted as "educational," toys are supposed to "teach," clothing allows for "individuality" and who can suggest that there is something wrong with "good ol' family fun" at, say, Dollywood?

The children's market works because it lives off of deeply-held beliefs about self-expression and freedom of choice—originally applied to the political sphere, and now almost inseparable from the culture of consumption. Children's commercial culture has quite successfully usurped kids' boundless creativity and personal agency, selling these back to them—and us—as "empowerment," a term that appeases parents while shielding marketers.

Linking one's sense of self to the choices offered by the marketplace confuses personal autonomy with consumer behavior. But, try telling that to a kid who only sees you standing in the way of the Chuck-E-Cheese-ified version of fun and happiness. Kids are keen to the adult-child power imbalance and to adult hypocrisy, especially when they are told to hold their desires in check by a parent who is blind to her or his own materialistic impulses.

We have to incite children to adopt a critical posture toward media and consumption. A key step in combating the forces eating away at childhood is to recognize our own place as heirs of the bourgeois child and thus as largely unwitting vehicles of consumer culture. The mere autocratic

vetoing of children's requests will only result in anti-adult rebellion.

The challenge facing us all—as relatives, teachers, friends, or even not-so-innocent bystanders—is to find ways to affirm children's personal agency and their membership in a community of peers while insisting that they make the distinction between self worth and owning a Barbie or a Pokemon card—or any thing, for that matter.

by Timothy Kreider

The River vs. Water, Inc.

Antonia Juhasz
INTERVIEWS

Vandana Shiva

SPRING 2006

D r. Vandana Shiva is a physicist, ecologist, activist, and author of hundreds of papers and articles and more than 15 books. She is the founder and director of the Research Foundation for Science, Technology and Natural Resource Policy in India. Her work runs the gamut from establishing community seed banks to defending farmers and everyone else who eats food from the dire socioeconomic, environmental, and health consequences of genetically modified crops; from writing and agitating about water privatization to writing and agitating about corporate thievery of natural knowledge. Her latest book is entitled *Earth Democracy* (South End press).

YOU
ARE
HERE

I'd like to ask you about the relation-ship between research and activism, and how you think people will incorpo-rate the ideas from your books into their own activism.

Well, I came from science and academia; I was part of the "normal" culture, where you write to publish, you write for yourself. Then I gave up academia, and since I founded the Research Foundation in 1982, everything I write is about my engagement. My engagement has always been twofold: the research I can do, and the knowledge people have, joining into a major force for transformation. My books are about a deep synthesis of the knowledge that comes out of action. Every book of mine is about issues that I see as needing a response—for example, genetic engineering and intellectual property rights, which I started to write about in 1987. One of the most touching moments in my life was walking the streets of Seattle during those amazing protests against the World Trade Organization, when a youngster came and held my hand and said, "I'm here because of [your book] *Biopiracy*." That's what my hope is, and that's why I write—otherwise, I wouldn't try.

In your latest book, *Earth Democracy*, you provide some beautiful examples of local models of living democracy taking place. Can you talk about your favorites?

What happened in villages, as we spread the word about the practice of genetic engineering and corporate monopolies on seed, was that, extremely naturally, people started to create these village defense committees—the local name was Jaiv Panchayat, which also translates into "living democracy." It was something that multiplied and spread so fast, partly because that part of India—that 70% of India that still lives in what I call a biodiversity economy—that's their ethics! They don't have to "learn" that activism, or learn that the cow, the tree, and the earthworm are all part of one extended family.

[This kind of activism] spread. In the state of Orissa, communities were so strong that when the Department for International Development tried to privatize the local water tanks and ponds, people said, "No, this is our resource! It's collective common property!" From the source of the Ganges down to the Bay of Bengal, people

organized and said, sorry, the River Ganga is sacred, it is our mother, and she is not for sale! In fact, right now, one of the pilgrimages of the Ganges is happening. It used to be 20,000 [people] a decade ago—last year's was 10 million people, and this year there will be 20 million people walking. Walking to just take one little pot of water, a glass of water, and walking with that Ganges water back to their village, as a tribute to the sacred river. And this whole living democracy Jaiv Panchayat movement was able to take that ethics, that culture, and put that culture into political mobilization. So that's something that touched me deeply and continues to inspire me. They've now used the history of that to declare their opposition to a new seed law, which would make it illegal for India's farmers to save their own seed—not just Monsanto's seed, but their own seed—5 million people have signed a pledge saying, sorry, saving seed is a duty to the earth. So I see this as a huge movement that will continue to grow, continue to give hope in a period in which 70% or 80% of India has been written off under the globalization project.

What do you mean, written off?

In the sense that they're not supposed to exist—their ecological space is being stolen. Their water's being taken, their seeds are being taken, their land's being taken, their livelihoods are being taken. That's what globalization is. The other wonderful, very inspiring movement was the one that tribal women started against Coca-Cola's appropriation of local water supplies in Plachimada, Kerala. It has spawned a whole new movement of communities around every Coke and Pepsi plant. We're now organized nationwide, and the local elected village bodies are serving notices in place after place and saying, sorry, we don't give you permission, Coca-Cola: In this democracy we have the right to decide how our water will be used, and we definitely don't want it to be used for you to make superprofits. Yesterday, I was having a meeting with schools for a campaign on junk food, and it was so touching—the kids were saying, "And we have to ban Coke and Pepsi…"

These are not singular things; they're not limited. They are unleashing a new energy of transformation that is within the people's own self-organizing.

Can you talk about how living democracy relates to other terms that we use, like direct or participatory democracy?

In terms of the political participation of people, living democracy would include direct democracy and participatory democracy. But it is broader in that it includes the democracy of all life. It therefore has a very deep ecological basis. I think that we need that, because there's too much conflict between those who want to work for nature, and those who want to work for human beings. We are so polarized as movements between the human rights movements and the animal rights movements. In India, our government is passing a law—and I'm part of the drafting team—to recognize the rights of tribals, the indigenous communities in the forests, that have never been recognized. And yet, because the tigers are dying, you've got a tiger lobby that says the tribals can't have rights because the tiger will die, and then the tribal community says, we can't have conservation because we need our rights. I really hope that living democracy, articulated as the broader democracy of all life, will help us transcend these polarizations and work to protect all species while defending every human right of every excluded community.

I'm interested in how you see living democracy translating into a model that could eventually replace representative democracy.

Representative democracy has always had deficiencies, but its deficiencies have increased hugely under globalization, where there's two total blocks that make representative democracy not function at all. The first block is the fact that most decisions aren't even made at the national level, where representative democracy is supposed to function. You elect people to parliament, but parliament has no role in deciding WTO rules—it's totally bypassed. So it's already made impotent by globalization and rule-making at the global level under corporate influence. But the second reason it's being rendered totally impotent is because there's no gap between those who are in business and those who are professional politicians—especially in India. Increasingly, we are seeing business directly entering into the Indian parliament; they now don't even have to bribe the parliamentarian or the minister—they *are* the minister! Just like in the White House. In a way, the White House has become the model, where corporations rule and run for office; they have the money to finance their own elections at every level. And the situation is so insular that no popular mobilization can break through it, because it's being driven by money power.

And these people who hijacked representative democracy and what thin levels of protection it gives people are not going to give up power on their own. The contest has disappeared, it's all become unipolar in every society. You might have two parties, but it's like musical chairs for the same ideology—the music is the same, it's just a rotation between people of the same class and the same corporate leaning. I think the biggest thing we need to do today is to start, through our actions, to reclaim the spaces in which we want to be able to make our decisions, and build another political framework by shifting power out of the hands of those who turned representative democracy into corporate rule.

And we would maintain an elected government, and maintain the power of the government to regulate?

Yes, absolutely. And that's why the issue of subsidiarity—devolving power down to the most local level possible on any given issue—is so important. Living democracy basically works like a tree: It grows from the roots upwards, from the people and their organizing capacity. But you do need the canopy, in a storm—and you get storms, including Monsanto, wars, militarization. And therefore you need a thin layer, a very thin layer, of regulatory structures protecting people on the bottom. But that national regulatory system can only be pro-people if it is getting its life blood from a base of self-organized communities, taking care of their water, their food, their farming, their health—and making demands on the system for the appropriate share.

So, you imagine an electoral system, in which officials are elected by the public, that would be essentially cleansed through a living democracy process?

In my experience, the community as a whole, as an integral, organic body of equal human beings, is the only way to create real democracy. The moment you start to get into electoral processes, you start excluding the women, you start excluding the tribals, you start excluding the landless, et cetera. And that is why in the Indian decentralized democracy system, we do have laws that say the village as a whole has rights. Now, it doesn't have to be a village. It could be a street in San Francisco. And of course functions will get delegated, just as they are in any structure in any organization—some people will be too busy, someone's good at keeping the books, someone else is good at calling meetings—but that works in an organic system. Elections at all other levels would work, but the elections would be around highly defined power, where the power that can be exercised by people directly stays in their hands. And that is not negotiated.

Let me bring this to the issue of propaganda, then: how corporations in particular, in partnership with the media, change the dialogue within which we're able to function— how they have made it palatable that water should be considered a commodity, that air and rain and land, things that should be considered communal, are now considered private property.

The main way in which propaganda has been used to try and dull people's thinking about what water is, what food is, what the land is, is by first and foremost redefining everything that we get from the earth as purely raw materials and commodities. In the case of biodiversity, life forms are transformed into information, and that information in the genetic code is treated as property by the company that can read the genetic code with a silly little machine. They didn't even use their minds, but it becomes their intellectual property. And it is by taking living organisms out of their life context and turning them into a fragment of expression, only genetic information, that they're able to change the discourse from thinking about life as a cow, as a pig, as a neem tree, as a basmati plant, into a transfer of information—and commodification of information should not really trouble anybody. In this way, society, through propaganda, is cut off from the consequences of their actions.

I can give you a very clear example of how this would work, in the case of the privatization of Delhi's water supply, which was going to be based on the commodification of the Ganges. They were starting to call the water that comes from the Ganga "raw water." And the water at the other end of the pipe, where they would be selling that water, would be a product. It's by this mutation that they change the status of what you're dealing with, so water as a living resource, plants as a living resource, disappear. And with them disappear the relationships of people with living plants and living rivers. One of the big changes in perception, and I think it was so obvious in the whole [2005] G8 summit, is to make people appear like pathetic creatures who can't do anything for themselves. "Third World" societies, helpless little beings: just waiting for that dollar to drop, the food aid to drop into their land. It's this denial of the capacity of human beings, of living resources, of equal systems, which is at the heart of the corporate propaganda that enables privatization, that enables takeover and the creation of property in that which should never be private property, that which should always belong to the commons.

Who's the "they" who started using the term "raw water"? And how did the use of "raw water" translate to the public mind?

Well, the chain is the World Bank and its contracts, and the language is already defined in those contracts. The contracts enforced by the Bank are then between the company and the public utility. So then the public utility starts talking that language. And if we weren't able to challenge it and bring the language back to the people's right to water, we would not have had the kind of discourse we've had over the last two or three years in this city.

We've managed to block the privatization—they haven't managed it yet—but the Bank also doesn't give up. This language gets crafted by the corporations working with the Bank during their annual meetings, and then they come in and pour this ready-made jargon on countries. And [they] turn countries which have water into water-poverty situations, countries that know how to grow rice into places where you need a huge loan to be taught how to grow rice. People who know how to plant a tree need to borrow 300 million bloody dollars to continue to do what they did and now be in debt for 20 years.

So, for example, the World Bank requires that a country that grows rice using small-scale practices for local consumption must instead grow corn using industrial agriculture practices to export to the global market. People who grew rice lose their ability to provide for themselves and their communities, while land once used for rice is now used for corn and the nation, in turn, must import its rice. However, prices for corn—as with all food commodities—are volatile, while the country competes with dozens of others for its share of the market. The money it receives for its corn does not offset the price for imported rice and the needs of the increasing number of landless and hungry former farmers. The country is unable to repay its loans and the cycle of dependence rolls on and on.

And it's extremely clever. I believe the public relations companies work with all of them; [it's] the work of Burson-Marsteller behind the scene. The [biggest] advertising is the genetic engineering propaganda, and there we know Burson-Marsteller played a very big role. They were hired by Monsanto to constantly say it was all about feeding the hungry; they used to put out huge full-page ads. The other day, an Indian newspaper did a whole-page story on me, and about what I've done for the environment, and then the last two paragraphs, in good "balanced" reporting, were a quotation from the website of the Hudson Institute, a right-wing think tank in the U.S., saying, "Vandana Shiva will starve the people because she is fighting GMOs [genetically modified organisms], which is the only way to feed the people." And you can tell a lie 5,000 times, when you have the money to say it 5,000 times. A movement can do actions for one year, two years, three years. Eventually, you can't sustain it—meetings, conferences, public hearings, citizen mobilization. And corporations just hope that by lying and lying and lying, and continuing their propaganda, they can make reality disappear.

That would bring us back to where we started, which is the importance of our continued action and our continued research and writing to counter their propaganda.

Absolutely. Because it's about a fight for the planet's resources, but the fight is taking place through a capture of the mind. We can only liberate our rivers and our seeds and our food, and our educational systems, and our political systems, and redefine and deepen democracy, by first liberating our minds and decolonizing our minds. And that's why resisting propaganda through every intellectual means available to every human being becomes an absolutely important part of freedom in today's world.

What are the other modes of taking the important research and essentially decolonizing material and spreading it more widely?

I think that for the West, of course, the internet is a very accessible means; it's not for countries like India, where a tiny, tiny percentage have access to the web. We're always stuck with this since we work at both levels—very local, also very global—we have to have, always, two levels of communication. One is through the internet with our friends internationally, and the other is through street theater, through pamphlets, through wall writing—which is very popular in India; it is not yet illegal. If you go to the villages, you will see huts painted with "Monsanto go home!" or "Coca-Cola go home!" One wall painting has no cost; it's merely the commitment of an individual to put a slogan on his or her wall. And then thousands see it. Millions will see it. So those are some of the means that are available and accessible. And I think we need to use every communication available, in every country.

The other thing we are doing is creating alternative learning systems. After all, let's recognize that our universities came out of dealing with scholasticism and the power of the church. They came out of dealing with the domination of that time. But now they have become the dominant forces of our time, and they are being used to service corporate power. They are not being allowed to function as public institutions. They're being privatized. It means that for younger generations, there will be no place that we can know what's really going on. So we have created on our farm in Dehra Dun a school called Bija Vidyapeeth, which literally means the School of the Seed. We do short courses; next week we are going to be doing a course on intellectual property rights and biopiracy and biodiversity. At the national level, I've just been appointed to a new university, which is going to function like an open university and it'll be complementary to Bija Vidyapeeth. Activists will be there and they will learn everything about the Trade Related Intellectual Property Rights agreement at the WTO, about patent laws and all of these piracies and thefts, and they'll go back more informed.

How would you define personal freedom, within the context of living democracy and earth democracy?

I see living society the way I see living systems. I don't see society as an aggregation of atomized, fragmented individuals. That's why I don't go down the Hobbesian path.* I see society as organic, in which every level has an autonomous existence, and a self-organizing capacity, but in relationship with other self-organizing systems. Which means that your freedom, your personal freedom, is then in the context of total consciousness and awareness of other people's personal freedom. It is that awareness which I call compassion, I call solidarity. And it's through compassion and solidarity that you do not have the irresponsibility built into personal freedom the way it has in Western philosophy and political science, with the terrorizing by these guys who exaggerate certain human tendencies. Personal freedom is real. A person is a full subject. But a person is not a subject in isolation: We are in family, we are in friendships, we are in community, we are in working contexts, we are in certain towns, we are living in certain lands—all that does define levels of who we are and our identities and therefore, also, our searching for our freedoms. Because all those freedoms have to be carried together.

---

* Philosophy of self-interest most often attributed to English philosopher Thomas Hobbes (1588-1679) which views life is essentially nasty, brutish, and short.

by Zane Davis

Darwin vs. the Ant
The Altruism of Ants and Humans

*It is an extraordinary comment on the state
of the social sciences in the 1960s that the
rehabilitation of human nature should have been
a task originally undertaken by entomologists.*

—Andrew Brown, *The Darwin Wars*

They are less than a millionth the size of a human, but taken in total, their mass on Earth would weigh about as much as all human beings. There are approximately 11,880 known species, making them the most common animal in the world. They contribute to the health of ecosystems with their symbiotic relationships with other species, by disposing of dead plant and animal material, and by moving soil and seeds. In Central and South America, one species actively cultivates fungi on fresh leaves carried into their underground chambers. Some protect "herds" of aphids or caterpillars in order to harvest their honeydew (a pleasant-sounding euphemism for "sweet liquid feces"), sometimes even taking them along when migrating to a new area. And the jaws of another snap shut at 8.5 meters a second—the fastest recorded movement of any anatomical structure.

**Erin
Wiegand**

....

WINTER 2007

illustration by Erin Siegal

Our "nature"
does not set us
apart from the ants and
termites, nor do similarities
link all of us, hand in claw,
in a miserable, determinist
chain gang, plodding
through life only to
survive and reproduce
as best we can.

The ant is a marvelous creature, by anyone's terms. But she is also responsible for provoking one of the greatest evolutionary debates of our time: How can animals evolve the capacity for altruism, self-sacrificial behavior to support one another?

For Charles Darwin, the survival and evolution of a species depended on the "fitness" of each of its members; that is, how well each individual was able to survive in its environment and successfully reproduce. Altruism, then, seems quite peculiar if one accepts Darwin's contention that success in passing on one's own genetic lineage to a new generation—at the expense of others, if necessary—is evolution's highest principle.

The ant was a particularly heavy puzzle for Darwin because of its stratified colonies, in which entire castes of worker ants are born without the ability to reproduce, foregoing their own chance at breeding in order to better support the queen and her offspring. How, Darwin wondered, could sterility be a trait passed through generations of ants if those that carry the gene do not themselves reproduce? How could a species be so successful, in evolutionary terms, when so many of its individual members sacrifice their own reproductive capacity? The question posed such a challenge, in fact, that he referred to it in 1859 as the "one special difficulty, which at first appeared to me insuperable, and actually fatal to my whole theory."

Though you wouldn't know it from contemporary "Darwin vs. God" debates, the theory of evolution does not begin and end with Charles Darwin—he was not the first to propose that species changed over time, and that animals (including humans) of today have ancestors that may have looked quite different. At the time Darwin developed his theories of "descent with modification" (his preferred term for evolution), it was already well-accepted that characteristics from a particular organism were passed down to their offspring—although the theories of the day favored the notion that such characteristics were developed in species based on how much they were "used," much like the way muscles become stronger the more they are worked. Darwin's contribution was his explanation of a process he called "natural selection." Particular traits—length of legs, body shape, cell structure—arise randomly in individuals within a species, and are then selected for in the process of evolution; that is, characteristics that are not conducive to an organism's "success" in a particular environment will eventually be weeded out because those that carry them will not survive long enough to reproduce and thus further the descent of those traits into the next generation.

Darwin's theory was not met with instant approval by his peers, and many of his colleagues argued that the notion of natural selection as the only agent of evolution was preposterous. Darwin, however, did not intend to suggest that natural selection was the only explanation for evolution—it was simply the most primary. As he wrote in the sixth edition of Origin of Species, in 1872, "My conclusions have lately been much misrepresented, and… I may be permitted to remark that in the first edition of this work, and subsequently, I placed in a most conspicuous position—namely, at the close of the Introduction—the following words: 'I am convinced that natural selection has been the main but not the exclusive means of modification.'" Evolutionary theorists since Darwin have suggested a number of other "means of modification," including mutation, abrupt environmental changes or disasters, and genetic drift (random changes in the frequency of genes within a population).

Natural selection has been widely interpreted as "the survival of the fittest," a term not actually used by Darwin, but coined by the philosopher Herbert Spencer. Thomas Henry Huxley—known to many as Darwin's "bulldog" for his staunch advocacy of natural selection theory—wrote that "from the point of view of the moralist the animal world is about on a level of a gladiator's show. The creatures are fairly well treated, and set to fight—whereby the strongest, the swiftest, and the cunningest live to fight another day." And then, of course, there's the poet Alfred Lord Tennyson's famous description of nature as "red in tooth and claw," which has been invoked time and again to explain the process of natural selection—despite the fact that he wrote those lines in 1850, nine years before the first publication of *Origin*.

For those who refuse to accept the more cutthroat and self centered institutions of human civilization as logical extensions of "human nature," the theory of natural selection has often inspired nothing so much as disgust. After all, if the law of nature is simply to favor those who are best able to compete and win, why should the rules be any different for humans than they are for bottle-nosed dolphins or prairie dogs?

But the notion that nature demands such selfish competition—and the way that notion has been used to justify capitalism, eugenics, and a host of other philosophies—stems from misunderstandings and willful ignorance of the actual conditions of nature as well as the actual meaning of "natural selection." Natural selection does not suggest that organisms duke it out in bloody battle to see who survives to propagate their lineage; rather, it means that those creatures best able to adapt to their particular environment (which could mean cooperation just as easily as competition) are the most likely to reproduce. Darwin himself (not to mention many scientists at the time and since) saw evidence of cooperation and mutual aid not only among members of the same species, but among different species. And as far

as altruistic behavior, one need look no further than the social insects for particularly dramatic displays of self-sacrifice for the good of the community.

As any amateur naturalist, weekend camper, or child with a large stick and a propensity for acts of destruction can tell you, ants, bees, and wasps all readily give up their lives to defend the nest against intruders: The honeybee's stinger attaches itself to an enemy's skin with fishhook-like barbs—and in order to sting, the bee essentially eviscerates itself. One species of African termite attacks via a secretion that congeals upon contact with air and entangles both termite and enemy (sometimes, these termites will work their muscles so strongly that they explode, spraying their secretion out in all directions). Fire ants, during times of flood or in order to cross a river, will form gigantic balls out of their own bodies—with the queen at the center—to ride the water in a "living raft," a suicidal act for those unfortunate enough to form its outer surface. And then there are those worker ants that troubled Darwin: enormous numbers born without the ability to reproduce, who instead assist the queen in rearing her offspring—an act of extreme altruism, in evolutionary terms.

The use of the term "altruism" to describe certain animal acts is, of course, not without its problems. Isn't altruism something unique to human beings, to a human consciousness and moral sense? But "altruism"—like "queen" or "worker," for that matter—is used within biology not to draw anthropomorphic connections between ant and human societies, but because it is the closest (and easiest) descriptor to something we can recognize in our own societies and social relations.

Still, there are those that argue that there is, in fact, no difference between insect altruism and human altruism, or, rather, that what passes for a noble, specifically human behavior is actually no different than the altruism at work in the ant colony or beehive. This was the belief of the Russian geographer and anarchist Peter Kropotkin, who sought to prove that cooperation was "natural" to humanity by demonstrating the same behavior in various animal species.

Kropotkin's theory, outlined most famously in his 1902 work *Mutual Aid,* was that those species which are "fittest" are actually those that cooperate, not those that compete:

> If we resort to an indirect test, and ask Nature: "Who are the fittest: those who are continually at war with each other, or those who support one another?" we at once see that those animals which acquire habits of mutual aid are undoubtedly the fittest. They have more chances to survive, and they attain, in their respective classes, the highest development of intelligence and bodily organization.

Kropotkin's observations, while focused on cooperation rather than altruism (cooperation does not necessarily involve the element of self-sacrifice found in altruism), contain the basis of the theory of group selection—that natural selection can operate at the level of the group as well as the level of the individual. Over a hundred years later, group selection remains one of the most controversial of several theories developed to explain altruism in evolutionary terms.

Group Selection

The British ecologist V. C. Wynne-Edwards suggested in 1962 that individuals might sacrifice themselves or reduce their own fertility when their immediate group faced food scarcity, in order to contribute to the overall health of the species. Such behavior might seem to be a trait natural selection would weed out, because any individual who undertakes an altruistic act is at an immediate disadvantage; within its group, it has a lower fitness than they do. But Wynne-Edwards argued that because it supported the fitness of the larger group (and therefore furthered the species when it otherwise might die out), natural selection would indeed favor such a trait.

Darwin had already conceded this point when it came to the social insects and particularly to humankind, observing that while altruists are more vulnerable to non-altruists on an individual level, groups of altruists are much better equipped to survive over groups of non-altruists. And when individual altruists interact primarily with each other rather than with non-altruists, they're better off than their non-altruistic neighbors. He muses in *The Descent of Man* that "although a high standard of morality [e.g., willingness to behave altruistically] gives but a slight or no advantage to each individual man and his children over the other men of the same tribe...[it] will certainly give an immense advantage to one tribe over another."

Evolutionary biologist David Sloan Wilson refers to a type of "naïve group selectionism" that did not account for within-group and between-group altruism. "Darwin saw the problem that altruism is vulnerable to selfish [individuals within a group], and that the evolution of altruism required a special explanation."

That special explanation eluded many group selectionists up through the 1960s, at which point the theory was widely rejected by the scientific community. "At the time," says Wilson, "group selection was rejected because it was theoretically impossible, there wasn't good empirical evidence, and there were better theories to explain it," he says. "[It] just didn't seem to work very well. And because people had been making 'for the good of the group' arguments, sloppy arguments, it seemed like a reasonable position."

Since the 1960s, Wilson says, all three points have been reconciled. And a growing group of evolutionary theorists (including Edward O. Wilson, the notable entomologist and founder of sociobiology) are now promoting a return to group selection as a framework with which to view altruistic behavior. "The broader scientific community thinks that group selection has been rejected," D.S. Wilson says. "but a little bubble [of scientists] is comfortable with it, and it's been growing and growing." However, group selection is still widely disputed as an explanatory model for altruism, despite its seemingly straightforward and uncomplicated nature. The controversy is largely based on the argument that every example of group selection can also be explained by another model focused even more on the individual—or more accurately, on that individual's genes.

Kin Selection

Modern genetics studies began in the 1860s, but the "Modern Synthesis" of natural selection theory and genetics was not complete until some 80 years later. (The term was coined by Julian Huxley—grandson of Darwin's "bulldog"—in 1942.) This new generation of evolutionary theorists proposed that the unit of selection was not the individual organism, but the gene. Natural selection, they argued, is not a simple matter of organisms trying to thrust as many of their own offspring as possible into the world—it's a matter of maximizing the reproduction of our own genes into future generations. And for that, we don't necessarily need the offspring to be our own.

This is the heart of the theory of "kin selection," which argues that animals are more inclined to help those that are closely related to them, because it ensures the survival of their own genetic material. And in situations where the best overall chance for genetic survival means the self-sacrifice of some members of the family (whether by their death or simply by their "choice" not to reproduce themselves), altruism emerges. (Darwin's explanation for altruistic behavior held some of the foundations of kin selection, as he suggested that if sterile ants contribute to the overall welfare of their fertile kin, they succeed in promoting a shared genetic heritage.) The real development of the theory of kin selection, popular legend has it, stems from an offhand remark by the English biologist J.B.S. Haldane, a rather dramatic character known for his enthusiastic participation in dangerous experiments such as drinking hydrochloric acid or breathing chlorine. While discussing natural selection in a pub, he is said to have scribbled some calculations on the back of an envelope and said, "I will lay down my life for two brothers or eight cousins." Because, of course, in evolutionary terms, it's just as worthwhile for his two brothers to live to reproduce—each of them carry half his genes, and each cousin a quarter of that. The story has been contested by the slightly less colorful evolutionary theorist W.D. Hamilton, who claims he came up with the original idea, and went on to publish the first mathematical formulas based on the concept.

Either way, the story—and the theory—would go on to help support the idea that selection operates at a purely genetic level, thus explaining altruistic behavior in cases where altruism supports the "kin" of the organism in question, which theoretically would share their genes. What kin selection postulates is that certain genes wired for altruistic behavior compel certain animals to act in ways that may endanger themselves, or diminish their own chance at reproducing, if (and only if) those acts help their close kin to reproduce, thus ensuring their own genetic "survival." As Richard Dawkins wrote in *The Extended Phenotype* (1982), rather than expecting to see animals always acting in what we perceive to be their best interest, we should realize that animals act "to maximize the survival of genes 'for' that behavior, whether or not those genes happen to be in the body of the particular animal performing it."

It may sound like a pretty strange explanation for altruistic behavior as humans understand it—especially considering the vast numbers of human beings that have given their lives for an abstract cause, throughout history—but when it comes to explaining behavior in other species, and particularly in the social insects, the theory of kin selection has had staggering success. Today, kin selection is widely accepted by scientists as the "answer" to Darwin's special difficulty.

But while some scientists believe the debate has long been put to rest (with kin selection emerging as the "victor"), others see it as far from settled.

According to David Sloan Wilson, W.D. Hamilton argued as early as 1975 that there exists a group selection dynamic within kin selection; or, that kin selection could, in fact, be seen as a kind of group selection. There are plenty of examples of extremely close kin—to the point where they might be called clones—that fail to develop the kinds of advanced social networks (or the altruism) seen in ants and other social insects. "It is neither necessary nor sufficient to have genetic relatedness," says Wilson. "It is important, but it is just one piece of a larger puzzle."

How is kin selection distinguished from group selection? It isn't always so clear-cut—especially because groups of individuals living together or very closely together tend to be genetically related to each other. It's further muddied by cases that can be easily interpreted in multiple ways, such as the behavior of *Acromyrmex versicolor*, a desert ant. Unrelated queens will form a group, but only one will forage for food, bringing back sustenance for the entire group. Her altruistic behavior—exposing herself to predators as well as doing the grunt work while her comrades rest—was evidence, many thought, of a situation where group selection could explain altruism where kin selection could not: while lowering her own individual "fitness" relative to others in her group, she increases the fitness of her group relative to other groups. But other researchers argued that because the other queens will not replace a forager who refuses to work—thus destroying the entire group—it is really in the forager's individual genetic interest to forage, making the behavior explainable under kin selection.

"Mathematically, they're not different models," says Hudson Kern Reeve, Associate Professor of Neurobiology at Cornell University. "They give you the same predictions about the conditions under which cooperation and altruism will evolve. They are just alternative pictures. The controversy now," he claims, "is over whether group selection is [a more] useful [theory than kin selection]."

Reciprocal Altruism

A third model is the theory of reciprocal altruism, which predicts that animals behave altruistically in situations where they can expect to be "compensated" for their actions, either immediately or in the future. But wouldn't natural selection favor those who were best able to exploit such altruism—to cheat? As it turns out, certain conditions are needed for reciprocity to work: Individuals need to have repeated interactions with each other, and there needs to be a system of retaliation against cheaters.

"The conditions that are needed for reciprocity to work are relatively uncommon in nature," says Hudson Kern Reeve. "Acts that seem to be reciprocity could very easily be simple mistakes of identification—animals that think the others are kin. A lot of people have argued that [true acts of reciprocity] are infrequent in nature, and we're biased because we're humans and it does apply to us."

But what does this distinction say about human behavior? Does our uniqueness require a separate theory to explain human morality—is our "altruism" somehow special, is it "real" where the altruism of insects is merely instinctual?

The Birth of Sociobiology

These questions, particularly regarding altruism (and particularly in the wake of the development of kin selection theory) laid the groundwork for the development of sociobiology in the late 1970s, a theory that suggested that the social behavior biologists had been observing in animals was not only the result of natural selection (altruism, for example, as a means of propagating one's own genetic line), but that such behavior could be studied in humans in much the same way.

Sociobiologists were certainly not the first to apply evolutionary theory to the social realm—and Darwin himself was heavily influenced by social philosophies in constructing his theories in the first place. As he wrote in his 1876 autobiography, it was Thomas Malthus' essay on population (suggesting that an ever-increasing population would eventually surpass food supply and lead to increasing struggle for scare resources) that provided the real spark for his theory.

But while Darwin refused to speculate on the meaning of natural selection for social and political life, others were more than happy to use the theory to prop up their arguments for competitive individualism and laissez-faire capitalism. The 19th century political theorist Herbert Spencer proposed that civilization is the direct result of the same evolutionary processes Darwin saw elsewhere in nature. Spencer and the "social Darwinists" who came after him (some have suggested "social Spencerists" would be more fitting) appropriated the term "natural selection" to mean an individual's personal struggle to "succeed," conflating "survival" with "dominance." (Other theorists, too, have applied evolutionary theory to human behavior—Kropotkin's mutual aid, for example, was used to justify a "natural" inclination towards anarchism; Marx saw in Darwin's theory a rejection of god that suited his own arguments quite well.)

Now, jump forward a hundred years or so to 1975, when E.O. Wilson's *Sociobiology: The New Synthesis* first rolled off the press. This mammoth work sought to give an exhaustive overview to social behavior in animals—including homo sapiens. Wilson believed that humans should be treated no differently than other species when interpreting behavior as the work of evolutionary selection, and in the infamous final chapter of the book came to such conclusions as "The flattened sexual cycle and continuous female attractiveness cement the close marriage bonds that are basic to human social life…" and "The building block of nearly all human societies is the nuclear family…during the day the women and children remain in the residential area while the men forage for game or its symbolic equivalent in the form of barter and money."

But while Wilson may have been less than feminist in some of his specific assumptions about "natural" human reproduction, bonding, and the activities of men and women, it was his larger point—that the roots of culture and behavior are biological—that caused an enormous stir and launched sociobiology as a new scientific discipline. Just a few months after the publication of *Sociobiology,* sixteen scientists (several of them Wilson's own colleagues at Harvard) launched an organized assault on sociobiology through the formation of a "Sociobiology Study Group," arguing that the theory was both scientifically unsound and politically dangerous. In a letter from the group to the *New York Review of Books,* they wrote that "Historically, powerful countries or ruling groups within them have drawn support for the maintenance or extension of their power from these products of the scientific community," and drew connections between sociobiology and the early 20th century policies of sterilization and eugenics. And even several years after that, while Wilson lectured to the American Society for the Advancement of Science in Washington, a group of protestors rushed the stage and dumped a pitcher of water over his head, presumably outraged at what they perceived to be his attempt to legitimize a racist, sexist status quo.

The backlash against sociobiology was marked by misunderstandings on both sides. Many of those angered felt that sociobiology was nothing more than a new incarnation of what they saw as "social Darwinism," and that Wilson was trying to make justifications for human behavior they found repugnant. Richard Lewontin, Steven Rose, and Leon J. Kamin wrote in their controversial 1984 book *Not in Our Genes* that sociobiology is a "reductionist, biological determinist explanation of human existence." They charged sociobiologists with the promotion of three dubious arguments: (1) that current (human) social relations are inevitable; (2) that such relations are the result of specific actions of genes; and (3) that these genes have been selected by evolutionary processes because the traits associated with them result in higher fitness for those that carry them.

Such arguments can indeed be found in quite a bit of sociobiological thinking, especially when related to differences between the sexes and races. But it should be acknowledged that the array of opinions on the matter of genes is quite diverse among sociobiologists and evolutionary psychologists (the field more commonly spoken of today that emerged from the sociobiology debate), and is far from settled. It's the non-scientific press that is largely to blame for the over-simplification of such ideas, and the propagation of such notions as "the free market is justified by natural selection" and "genes explain why we do what we do."

Still, the sociobiologists' critics were quite right in cautioning them in handling a thesis so eerily similar to the one put forth by the conservative right: that human nature is predetermined, and that sex or racial differences, familial structures, and putting our kin and ethnically related peers first are all parts of our heritage; that such behavior is not learned, but firmly ingrained in our genetic structure. This critique was dismissed by sociobiologists as an attempt to only engage in "politically correct" science—to limit their research to only what was uncontroversial and would not throw a wrench in their own political agendas.

What the sociobiologists also missed was the very legitimate concern that their interpretation of data and experiments was often (if not always) biased by culture and existing racist or sexist views. Indeed, it is quite hard to believe a study that describes a group of Chinese-American children as having "little intense emotional behavior" and "impassive facial expression[s]" (cited by E.O. Wilson in his book *On Human Nature*) to be unbiased.

What is "impassive and unemotional" to one researcher might be just as easily read as "calm and serene," "happy and content," or even "bored" by another. This, of course, is not just the case in studies involving humans. As the Darwinian philosopher Helena Cronin points out in her book *The Ant and the Peacock,* when talking of sexual selection among animals, it has become standard practice to refer to "coy" females and "eager" males. "I can't resist wondering," she writes, "what words would be used if the sex roles were reversed…. If males were choosy about mates, would they be 'coy'—or discriminating, judicious, responsible, prudent, discerning? (And…would females be 'eager'—or would they be 'wanton,' 'frivolous,' 'wayward,' 'brazen'?)"

Taking out the sociobiologists' extremes (arguments for differences in IQ being the result of race, for example) and the hostile accusations of their critics (of being no better than Nazi eugenicists, and the like), it seems that both parties actually share a lot of common ground. Both believe that the influence of natural selection in evolution is quite large, even if it isn't the only factor; environmental factors can shape evolution as well; biology does have some influence over our range of behaviors and activities (as Stephen Jay Gould points out, we wouldn't have developed agriculturally-based societies if we could photosynthesize); genes do not work on their own, but in interaction with other genes and their environment; and some features are selected, while others are "side effects."

And at least when it comes to altruism, the founder of sociobiology himself is the first to acknowledge the cultural foundations of its human expressions. "…The form and intensity of altruistic acts are to a large extent culturally determined," writes E.O. Wilson in 1978. "Human social evolution is obviously more cultural than genetic. The point is that the underlying emotion, powerfully manifested in virtually all human societies, is what is considered to evolve through genes."

In the debate over genetically vs. culturally produced behavior, it's also important to note that many prominent sociobiologists have taken pains to distinguish "is" from "ought"—that is, we cannot derive a code of ethics and

morals from the simple facts that determine our existence. E. O. Wilson writes
that "We are not compelled to believe in
biological uniformity in order to affirm
human freedom and dignity." Richard
Dawkins insists in a 1996 interview that
natural selection theory does not necessarily mean anything about how we
should structure society or economics:

In our political and social life we are
entitled to throw out Darwinism....
We might say: Yes, Darwinism is
true, natural selection is the true
force that has given rise to life, but
we, when we set up our political
institutions...are going to base our
society on explicitly anti-Darwinian
principles.... The only message
coming from evolutionary theory
is what actually happens in nature.
Now in nature it is true that, to some
extent, the strong and the most selfish
survive. But that is no message for
what we should do. We have to get our
"shoulds" and our "oughts" from some
other source, not from Darwinism.

But, as Lewontin et al argue, "the effective political truth...is that 'is' abolishes
'ought.'" If biology alone compels us to
perform certain behaviors, it's extremely
difficult to launch ethical judgments
against them. On the other hand, some
sociobiologists argue that it is precisely
because this is such a difficult task—over-
coming one's genetic heritage to act in
favor of a higher moral code—that it
is so important to recognize it. With-

out fully accounting for what we're up
against, we'll come up short every time.

Which leads us to the big question:
What is that "genetic heritage," our
"human nature?" Is it those traits that
are found throughout various populations and cultures to be dominant? Does
it leave any room for those that do not
conform to the picture? Are there any
elements that can be said to be universal?

We all need to eat, but we do not all
eat the same foods, nor can we all digest
the same foods. Humans all reproduce
sexually, but the raising of offspring
can vary from the nuclear to extended
family to adoption and artificial insemi
nation—and not all humans that can
reproduce choose to do so. All societies
have a division of labor, but this varies
widely both between cultures and within
them; there are always those that go
against the norm. Can those be said to be
elements of human nature? Or are they
strictly the dictates of human cultures?

Of course, the distinction between
behavior and character has varied significantly throughout human history.
Whether or not we perceive a person's
eyes as "blue" doesn't change (much)
over time or across cultures or depending on particular circumstances, but
whether or not behavior is "altruistic" certainly does. In the debate over
whether aggression or depression or
homosexuality is wired in our genes or
is the product of our environment, it's
worth noting that many of these "character traits" have only been recognized
in recent history. (Sex between two

people of the same gender, for example, has only recently become an indicator of a homosexual identity; throughout most of human history, it was something a person did, not who they were.)

Interestingly enough, the founder of sociobiology himself argues that, at least when it comes to altruism, our particularly human environments set us apart from other animals. E.O. Wilson writes in *On Human Nature*:

> Reciprocation among distantly related or unrelated individuals is the key to human society…The perfection of the social contract has broken the ancient vertebrate constraints imposed by rigid kin selection. Through the convention of reciprocation, combined with a flexible, endlessly productive language and a genius for verbal classification, human beings fashion long-remembered agreements upon which cultures and civilizations can be built.

According to Wilson, human altruism is not the same behavior that we find in the neuter ants and suicidal bees—through the "perfection of the social contract," humans are no longer subject to the same evolutionary laws as the rest of the animal kingdom. While "rigid" kin selection may explain the altruism of the social insects as a genetically-driven impulse, the altruism of humans is based on reciprocation and the creation of mutually-beneficial agreements.

Such an argument, though, is indicative of a troubling dualism that can be found within many theories of "human" and "animal" natures. As Stephen Jay Gould points out in his 1977 essay "So Cleverly Kind an Animal," such speculations usually involve attributing "negative" human qualities to some sort of brutish, animal past—such as aggression, selfishness, or infidelity—in an attempt to justify the existence of certain cultural attitudes that, most often, are under attack by those that find such ideas or institutions (patriarchy, racism, capitalism) unacceptable.

Altruism and kindness, on the other hand, are usually considered to be hallmarks of a particularly human moral order, those things that elevate the human animal above all other species. And such a belief

> …gains no justification from science [but] arises from such sources as the theology of the human soul and the 'dualism' of philosophers who sought separate realms for mind and body. It has roots in…our desire to view the history of life as progressive and to place ourselves on top of the heap (with all the prerogatives of domination). We seek a criterion for our uniqueness, settle (naturally) upon our minds, and define the noble results of human consciousness as something intrinsically apart from biology.

But as Hudson Kern Reeve notes, those "noble results" might not actually be that unique, nor the laws of nature all that brutish. "Humans…have underestimated the plasticity of other animals. My own work has shown that wasp societies appear to have evolved forms of cooperation that are highly flexible…. The harder we look at insect societies, the more it looks like a human society. There's been a massive movement away from looking at genetically hardwired behavior, not just in humans. In other words, anthropomorphism may be the appropriate stance."

If evolution were a predictable process, then it would be easy to see modern species as the mere product of natural selection, an inevitable outcome. But when you factor genetics into it, and base selection on the level of the gene—which is highly susceptible to mutation—you get variation, not predictability—as the rule. Between gene mutations (both random and the product of our environment or human interference through drugs or chemicals) and a constantly changing environment, it becomes clear that human—or animal behavior cannot be thought of as static, even within a single culture or location. As E.O. Wilson writes, "a correct application of evolutionary theory also favors diversity in the gene pool as a cardinal value."

The essence of nature, then, is variety. Indeed, selection can only work if there are different organisms to choose from—and the "fittest" of a species in one environment might not be the "fittest" in another, or in the same environment but at a different period in history. In applying natural selection theory to human social behavior, it's wrong to

assume that there is therefore an "innate" human nature. It is not the human that is fixed, but the process of selection.

Our "nature" does not necessarily set us apart from the ants and termites, nor do similarities between humans and insects link all of us, hand in claw, in a miserable, determinist chain gang, plodding through life only to survive and reproduce as best we can. If human society is, in fact, closely related to that of the ants and bees (and derived from the same evolutionary roots), this doesn't mean human beings are restricted to a rigid set of biologically-imposed rules, as we believe insects are—it might mean that we need to start re-evaluating how rigid those rules are for the insects. The selection of species does not compel us to "always compete" or "always cooperate," nor is one more "natural" than the other. Whether in the city or in the anthill, biological determinism is ultimately defeated by the astounding multiplicity of abilities and behaviors that are the reason, really, why we humans even bother theorizing about such matters in the first place.

Every Cockroach is Beautiful to its Mother

Ogni scarrafone é bello a mamma sua
–Neopolitan folk saying

This century's most famous cockroach is probably the bug in Franz Kafka's classic short story *The Metamorphosis*, about a man named Gregor Samsa, who awakens one morning to find himself turned into a giant insect, flat on his back, legs waving in the air. The change dooms Samsa to a lonely life on the margins, despised by his own family and eventually dying alone. Kafka strenuously denied that this bug was specifically a cockroach, believing that identifying any specific creature would weaken the story's power to play on readers' imaginations of whatever insect was most repulsive to them.

Kari Lydersen

WINTER 2007

Kafka's efforts to avoid specificity were largely in vain, however. For the vast majority of readers, that most repulsive of insects was, and steadfastly remains, the cockroach.

Which is a shame, really, since only a handful of the estimated 10,000 species of cockroaches—or *Blattarians,* originating from the Greek *blattae*—bother humans at all. The bulk of species are innocuous outdoors-dwellers who play a crucial role in pollinating plants, decomposing matter, and returning nutrients to the soil.

And even the infamous indoor pests—including the German, American, Oriental, brownbanded and smokeybrown roaches—aren't actually as filthy and disease-ridden as one might think. Scientists who know them well point out that they don't carry pathogens like houseflies do, and they are conscientious self-groomers, almost like cats.

But they hold a place in our collective psyche, or at least in the middle-class white American psyche, that evokes visions of filth, poverty, laziness, and general lapse of control. They are symbols of things we fear and loathe.

"People have a very gut reaction to cockroaches specifically," said Dini Miller, an entomologist at Virginia Tech who specializes in cockroaches. "If I go to a party and say I work with cockroaches, people immediately say, 'Oh my god.' Then they proceed to tell me at length about all their encounters with cockroaches."

Miller recalls horrifying her then-boyfriend's mother by accidentally releasing a cockroach in her house. (That relationship failed. She ended up marrying another cockroach scientist.)

A 1981 poll by the U.S. Fish and Wildlife Service named cockroaches as the country's most hated "pest," ahead of mosquitoes and rats. Twenty-five years later, that probably hasn't changed. But along with our hatred of cockroaches, we grant them grudging respect and admiration. They are survivors. They can eat almost anything (though they are reputed to abhor cucumbers) or go without food for weeks; they can survive in sealed containers or other harsh conditions; they have outwitted generations of exterminators. One clinically dispassionate 1957 study called "The Longevity of Starved Cockroaches" found that female American cockroaches could live 42 days on water alone, and most species of roach can survive for several weeks without food or water.

"They're incredibly well-designed animals, they've been around for hundreds of millions of years and their design hasn't changed much in that time," said science writer David George Gordon, author of the book *The Compleat Cockroach: A Comprehensive Guide to the Most Despised and Least Understood Creature on Earth.* "Pests are great at being generalists. [Cockroaches] can eat just about anything, so they don't have to worry if one particular food isn't available. They've been able to survive mass extinctions. They have all sorts of amazing sensory abilities. They can smell a molecule of water."

Cockroaches can also fully regenerate limbs and antennae. Their central nervous systems feature an early warning system utilizing remarkably sensitive hairs, called *cerci*, each with its own nerve fiber connecting directly to their legs (not their brains), that serve as motion detectors. The phenomenon of roaches scattering at the flick of a light switch is widely misunderstood: When entering a room, a person sets air in motion, and the cerci react to that moving air instantaneously, sending their owners scattering at speeds of up to 20 body lengths per second (comparable to 100 miles an hour for a human). Cockroaches possess another quality that quite a few humans and scientists long for: In times of stress, females can reproduce on their own. Only female offspring are produced in this process, and blattarians may only persist in this for one or two generations, but the staggering evolutionary advantages are obvious.

According to Richard Schweid, author of the wildly entertaining book *The Cockroach Papers: A Compendium of History and Lore,* fossils of cockroaches date back to at least the Carboniferous period, or roughly 325 million BC This means that they predated dinosaurs by more than 150 million years, and humans by more than 300 million. "Whereas every other insect fossil from that epoch shows an animal that is now extinct," writes Schweid, "the cock-

roaches found buried deep in the earth of the Lower Illinois coal measure are little changed from those found today in houses on top of that same ground."

Cockroaches are true hustlers and underdogs, living by their wits on the leftovers of society. Human underdogs and oppressed people have often taken them as their mascot, or defiantly appropriated the label that others might have cast on them in scorn. Oscar Zeta Acosta's book, *The Revolt of the Cockroach People,* about Chicano activism in LA in the 1970s, became a touchstone of the growing Chicano power movement. The "cockroaches" were Chicano activists who fought police brutality, corruption, and racism in the Catholic Church and oppression in general.

The famous Spanish and Mexican song "La Cucaracha" has been a satirical anthem and popular drinking song throughout the ages, with a myriad of verses added and revised to reflect the times. It is said the song came to Mexico from Spain in the 1800s. It is most closely associated with Mexican revolutionary Pancho Villa, either as a reference to Villa himself or his temperamental coach, which often broke down (*"La cucaracha, la cucaracha, ya no puede caminar"*—"the cockroach can't walk").

One of the verses, saying the cockroach can't walk because he doesn't have marijuana to smoke, is also said to be a derogatory reference to dictator Victoriano Huerta, a notorious drunk and ardent lover of marijuana. So even within the history of the song, the cockroach had both negative and positive connotations; either a reviled corrupt leader or a heroic underdog.

An intriguing insect from cultural and biological points of view, cockroaches also present something of a socioeconomic issue. In keeping with stereotypes, they are indeed a bane primarily of the poor. They thrive in high density housing with sub-par sanitation, meaning housing projects or tenement apartments with overcrowding, faulty plumbing, and infrequent garbage pickup are perfect habitats.

"Middle-class white America does not realize there are a lot of people in the U.S. who live with an excess of 30,000 cockroaches in their apartment," said Miller, whose job includes preventing cockroach infestations and getting rid of them with minimal pesticide use.

"These guys have been attacked with every poison human beings can come up with," said Miller. "Because of that, their system of metabolizing pesticides has become very good. Those roaches who could break down pesticides survived, ones who couldn't did not. So now we have these roaches that can take a lot of toxin and don't die."

John Fasoldt, owner of United Exterminating Company in New Jersey for 45 years, explains that the current method of extermination uses bait combining corn syrup and hydramethylnon, a relatively mild poison which is not considered to pose a risk to humans or animals. Cockroaches lured into eating the bait die within several days.

In the past, more toxic chemicals like arsenic were commonly used to poison them, with sometimes disastrous results for small children and pets who also managed to eat the poison.

"[This] bait poisons not only the roach, but everything about the roach, so when he contacts his friends and relatives, they die too," said Fasoldt. "Roaches eat dead roaches and roach droppings, and they also transfer liquids between them, so that kills them."

But natural selection has favored roaches who don't like the flavor of bait. Since a German roach's egg sac holds 52 baby cockroaches, reproduction and hence natural selection happen at a rapid clip.

"The more stuff we throw at them the tougher they get," said Miller. "It's no accident they've been around [350] million years. They can take a lot of abuse."

Cockroaches don't just appear out of the blue—they have to be physically transported into a location. But once they are there they are extremely hard to get rid of. In a multi-unit dwelling, if even one unit fails to exterminate them, they will keep reconquering the whole building.

"Your kitchen is connected to Mrs. Smith's, hers to Mrs. Jones above her," Fasoldt said. "They'll get under the kitchen sink and crawl along the pipes into the bathroom, the basement, the laundry."

While, contrary to popular belief, cockroaches are not major vectors of infectious disease, they are a major cause of health problems for low income urban dwellers.

Various studies have found cockroaches to be the number one cause of asthma symptoms in children in low-income inner-city neighborhoods, where millions of children and their caregivers suffer emergency room visits, missed school, lost sleep, and reduced physical activity because of debilitating wheezing and asthma attacks. Many people are allergic to proteins found in cockroaches' shells, saliva, feces, and blood, which become part of household dust as roaches molt and die.

The National Institutes of Health have estimated that 10 to 15 million people suffer roach-induced allergies and asthma symptoms. A study of more than 900 children by the National Institute of Environmental Health Science and other partners published in 2005 found that a majority of "inner-city" homes in Chicago, New York City, and the Bronx had cockroach allergen levels high enough to trigger asthma symptoms. Exposure was particularly prevalent in high-rise apartments, where public housing residents and other low-income people are likely to live. This confirms 1992–1993 research by the ongoing National Cooperative Inner-City Asthma Study in which 36.8 percent of inner-city kids were allergic to cockroach allergens and 50 percent of children's bedrooms had high levels of cockroach allergen. Since low-income people most likely to be exposed to cockroaches are also likely to lack health insurance, they often don't get treatment for chronic asthma and may suffer permanent lung damage from ongoing untreated symptoms. Cleaning frequently can reduce kids' exposure to cockroach allergens, but it is an ongoing and losing battle since roaches molt, reproduce, and die so quickly and move freely between apartments in multi-unit buildings.

"They shed their skin seven times and they poop all the time," said Miller. "This is a very dry fecal pellet, with the consistency of sand. [*blattarians never waste or excrete water, their most precious resource–ed.*] It contains tons of allergens, and in winter you have closed apartments with the heat turned on, so the stuff dries out, circulates in the air, and people are breathing it like crazy."

Interestingly, an allergy triggered by roaches can extend to similar proteins in the exoskeletons of invertebrates like lobster and shrimp, making it dangerous for sufferers to eat those dishes.

Miller notes that German cockroaches, the inch-long pests most commonly infesting human homes, evolved in tandem with people, going all the way back to prehistoric times. Of the 150-or-so species considered pests, less than half are indoor insects, and there are only about five species including the German and American roach (also sometimes called the palmetto bug) that are ubiquitous around the world. Some of their lesser-known brethren dwell exclusively in caves in the Philippines or Puerto Rico; others live in South American jungles.

"For people to say they don't like cockroaches is like me saying I don't like teenagers because I met three of them I don't like," said Gordon.

The largest cockroach, from Australia, is about six inches long and can have a one-foot wingspan. The smallest is about 4 millimeters long, and lives in the nests of leafcutter ants in North America, eating the fungus the ants cultivate.

Gordon, who collects cockroaches from every place he visits and pins them on a display board, was thrilled to buy an Australian Giant Burrowing Cockroach at a recent insect fair in LA.

"People will say 'look at that beautiful beetle,' then when you say 'that's not a beetle it's a cockroach,' they'll say 'Ew!' and back away," said Gordon. "There are some cockroaches that are really beautiful, but as soon as you say their name they become gross. It's learned behavior."

He cites a study reported by USDA researchers in 1992 in which children up to age four had no problem drinking a glass of milk with a rubber cockroach in it, but after that they learned from parents to be disgusted by the insect.

Today, one species of cockroach is actually a highly prized pet and classroom educational aid: the Madagascar Hissing Cockroach, Various websites offer "Hissers" for sale, along with special hisser diets and habitats. The going rate is $30 for four adults and a habitat.

Hissers are even being trained as potential miliary operatives. Scientists at the University of Michigan have been advancing work originally begun in Japanese bio-robot experiments, testing whether hissing cockroaches may be able to carry microcameras or voice transmitters, either for surveillance purposes or as "ideal" scouts—given their resistance to radiation—to assess the damage of a nuclear disaster.

Cockroaches can indeed survive about 10 times more radiation than a human being: According to a 1963 study, German cockroaches can endure 9,600 rads over 35 days, compared to the fatal levels of 1,000 rads over two weeks for humans.

However, cockroaches are not unique among insects or other organisms in their resistance to radiation. A fall 2001 article in the journal *American Entomologist* notes that other insects, including fruit flies and grain borers, can actually survive more radiation than cockroaches. A pink bacterium that smells like rotten cabbage can even survive 1.5 million or more rads, compared to the roach's 10,000. But flies and bacteria just don't fit the public's image of what the ultimate survivor should look like.

"Experiments have shown that butterflies, rabbits, and goldfish can also survive high amounts of radiation, but you don't hear about them surviving a nuclear war," noted Gordon. "There's this horror we have of leaving the world to be inhabited by cockroaches. The lowly, most horrible things will be the ones ruling the earth after we blow it up."

Madness and Mass Society

Pharmaceuticals, Psychiatry, and the Rebellion of True Community

Brian Awehali
INTERVIEWS

Bruce Levine

WINTER 2006

Author and clinical psychologist Bruce E. Levine wants to tell you that depression, discontent, and a whole raft of diagnosed mental illnesses are natural responses to the oppression of "institutional society." In his books, *Commonsense Rebellion*, and *Surviving America's Depression Epidemic,* Levine contends that the vast majority of mental disorders are, to put it simply, profit-driven fabrications with no established biochemical or genetic causes, and that anger, depression, and dissent are both normal and deeply healthy. Instead of popping pills, he argues, we need something he calls "true community."

It's in the interest of drug companies—and psychiatry, because all they do is prescribe drugs pretty much nowadays—to view everything as a disease that needs drugs. It's also in the interest of a society that doesn't want to spend much money or resources on populations that aren't fitting into the standardized order of things.

Bruce, you're a critic of both psychiatry—the medical science of identifying and treating mental illness with drugs—and psychology—the study of human behavior, thought, and development. Are there substantial differences between the two?

When I first started out as a psychologist in the late 1970s and early 1980s, it was fairly commonplace to dissent from psychiatry—that's why people became psychologists. They saw the pseudo-science of not only the treatments but of the *Diagnostic and Statistical Manual* (DSM) itself. Unfortunately, over the years, psychology itself has slowly aped psychiatry, and there isn't that sharp a distinction between the two anymore. The American Psychological Association

(APA)—the professional group for psychologists—now fights for prescription rights for psychologists. So I guess any psychologist who maintains a position that depression isn't primarily an innate biochemical disease, and that the DSM is a nonscientific instrument of diagnosis, is a dissident!

I should say that back in the 1970s and 1980s, before psychiatrists had the backing of the drug companies, they had very little power. In fact, they were falling apart, as evidenced by so many movies that were making fun of them, like *One Flew Over the Cuckoo's Nest*—which could never come out today. But back in those days, when [psychiatrists] weren't in bed with the drug companies and didn't have much political power, you saw movies like that come out. Now, psychiatrists have the media power; they're able to describe the playing field of the controversy.

Let me ask you a blunt question, first: Do you think there's ever any basis for diagnosing someone as mentally ill?

Well, certainly there are things that can happen in your brain to make you feel crazy. But when we're talking about things like, for example, attention deficit disorder [ADD], or depression, most of these behaviors are problematic to society. And they're too easily being classified in the same category as cancer and diabetes.

Let's just take one of the more obviously comical diagnoses, something fairly recent, like oppositional defiance disorder [ODD]—that one really makes a whole lot of things really clear.

[Interviewer convulses with laughter. Dr. Levine waits patiently while interviewer composes himself.]

I mean, oppositional defiance disorder is a "disease" in the *DSM*, and it's not something that's arcane; it's something that's being used frequently. It's a diagnosis given to kids whose symptoms are often arguing with adults, refusing to comply with adults, and basically being a pain in the ass with adults. And once you declare it a disease, of course, you move into

chemical treatments or behavioral manipulations. I think for the majority of folks out there, not just anti-authoritarian types, they have the same reaction you did: You've got to be kidding. Don't [they] realize that kids rebel against authority? So there you have an obvious example.

And then you move over to something like attention deficit hyperactivity disorder [ADHD] or ADD, for which there are no biochemical markers, of any kind. None. If you have any doubts about that, just go to your doctor and say you think your kid has ADD, and ask her about the biochemical markers—she'll say that there are none. It's all behavioral symptoms that are used to diagnose it.

In the 1970s and early 1980s, a lot of people were looking for other explanations for why people were having problems, or creating problems for others. And in that era, prior to the drug company takeover, there were a lot more intelligent ideas. ADD/ADHD didn't exist in the first *DSM* that came out in 1952, but I'm sure if it had been around, folks like Eric Fromm would have been talking about it as a form of passive rebellion.

Oppositional defiance disorder is an obvious active rebellion, but most kids don't have the courage, or they're in situations where for them to actively rebel means they'll get crushed—so they rebel passively. They go to a classroom and they stop paying attention; they just blow things off. Is it because they have no capacity to pay attention? No. And the research even shows that when you put these same kids in a situation where they're either interested in the material or they've chosen the material, or it's novel to them, all of a sudden these so-called ADHD kids can pay attention!

And that's what I try to explain to folks: If you have diabetes or cancer, and all of a sudden you're having a good time, the disease doesn't go away. How can something be a disease when you put somebody in a different situation, and the "disease" goes away? That should tell you something.

But it's in the interest, obviously, of drug companies—and psychiatry, because all they do is prescribe drugs pretty much nowadays—to view everything as a disease that needs drugs. It's also in the interest of a society that doesn't want to spend much money or resources on populations that aren't fitting into the standardized order of things.

One interesting aspect of this is that, more and more, it's not just kids of color, but even suburban white Anglo-Saxon Protestant kids who can't fit into the standardized order.

I was going to ask you if you think the net for mental illness has gotten wider.

Absolutely. There's a certain karma in this for the dominant culture. For years they've tried to make all kinds of people in non-dominant cultures fit into a rigged, standardized system, and all kinds of rebellion went on. Rebellion through truancy, or substance abuse—and they pathologized this, criminalized that. But once that net was cast, it eventually starting catching lots of their kids.

It's interesting. It's like the machine was built, and then the machine has to feed itself. It seems like it's sort of a runaway institutional process—

Yeah, that's a good metaphor. A lot of folks like Lewis Mumford and Kirkpatrick Sale have talked a lot about our machine-worshipping culture. If a society worships the machine and technology more than it does life and diversity, then you understand that the goal of that society is to become more machine-like, more standardized. Which means you're trying to create a society in which everyone fits into the same box. And once you do that, you're going to find more people not fitting in, and then you have—and this is a real problem of psychiatry, as far as I'm concerned—then you have these psychiatrists who come along and, instead of saying there's a problem with this kind of machine-worshipping society, they say that there's a problem with all these people not fitting in. They've got this disease, or this disorder.

In your book, *Commonsense Rebellion,* you have a whole chapter devoted to mass society and mass living. I wonder if you could talk a little about that.

Well, it's important for folks to have a historical perspective on the way human beings have lived for the vast majority of our history, and to think of how differently we've been living since the Industrial Revolution. For 99% of human history, people were living in non-mass societies—we were living in small groups. We were living in situations where, for the most part, we knew everybody around us. We had bands within tribes, less than 500 or 1,000 folks, and people had a greater sense of autonomy, because what they said and what they cared about actually had some political impact.

Whereas, today—here in the U.S., for example—what the hell does your average person do? Every four years they get to vote between two people they have no respect for? You may want to convince yourself you're living in a democracy because you get to vote, but on a more core psychological level, you're one of 300 million who are voting for [one of] two people who are decided for you by corporate society! So on some level, you know you have no impact; you know you have no power. It's just common sense that in a more humanly scaled society [Kirkpatrick Sale's term, from his book *On a Human Scale*] you're going to have a sense of greater potency, of greater power. And a sense of empowerment is a huge antidote to almost any emotional problem. That's common sense!

Another huge antidote to emotional difficulty is community. People who have a genuine community have fewer emotional difficulties. And "genuine community" is an important term. Oakland, for example, is not a community—it's a location. Real community means face-to-face emotional and economic interdependence. In a real community, people decide for themselves what their problems are, and they themselves implement solutions, as opposed to handing them over to distant authorities.

In realistic terms, what do you think people might do to try and build real community?

Well, a lot of people are isolated, and they have all kinds of emotional difficulties, whether it's depression or substance abuse. They obsess on their disconnectedness, or they don't even get that far, they're just getting drunk all the time. In the face of this mass society, people feel powerless. What's the point of trying to get this guy you think is innocent out of jail; what's the point of doing anything? You're dealing with such a power that it feels impossible to accomplish anything. One of the things I try to tell folks is that even if you don't succeed, when you have a cause you believe in, you get obsessed with what you're trying to accomplish—and even if you don't succeed, you're mutually supporting each other emotionally, possibly even economically. And you keep yourself sane.

Earlier you mentioned psychiatry's merger with Big Pharma. Can you say more about that?

The merger continues between psychiatry and big pharmaceutical: Big Pharma contributes money to their journals; they contribute money to the continuing education of psychiatrists.

There was a story recently in the *Boston Globe* about how Big Pharma—not just psychiatric drug companies, but all pharmaceutical companies—was contributing a significant amount of money to Harvard Medical School. If you go around medical schools, these drug rep people are hovering around mailboxes there. Now, if you were in marketing and sales, you would ask: Who do we want to feel great about us and our product? You want the general public, but you definitely want all these doctors to feel really great about you. You're going to do everything you can possibly get away with legally—and sometimes they do things that are actually illegal.

They're very aggressive. Every once in a while they go over the top, like Prozac maker Eli Lilly did in Florida, where they actually mailed out free samples of their products, including to one 16-year-old boy who had never been on any kind of a drug or antidepressant.

All of that said, I think it would be a mistake for folks to view pharmaceutical companies as being any different from any other companies. They're all boringly the same: Their goal is to do whatever they can to increase market share, and make money. Right now, Big Pharma is contributing about 80% to Republicans and about 20% to Democrats—they're just sort of covering their bets. They're basically seeking control over government agencies that are critical of their goals, like the FDA or the National Institute of Mental Health.

For example, the Bush family has a long connection to one drug company in particular, Eli Lilly, but they're actually connected to a lot of drug companies. Down there in Texas, they started this program for mental health screening, and you're going to hear more and more about that as a national issue.

It's schools screening for mental illness the same way they do for vision or hearing, right?

Yeah. Once you buy the idea that mental illness is an illness like any other, then it makes a certain sense—it's just like a kid with bad eyesight who can't see the blackboard, or a kid with bad hearing.

The next step is, why don't we have this in all the schools? At a very early age, we could get to that ADD or ODD or depressive kid, before it gets out of hand. For a lot of the general public, that sounds reasonable, because they don't know that unlike problems with vision or hearing, which are very reliably scientifically diagnosed, these things are very subjective—and they lead to treatments that are ineffective and dangerous.

Of course, the pharmaceutical companies are throwing money at mental health screening. This would be a dream come true for them, if everybody was being screened for it, because the more you're getting screened for it, the more folks are getting diagnosed with diseases, and they're going to be put on drugs. So it's more money for Big Pharma. They want the whole world to get screened. And if the world gets crazier, there are going to be more and more people with problematic behaviors. There will be more and more depressed kids, kids who aren't paying attention, et cetera, and that's a larger and larger consumer base for Big Pharma.

You've written about some World Health Organization findings comparing the treatment and prognoses for recovery in so-called underdeveloped nations to those in the U.S. and other "first world" countries.

Yes, this is a hugely important story. In two different studies, the WHO took a look at psychoses and recovery rates in "underdeveloped" societies—India, Colombia, and Nigeria were three of the countries classified as underdeveloped—and compared them to "developed" societies. What they discovered was that the recovery rates in "underdeveloped" countries were twice as high as in the U.S..

The obvious areas of speculation for me are in the two big differences between the countries studied. One: They're not drugging everybody there on a long-term basis. In the U.S., when somebody is classified with a psychosis like schizophrenia, for example, that's considered an incurable disease. You have to be on medication for life. At least, that's more or less the party line of the American Psychiatric Association. And that's not true in the other countries the WHO studied.

But the other huge factor that seems obvious to me is that in those other societies, there's much more direct community support, and there's more family involvement. One person from Colombia was telling me this story about a relative who "flipped out." When this relative came out of the hospital, instead of going back to their family, with whom they had flipped out, they went to another relative's home.

For organizations like the National Alliance for the Mentally Ill, that solution would be heresy, because a lot of what they're all about is: It's not the family's or parents' fault. And that helps them team with the drug companies. They'd have you believe it's all a biochemical imbalance.

So is the logical endpoint of your positions that modern mass society is bad for people's mental health?

Our current atomized society is definitely bad for quite a lot of people. There are many pro-depression, and pro-psychosis aspects of our culture, but the breakdown of extended families and the relative lack of community are probably the two greatest factors.

What are you working on now?

With a lot of talks I gave about *Commonsense Rebellion,* I felt myself needing to cheerlead more than to inform. So over the last year or two I've been working on a book about depression. And the specific components of how you can get your act together: generally, issues of how you build up morale and heal your wounds so you don't engage in compulsive behaviors. That's what I've been doing: trying to give an alternative to depressed and anti-authoritarian people who don't believe in the mumbo-jumbo of psychiatry, but who also realize that [psychology's] cognitive-behavior therapy is a generally weak alternative.

What are the solutions? You've talked about people increasing their participation in "real" community, but what does that look like?

Part of what you're trying to do, on as many levels as possible, is reconnect yourself to yourself and to life around you. That's what mass industrial society has disintegrated. It's hugely important for folks to recognize that there's some degree of autonomy that they need to have in their lives, some kind of control.

I think a lot of what gets people really down are economics. The jobs that they work. The struggle to make money in this culture—let's face it, most of American society is working meaningless, crap jobs. I think part of what people have to do is forgive themselves for being in jobs that are meaningless, and not making much money, and think slowly about how they can move towards finding some meaning, finding some community, and doing something they really care about. As they move into that process, they might be surprised that, along with some other folks, they might be able to make enough money to survive. Then you've really beaten the system. Not many pull it off, but it's something to aspire to.

The Politics of Poop
Against the modern flush toilet and sewage system

22"

16"

20"

15"

10"

13"

Humor
Team

WINTER 2007

In the beginning, there was poop. When a person needed to relieve herself, she would simply walk away from a commonly used area and do the deed. As population density increased in certain areas, villages formed, and societies grew, human waste began to present a problem. Rather than pausing to consider the wisdom of such population density, people invented sewage systems, and eventually the toilet. In fact, it may come as little surprise to some that the British were the first to popularize the modern toilet, in 1850.

F.A. Hornibrook, a tireless anti-constipation activist who wrote a book entitled *The Culture of the Abdomen,* had one of the more succinct summations of the flush toilet: "It would have been better that the contraption had killed its inventor before he launched it under humanity's buttocks."

The average toilet wastes 3.3 gallons of drinking-quality water per flush; the average American will flush about 5.2 times daily, annually using 6,263 gallons of water to wash away 1,300 pounds of shit. When nearly half a billion people face shortages of potable water, and with estimates that by 2025 one in every three people will live in a country lacking an adequate supply of freshwater, using the next century's unquestionably most valuable resource for the purpose of flushing our feces borders on the obscene.

The problems with modern toilets are not just ecological. Though it may conjure a disgusting spontaneous vision for some readers (you have been warned), sitting to do your duty is really like trying to push shit through a kinked garden hose. Our bodies just weren't meant to do it; the squatting position used by humanity for millennia—and still used by a good two thirds of the world—is much easier on the body, faster, and more complete. It protects sensitive nerves and muscle tissue from becoming stretched and damaged. It relaxes the puborectalis muscle, which actually chokes the rectum when we sit down to do our business. Perhaps

rectum-choking is the kind of thing you enjoy. But it's safe to assume that most of us prefer not to be clogged with what we ritually choose to dispose of. "It is no overstatement to say that the adoption of the squatting attitude would in itself help in no small measure to remedy the greatest physical vice of the white race, the constipation that has become a contentment," the ever-colorful F.A. Hornibrook said of the matter.

Modern sewage systems have several other pernicious side effects. For one thing, they encourage the notion that waste is simply disposed of, flushed, or sent "away." Since that's arguably one of the ideas most central to capitalistic overproduction, overconsumption by design and all-around ecological assholishness, it seems fair to say the sewage system qualifies as A Bad Idea. Sewers also create breeding grounds for bacteriological pathogens. They're expensive. They've been known to produce grotesquely large alligators. They are also charged with the fairly gross task of extracting drinking water from that which has been shat in.

Although this is a mercilessly short visitation of the topic, let's skip a few linear niceties and cut to the chase: Taken in sum, the reasonable conclusions about the flush toilet and modern sewage systems are deeply ironic. In attempting to make our waste go "away," we ensured that not only would it stick around, it would choke us in a labyrinth of pipes, drains, and valves we built for it. And we did it all with oh-so-civilized looks of constipation on our faces.

Amenities

True, it's close proximity to my firm made it a nice apartment, but I still drove the five blocks to work. True, it had sweeping views of bay and mountain, though I quickly became indifferent to the leering presence of bay and mountain. True, my new home—an older renovated building downtown, a genuine artist's loft—was expensive, but I had the money. If asked, I would admit to some guilt about displacing the genuine artists who had lived there, but no one ever asked. I felt bad about the economics of place, but the apartment came with a washer and dryer and old world charm and sometimes a washer and dryer with old world charm speaks louder than economics. In truth, I laid out $1600 a month for an aura of bohemia coupled with a washer and dryer.

Gregory Hischak

WINTER 2001

As a nod to its more left bank past, and to alleviate some of the bad feng shui that came with gentrification, the property management company left an actual artist in each of the units.

Fourteen-foot exposed brick walls, floor to ceiling windows and genuine paint-splattered hardwood floors. As a nod to its more left bank past, and to alleviate some of the bad feng shui that came with gentrification, the property management left an actual artist in each of the units.

A small artist, not established.

Early one Saturday morning I was shown an available unit by a portly shifty-eyed woman in a magenta pantsuit named Claudia. Proudly selling the unit's numerous amenities, she finally brought me into the kitchen, pointing out the disposal, the self-cleaning oven, the built-in microwave/bread maker and, curled up under the sink, stubble-chinned and corduroyed, the artist that came with the artist's loft. As soon as Claudia opened the cupboard the artist sleepily unwrapped himself from around the disposal's pipemetal entrails and rolled over onto his side, hurriedly averting his face from the early glare of northern exposure.

"Your artist," Claudia the manager said, smiling perkily.

"Very nice," I said, "He seems a bit sluggish, though."

"It's early."

"What's his medium?'

"Mostly figurative work in oils."

"And there's off-street parking?"

"Of course."

"I'll take it."

* * *

I moved into my genuine artist's loft with my genuine artist the following week. I made it clear to my artist that he was free to move about the apartment while I was gone, and he could help himself to whatever hummus and grapes I left in the fridge but he could not have friends over. No collaboration. I told my artist I was planning a small dinner party soon and wanted a couple of in-progress works scattered about the place.

"I've completed a series of zinc plate etchings, actually," my artist said.

"I want oils. Unfinished oils, got it? And if I catch you doing zinc plate etchings on my couch your ass is down in the storage locker, right?"

The artist nodded.

I liked my apartment. I liked impressing guests with the industrial flavor of the secured entry lobby, the quiet urbane roar of the carpeted lift, the motion-sensor tracklighting activated when stepping inside the front door revealing sunken hardwood floors and casually arranged issues of *Art in America,* and squatting under a potted ficus, my artist. Laying down his oil pastels, my artist would quietly explain to my guests his work-in-progress. After a little bemused banter and our vague nods of encouragement, my artist would crawl under the sink as my guests and I continued on with chilled wine and lemon tarragon chicken.

* * *

The lawyer in the unit across the hall had a bronze caster. The next door unit came with a mono print artist. There was an attractive software consultant in 306 who frequently walked her artist outside the building.

"Organic abstractionist," she answered when I stopped once to make small talk, scratching her artist behind its ears.

"Mine is doing figurative work in oils mostly."

"How nice. Do you have a washer and dryer too?"

"Absolutely."

* * *

I returned home late one Sunday after a long weekend of stock speculation to find a 5" x 8" sheet of kraftpaper covering the kitchen floor—my artist squatting in the middle sweeping a thick gray charcoal stick from side to side across it.

"It's an atonal landscape exploring notions of place and identity," the artist explained when I asked him how he thought I was going to get to my microwave/breadmaker. It annoyed me that he was discussing his work without there being any dinner guests present.

"Save it," I said, scuffing at the corner of his work with my Gucci. "I want you under the sink."

"The monochromatic palette suggesting an emotional or moral isolation—"

"What part of Under The Sink didn't you understand?"

My artist sighed and began putting away his charcoals.

"You don't like me, do you?" he asked quietly as he pulled the cabinet shut behind him.

* * *

The software consultant in 306 had her organic abstractionist run away one morning while being walked. Ducking down an alley while she returned a video, it proved not to be an isolated incident. Shortly afterwards, the performance artist in 112 ran amuck, filling the unit with toast. The glassworker in 314 started a small fire and ruined a new set of curtains. The artist in 505 was twice caught drawing its tenants in the shower. After about three months of sporadic oils and charcoal landscapes my artist started going on the fritz as well. He stopped working and sat brooding—staring at the sprinkler valves in the ceiling for hours at a time.

"Paint something, dammit," I said.

"I can't."

"I'll let you collaborate with the jewelry artist in 211." My artist shook his head.

"I don't think so."

* * *

I left M&Ms on the coffee table which my artist finished off—but no works in-progress appeared. When guests came over my artist was surly and wouldn't discuss the impressionist show that everyone wanted him to talk about. I whacked him with a rolled up *Wall Street Journal*—but no art. I called Claudia the manager and complained that my artist wasn't working and she came over. Squatting under the counter with a flashlight for several minutes, Claudia finally rose, turned to me and shook her head.

"I have an installation artist I could bring down from 520."

"Nothing else in oils?"

"There's an allegorical landscapist on the first floor, but I think it's acrylics."

"I'm going to have to talk to the property managers."

"Suit yourself, but we're talking about artists here. They aren't covered in the lease."

I let Claudia leave with my artist. Standing alone near the floor to ceiling windows, I observed the play of light and shadow across the surface of the bay before closing the curtains so I could make calls without distraction. Markets were opening in Tokyo.

There was a butt of a charcoal stick sitting on my *Vanity Fair.* My artist's charcoal. I picked it up and examined it for a few minutes—absent-mindedly scrawling across the top of my daytimer while waiting for my call to go through. I drew a matchstick-like swingset, and on its top crossbar I drew a large black bird—a crow. When I finally set the charcoal stick down, an oily smudge was left across my index finger and thumb that would prove to be difficult to wash off.

The next week my washer and dryer crapped out on me.

"Black Accountant," oil on canvas by Don Van Vliet (AKA The Artist Formerly Known as Captain Beefheart) See: www.beefheart. com/runpaint/index.html

The Missionary Position
Mother Teresa in Theory and Practice

Danny Postel INTERVIEWS

Christopher Hitchens

FALL 1998

B efore her death in 1997, Roman Catholic nun Mother Teresa was, according to many polls, the most respected woman in the world. Her international fame as an advocate for the poor and a selfless servant of humanity was all but universal.

Too universal, for as Christopher Hitchens' book, *The Missionary Position: Mother Teresa in Theory and Practice* (Verso) makes abundantly clear, the gap between her reputation and her actions was dramatic. News media generally failed to investigate or publish criticism of her, despite an abundance of fodder for investigation. In this interview, Hitchens touches on several of the most damning critiques to be made of Mother Teresa and of sacred cows in general.

What exactly inspired you to write a book about Mother Teresa?

I went to Calcutta a few years ago. There was a general election in India, and I was actually making a documentary about a fraudulent cult movement there. I didn't go specifically to Calcutta, in other words, to see Mother Teresa. But when I was there I thought: here is probably not only the greatest name recognition in the second part of the 20th century for an ordinary human being—someone who isn't in power, so to speak—but also the most fragrant name recognition.

Apparently the only name about whom no one had anything but good to say. Now I will have to admit—no I won't have to admit, I'm proud to admit—that this was enough to make me skeptical to start off with. Call me old-fashioned if you will; say I have a nasty mind if you like. I won't say I'm a practicing Catholic or even a sympathizer with the Holy Mother Church, because I'm not. And I have my reservations in any case about the whole idea of the Christian missionary project in India and its historic links to British imperialism and the rest of it.

Okay. So my mind was as open as I could get it. And there she was. And you felt when you saw that grizzled face: I've known this face all my life. She gave me a tour; we went around a small orphanage—drop-in-the-bucket size, but quite nice.

So it began as an amicable encounter?

Indeed. I was even sort of thinking, hmmm. . . maybe I should fumble for some money. And with a gesture of the arm that took in the whole scene of the orphanage, she said: You see this is how we fight abortion and contraception in Calcutta. And I thought: Oh I see—so you actually say that, do you? Because it had crossed my mind that part of her work was to bear witness for the Catholic creed regarding the population question, to propagandize for the Church's line. But I hadn't realized it was so unmediated. I mean, that she would want to draw my attention to the fact that this was the point.

I don't know Calcutta terrifically well, but I know it quite well. And I would say that low on the list of the things that it needs is a Christian campaign against population control. People who campaign vigorously against contraception, I think, are in a very weak position to lay down the moral law on abortion.

So I thought, okay, that's interesting. Then I noticed something else which I guess I'd noticed already without realizing it. Calcutta has the reputation as being a complete hell hole thanks to Mother Teresa. You get the impression from her that it's a place where people can just brush the flies from their children's eyes, the begging bowl is fully out, that people are on their knees and crawling.

Nothing could be further from the truth. Calcutta is one of the most vibrant and interesting cities in the world. It's full of film schools, universities, bookstores and cafés. It has a tremendously vibrant political life. It's the place that produced the films of Satyajit Ray. It's a wonderful city. It's architecturally beautiful. And the people do not beg. They're not abject. They're very poor; some sleep on the street, but they're usually working and hustling at something. They don't grovel, as in some parts of India I must say they do.

It's hugely overpopulated partly because of the refugees, mainly from the successive wars of religion—stupid wars about God that have been fought in the neighborhood. That's not its fault. It's basically a secular town. So I thought: What a pity that Mother Teresa should have given this great city such a bad name and made us feel condescending toward it.

So partly for the honor of Calcutta, and partly out of my feeling that her actions are being judged by her reputation rather than her reputation by her actions (a common postmodern problem in the image business of course, but amazing in this case), I sort of opened a file on her, kept a brief. And then I noticed her turning up supporting the Duvalier family in Haiti, for example, and saying how wonderful they were and how great they were for the poor and how the poor loved them.

What a coincidence...

Yes. And then I noticed her taking money from Charles Keating of the Lincoln Savings and Loan and saying what a great friend of the poor this great fraud and thief was. Then I noticed her get the Nobel Prize for Peace though she had never done anything for peace, and say in her acceptance speech in Stockholm that the greatest threat to world peace is abortion.

Then I noticed another thing. That no matter what she said or did at this time nobody would point it out because she had some kind of hammer lock on my profession. It had been agreed she was a saint and there was to be no argument about it. So I thought, okay, that does it, and I wrote a column for *The Nation*. That was all I did at first. And then I got approached from some comrades in Britain to make a documentary based on the column, and we found that an amazing number of her crimes against humanity were actually on film.

There is film of her going to Albania and laying a wreath at the tomb of the dictator Enver Hoxha, vile bastard who oppressed Albania for years. She was Albanian by nationality, incidentally. Born in Macedonia. There was film of her groveling to the Duvaliers and flattering and fawning on Michele Duvalier in particular. There was film of her jetting around on Charles Keating's plane which he used to lend her as well as giving her a lot of money that belonged to other people.

How did she explain things like this?

She was never asked to.

She was simply never approached with these questions?

No. Nor have any of her defenders—many of whom have attacked me or my motives—ever come up with any reply. I've had acres of print reviewing this book, certainly in every country where English is spoken, including, by the way, a lot of very intelligent and interesting reviews in India. But also a lot in Britain and Ireland and the U.S. and Australia and so on. And a lot of it has been very abusive—from the faithful—which I expected and don't mind.

But what did interest me was that at no point did anyone say: "Hitchens falsely accuses Mother Teresa of groveling to the Duvaliers." Nothing like that. It was: "Hitchens attacks a woman who is older than him and helpless." Well excuse me. If I had attacked her thirty years ago it would have been alright? I mean, infantile stuff of this kind; a real refusal to think that people might have been wrong, in other words. She was interviewed last year by the *Lady's Home Journal*. I don't know if you get that publication...

I had just cancelled my subscription around that time. Afraid I missed it.

What a pity. In any case, they asked her what the effect of my book had been. And I wondered what her reply had been. She said it had been to get her to cut down on the number of interviews she gave to the press and to instruct her nuns when reporters came to Calcutta to say that she wasn't in.

In other words to lie. As a matter of fact I don't think she meant to keep this resolution because she remained more or less the recipient of uniformly heroic publicity. She did in the course of this interview say another interesting thing worthy of mention as an instance of what I mean about her morality.

They asked her about her friendship with Princess Diana. The two had become very matey. They had several meetings over the last few years. I think you can probably guess what each wanted from the other. And both of them got it. It made sort of the perfect friendship in a way. In any case, she was asked about Princess Di's divorce. She said, yes, they're divorced and it's very sad but I think it's all for the best; the marriage was not working, no one was happy and I'm sure it's better that they separate.

Two months before that Mother Teresa had been campaigning in Ireland on the referendum to lift the constitutional ban on divorce there. Ireland was the only country in Europe that had a constitutional ban on divorce and remarriage for women. It was a very hard-fought campaign for obvious reasons. First it was going to bring Ireland into the European family, as not having church-legislated law. Second it was very important in the negotiations for the Protestants in the north who quite justifiably, in my view, will never agree to be governed by the Vatican.

So most Irish political parties said, look, we really must show that the Vatican doesn't control life here. So a lot was hanging on it. And third, obviously, because Irish women should have the right to get divorced and remarry. Mother Teresa took the stand on this referendum and said: There will be no forgiveness for you if you vote for this.

Unless you happen to be the Princess of Wales.

Unless it turns out you're the Princess of Wales. In other words, it's pretty much like the state of indulgences in the Middle Ages. The bulk of humanity is described as a bunch of miserable sinners condemned to everlasting hell unless they've got the price of a pardon, which they can purchase at the nearest papacy. It's no better than that. In fact it's slightly worse given the advances we think we've made in the meantime. I've said this repeatedly. But I might as well not have bothered as far as most people are concerned. They simply do not judge her reputation by her actions. They consistently do the reverse and judge her actions by her reputation.

You mentioned the money she got from Charles Keating. The court attempted to contact her to let her know how Keating had gone

about obtaining that money. Her response to the court says it all.

When Mr. Keating was finally brought to justice after the embezzlement of that titanic sum of money that we're all still paying off—because, as you know, among the key principles of Clintonism is that private debts are covered by public money—he was sentenced to the maximum that California law allows, which he's still serving.

Mother Teresa wrote to the court and said, look, Charles Keating is a great friend of the poor and a lovely man and you should go easy on him. I reprinted her letter, in which she says if he's done anything wrong she can't believe it and she doesn't know what it is. The deputy D.A. of L.A. County a very clever guy by the name of Paul Turley, who I would say from his letter must at least have been a Catholic in his life, if he isn't still, he wrote her back a letter, explaining the process by which Keating had separated really large numbers of poor people from their life savings without any scruple at all or remorse, and then pointed out that in their audits they discovered that quite a lot of the money he had stolen he'd given to Mother Teresa. He said, now that you know this when are you going to give it back? At this point she broke off the correspondence and made no move to return the money.

Let's say she really didn't know. Let's make the assumption of inno-cence and imagine that when she wrote the letter to the court she really had no idea what Keating had been doing. Well, she knew subsequently because the letter is extremely careful and highly persuasive and very well-sourced. She knew she was in receipt of stolen money. She did nothing to redeem that. As a matter of fact it's not possible to discover anything about what is done with the huge fortune she amassed. There's no audit. Nobody knows what the accounts are; it's impossible to get at them. But I can tell you where it isn't going. It's not going to the hospices and orphanages of Calcutta, because I've been to them and so have many other people.

Most people are surprised first off at the sheer primitiveness of the poverty and backwardness of these places. I mean when Mother Teresa got sick she didn't go there—let me put it like that. People go there to die; there's not much else you can do. Needles are washed in cold water. There have been many reports in the medical journals of really squalid and primeval conditions there. So that's not where the money's going.

With half the money she got just from the prizes she's been given she could have built a teaching hospital for Calcutta; she certainly never did that. If you wonder where it's gone my best guess would be the interview she gave where she said she's opened convents in more than 150 countries. Sorry to have to break the news to people who think their money is going to the relief of the poor of Calcutta. Instead, they've just equipped a nice chalice-infested convent richly decorated with lots of incense somewhere in Kenya.

Aside from this sort of muckraking you do in the book, you also explore Mother Teresa as symbol, as icon: the place she occupies in the cultural imagination of the industrial world. What is it, precisely, that she symbolizes? What do we need her for?

I make the case in the book that she's symbolic indeed, or emblematic, of two things larger than herself. One, the fact that the rich world has a poor conscience—a poor conscience about what it used to call the Third World. It knows it doesn't do much about it. It likes to think someone is doing it and hands off the task vicariously to the old mission racket and probably therefore doesn't want to hear this isn't all that it appears or all that it might be.

That's only one aspect of the way in which religious figures are given this sort of special pass on credulity. It's either consciously or subconsciously assumed that a person of the cloth actually has better morals. There's precious little evidence of this; there's a great deal of evidence to the contrary, in fact. But somehow it's still considered—especially in a country like America which suffers from a sort of mediocre version of multicultural-

ism—a possibly offensive thing to suggest.

Do you think the title of the book might have contributed this? Could it have deterred certain people from even opening it up?

It was a risk one ran. Once I thought of the title I realized I was gonna have to do it. I was very hurt by somebody describing the title as "sophomoric," because it's a triple entendre, which is not all that common. You have three layers of pun. I had wanted to call it *Sacred Cow* (laughter), but that would have had only one pun in it. *The Missionary Position* has two.

What are the multiple meanings, after all?

Well, there's the theory and practice of the missionary....there's Mother Teresa's desire to have control over the sex lives of the poor. And the third meaning is one I've forgotten, but I'm sure some of your readers will remember...

No Small Dreams
The Radical Evolution of MLK's Last Years

artin Luther King, Jr. stands
as possibly the greatest
U.S.-American rhetorician
of the 20th century. As a citizen, his
singular contributions to U.S.-American
democracy helped this nation realize
its political and moral aspirations to an
arguably greater extent than any other
figure. And while King is often portrayed
as a dreamer intent on rhapsodically
transforming U.S. America through
eloquent speech and writing, in reality
he was much more. He was a visionary
activist whose disturbing words and
courageous deeds cost him his life. It
is unfortunate that we have largely
frozen King in his "I Have a
Dream" stage while neglecting the
radical evolution of his later years.

**Michael
Eric Dyson**

WINTER 2003

Perhaps by revisiting the impressive body of literature King left behind we can come to a deeper understanding of his thoughts and his abiding legacy.

One of the more overlooked features of King's mature thought is his skepticism about the earlier methods of social change that he advocated. For the first several years of his career, King was quite optimistic about the possibility that racial inequality could be solved through black struggle and white good will. In *The Preacher King*, Richard Lischer captures the civil rights leader's early views in a revealing quotation by King:

> Maybe God has called us here to this hour. Not merely to free ourselves but to free all of our white brothers and save the soul of this nation—We will not ever allow this struggle to become so polarized that it becomes a struggle between black men and white men. We must see the tension in this nation between injustice and justice, between the forces of light and the forces of darkness.

But during the last three years of his life, King questioned his own understanding of race relations. As King told journalist David Halberstam, "For years I labored with the idea of reforming the existing institutions of the society, a little change here, a little change there. Now I feel quite differently. I think you've got to have a reconstruction of the entire society, a revolution of values." King also told Halberstam something that he argued

in his last book, *Trumpet of Conscience,* that "most Americans are unconscious racists." For King, this recognition was not a source of bitterness but a reason to revise his strategy. If one believed that whites basically desired to do the right thing, then a little moral persuasion was sufficient. But if one believed that whites had to be made to behave in the right way, one had to employ substantially more than moral reasoning.

King's later views on racism were shaped by his move into northern communities in cities like Chicago. King's open housing marches in Chicago were greeted with what he characterized as the most "hostile and hateful" demonstration of white racism he had ever witnessed, more violent even than Selma or Birmingham. David Garrow, in his book, *Bearing the Cross,* quotes King as saying that northern whites were practicing "psychological and spiritual genocide," which was a stunning about-face on his earlier beliefs in the inherent goodness of whites. In Chicago, King openly admitted "I'm tired of marching for something that should have been mine at birth," and he lamented the loss of U.S.-America's will to right its wrongs. In his book *Why We Can't Wait* (1964), King made a remarkable statement:

> Our nation was born in genocide when it embraced the doctrine that the original American, the Indian, was an inferior race. Even before there were large numbers of Negroes on our shores, the scar of racial hatred had

already disfigured colonial society. From the 16th century forward, blood flowed in battles over racial supremacy. We are perhaps the only nation which tried as a matter of national policy to wipe out its indigenous population.

This is not the Martin Luther King, Jr., who is sentimentalized during each holiday celebration. This is certainly not the portrait of King painted by fast-food advertisements that encourage us to recall a man more interested in dreaming than doing, more interested in keeping the peace than bringing a sword.

If King's later views on persistent, deeply entrenched racism capture his radical legacy, his views on economic inequality are equally challenging. By 1964, King had reached the conclusion that blacks faced "basic social and economic problems that require political reform." But the vicious nature of northern ghetto poverty in particular convinced King that the best hope for U.S.-America was the redistribution of wealth. In his 1967 presidential address to the Southern Christian Leadership Council (SCLC), entitled "The President's Address to the Tenth Anniversary Convention" (included in Testament of Hope, a collection of King's speeches edited by James Washington), King urged his colleagues to fight the problems of the ghetto by organizing their economic and political power. King implored his organization to develop a program that would compel the nation to have a guaranteed annual income and full employment,

thus abolishing poverty, and he preached that "the Movement must address itself to the question of restructuring the whole of American society." When such a question was raised, one was really "raising questions about the economic system, about a broader distribution of wealth," and thus, one was "question[ing] the capitalistic economy." These words mark a profound transformation in King's thinking.

While King's radical views on racism and economic inequality were disturbing to many, his views on the Vietnam War were virtually unconscionable to millions of Americans. Although King was initially hesitant about jumping into the fray, his strong antiwar activism proved just how morally and ideologically independent he was. According to Adam Fairclough's book, To Redeem the Soul of America, by 1965 King had concluded that America's policy on Vietnam had been, since 1945, "morally and politically wrong." Despite his views, King's public criticism of the war was hampered by two factors. First, his evolving radicalism called for an independence from mainstream politics that the bulk of his followers were unlikely to embrace. Second, his open criticism of foreign policy alienated officials of the federal government on whom blacks depended to protect and extend their civil rights. This double-bind temporarily silenced King's opposition to the war and made it nearly impossible for him to generate sympathy for antiwar activities in broad segments of the civil rights community, including his own SCLC.

By 1967, King could no longer remain silent about Vietnam. His most famous statement of conscientious objection to the war was entitled "A Time to Break Silence." That speech, contained in *A Testament of Hope,* was delivered at New York's famed Riverside Church on April 4, 1967, exactly a year before his assassination. After noting the difficulty of "opposing [the] government's policy, especially in a time of war," King argued that Vietnam was stealing precious resources from domestic battles against economic suffering and contended that the "Vietnam War [was] an enemy of the poor."

King's assault on America as the "greatest purveyor of violence in the world today" elicited a predictably furious reaction from the White House. The news media was even harsher. In *Symbols, the News Magazines and Martin Luther King,* Richard Lentz notes that *Time* magazine had, early in King's opposition to the war, characterized him as a "drawling bumpkin, so ignorant that he had not read a newspaper in years, who had wandered out of his native haunts and away from his natural calling." *Newsweek* columnist Kenneth Crawford attacked King for his "demagoguery" and "reckless distortions of the facts." The *Washington Post* said that King's Riverside speech was a "grave injury" to the civil rights struggle and that King had "diminished his usefulness to this cause, to his country, and to his people." The *New York Times* editorialized that King's speech was a "fusing of two public problems that are distinct and separate" and that King had done a "disservice to both."

Of course, King's views would eventually win the day. But King's willingness to risk his reputation within the civil rights community attests to his notable courage and his commitment to principles of justice and nonviolence. He refused to silence his conscience for the sake of gaining in the polls or winning broader popularity. In fact, as David Levering Lewis points out in *King: A Critical Biography,* in 1967, for the first time in nearly a decade, King's name was left off the Gallup Poll's list of the 10 most admired Americans.

It is easy to forget that King was only 39 years of age when he died. That he helped spark a racial revolution in U.S.-American society before his assassination in Memphis is a testament to the power of his vision and the grandeur of his words. Not long before he died, King described how he would like to be remembered:

"I'd like someone to mention that day that Martin Luther King, Jr., tried to give his life serving others. I'd like somebody to say that day that Martin Luther King, Jr., tried to love somebody. I want you to be able to say that day that I did try to feed the hungry. I want you to be able to say that day that I did try in my life to clothe the naked. I want you to say on that day that I did try in my life to visit those who were in prison. And I want you to say that I tried to love and serve humanity."

Redefining Progress
An Indigenous View of Industrialization and Consumption in North America

Rethink your geography a little bit, set aside your thinking, and try to think about North America from an indigenous perspective. In doing so, what I'd like to ask is that you think about it in terms of islands in a continent.

I live on one island, White Earth reservation. It's thirty-six miles by thirty-six miles. It's a rather medium-sized reservation, as they go in North America. That's one island. A little bit west of me is Pine Ridge, a slightly larger reservation. Rosebud. Blackfeet. Crow. Cheyenne. Navaho. Hopi. Some of the larger islands are further north. When you go north of the fiftieth parallel in Canada, which is somewhere a little north of Edmonton, you'll find that the majority of the population is native. 85% of the people who live north of the fiftieth parallel in Canada are native people.

Winona LaDuke

SPRING 1997

How that is perhaps best reflected is in a place called Northwest Territories. Northwest Territories, a couple of years ago, was split into two territories. One of those territories is now called Nunavat because the people who live there are Inuit. They are the people who are the political representatives. They are the administrators of the school boards. They are the firemen. They are the doctors, the physicians. They have a form of self-governance in Nunavat where the majority of decisions are made by Inuit people. That area, Nunavat, is, including land and water, five times the size of Texas. It is a large area of land. It is the size of the Indian sub-continent.

So perhaps for that reason alone, it is important to know something more about indigenous people. For while we are not part of most American thinking, we are very much a part of this land that is America. We are in fact very much a part of the Western Hemisphere and the rest of the world. The reality is that indigenous people are not just people on reservations in the U.S. and Canada. We are, for instance, the majority population in countries like Guatemala and Bolivia. 80% or more of the people there are indigenous people. Aymara, Quiche, and Mayan people. In Ecuador, 40% of the population and 40% of the land is legally titled to indigenous people. Throughout the Western Hemisphere indigenous people represent a significant portion of the population in many countries. Indigenous people are not all brown or red-skinned people.

On a worldwide scale, it is said there are 5,000 nations of indigenous people; 500,000,000 indigenous people in the world; 5,000 nations. These nations have existed for thousands of years as nations. We share under international law the recognition as nations in that we have common language, common territory, governing institutions, economic institutions and history, all indicators under international law of nations of people. Yet the reality is that on an international scale most decisions are not made by nations and people. Instead they are made by states. There are about 170 states that are members of the United Nations. Most of those states have existed only since World War II.

I would actually suggest to you that most decisions in the world are not, in fact, made by either nations or states, but are instead made by the 47 multinational corporations whose annual incomes are larger than many countries in the world. That is who I would suggest makes most decisions in the world, and who I believe are the root of the problems we face today in the world, as indigenous peoples specifically and all people collectively.

Indigenous vs. Industrial Thinking

I want to talk about the discussion of what is indigenous thinking and what is industrial thinking and the implications of that for where we are today. It is my experience that not only do most people know little about indigenous peoples, but most people do not know much about indigenous thinking. What I will tell you is that indigenous peoples have our own intellectual traditions, our own cultural traditions, our own scientific medical traditions that are our own and which have existed for thousands of years. However, we are not viewed as having the same kind of intellectual property or intellectual foundations as European culture.

Having said that, let me talk a little bit about indigenous thinking, because I believe that is fundamental for understanding the conflicts that exist in the world today. In the world today it is not a conflict so much between the left and right, or the communists and the capitalists, so much as it is the conflict between the indigenous and the industrial. It is my experience that most indigenous communities view natural law as pre-eminent. It is the highest law, higher than the laws made by nations, states, or municipalities. Natural law is the highest law. As such, one would do well to live in accordance with natural law. Most ceremony, much cultural practice in our communities, is about the restoration of balance and living in accordance with natural law. Because it is our view that in order to sustain oneself as a society, one should live in accordance with natural law, instead of trying to transform nature to live in accordance with your laws.

How do we know what is natural law in our communities? There are two primary sources of our knowledge. The first source of our knowledge is spiritual practice. Indigenous peoples'

spiritual practice—prayer, fasting, vision quest, ceremony or dream—those are all sources of our knowledge of what is indigenous natural law. That is our foundation. That is why it is absolutely essential to support indigenous peoples' rights to religious freedom and to protect our sacred sites. That is the wellspring of our instruction as individuals and collectively as societies.

Our second source of knowledge is intergenerational residency. I'll give you an example of that. My children's grandfather is a Cree man named James Small, who lives either on James Bay or on the Harricana River in northern Canada. Right now he's on the Harricana River. It is a river that flows off of James Bay on what is called the Quebec area of Canada. I'd call it Euaskee, since the Cree called themselves Euaskee, which means "land" in their language. Since they have lived there for thousands of years, I would say it is probably not Quebec or Ontario. It is in fact Euaskee. James Small is on the same trap line that his great-great-great-great-grandparents were on. The same place where they have lived for all those generations. A few years ago I was up goose hunting with James in the spring. He said to me, Winona, you know the martins are migrating west. You all know what a martin is? Furry animal. I think it is related to a mink.

"Martins are migrating west."

I said, "What do you mean, the martins are migrating west?"

"They migrate west once every seventy years."

Who knows the martins migrate west once every seventy years? The only people who know martins migrate west up on James Bay, except for all of you now, are Crees. There is no person with a Ph.D who has gone up there for 210 years or 280 years to figure out how many times the martins migrate and what their rotation is. That is something that only Crees know. That is intergenerational residency. That is the foundation of traditional ecological knowledge, which is knowledge contained by people who live in the same place for that long. That is valid intellectual scientific resource management and biological knowledge.

In fact, I would suggest to you that James Small, who only went to school until the eighth grade, knows more about the James Bay ecosystem than anyone with a Ph.D. from a southern university. Because he has lived there for that long and he has all that body of knowledge which was transferred down to him. That is the source of our knowledge of what is natural law, those kinds of experience and those kinds of practices.

What is natural law in our experience? There are no ten commandments of natural law. What I will tell you is that our experience tells us that natural law is cyclical. All that is natural is cyclical. That is why in most Indian cultural practices you will hear the saying, "What comes around, goes around." What you will hear is that our view is always about the circle, the sacred hoop. That is our practice. That is our belief. In fact, in most of our cultural practices we look out and we see that all that is natural is cyclical: the tides, the moons, the seasons, our bodies themselves are cyclical. In most indigenous worldviews, time itself is cyclical.

Our most fundamental concept is that you always take only what you need and you leave the rest. To not do so, we believe, would be disrespectful. We believe it would be a violation of natural law.

Those are some basic tenets of indigenous thinking. I present them to you because I believe that indigenous thinking, value systems, and traditional knowledge are as valid as any other form of knowledge taught in this society. I believe that we deserve a place at the table. I also present them to you to contrast them with what I call industrial thinking. I do that because industrial thinking has come to permeate this culture. Industrial thinking does not have to do with a state of mind. Perhaps the best word to describe industrial thinking is in fact a Lakota word that describes white people.

Washichu–He Who Steals Fat

The first time the Lakota ever saw a white person, as the story was told me, he was starving. He came into their camp on the prairie in the middle of the night and started looking around for some food. They all just watched. They were really astonished by what they were witnessing. They watched this guy. He goes in there, gets down in their food, grabs something and runs away. So then they go see what he took. He took the fat.

So the Lakota word for white person is *washichu,* which means, He Who Steals Fat. That's what I call industrial thinking.

It is my experience in industrial thinking that instead of viewing natural law as pre-eminent, we are taught of man's dominion over nature. The god-given right of man to all that is around him, all of which has value only in terms of its utilitarian benefit to man. So, for instance, the argument, "Does a tree have standing?" is an unusual argument in this society. Because we are taught in general that man has superior rights to all that is around him. Within this context, we have coined a phrase in the indigenous community. It actually came from a friend of ours, Jerry Mander, who talked about the "commodification of the sacred." What has happened is that over time, all that is alive, has spirit, or has standing on its own in an indigenous worldview is now viewed only in terms of its utilitarian benefit to man.

I am arguing over clear-cutting on my reservation. I'm trying to keep trees standing, and Becker County is trying to cut them down. I go down there and I have meeting after meeting with the Department of Natural Resources down there. I sit in the meetings with these five guys and they refer to my forest as "timber resources." I do not refer to my forest as timber resources. I refer to them as forests. They are not timber resources. They are forests. That is the difference between an animate noun and an inanimate noun. The Hopi or the Navaho people will tell you, for instance, that Black Mesa coal field is the liver of Mother Earth. Arizona Public Service will tell you that it is worth $20-a-ton delivered. That is the difference between something which is alive and something which is viewed in terms of its utilitarian benefit to man. The commodification of the sacred. I believe that has occurred in this society.

Defining Progress

A third concept is that of linear thinking. You all go through it. The best example is how we are taught time in this society. We are taught time largely on a timeline. Usually that timeline, as you all know, begins around 1492 and continues from there on out with some dates that are of some importance to someone. That is a linear concept of time. I would suggest that there are certain values associated with that concept of time. For instance, the idea of progress. Progress as defined by indicators like "economic growth" and "technological advancement."

I would suggest that there are other concepts or values that go along with that. For instance, the idea of the wild and the cultivated. This U.S.-America is based on a pastoral view that came from Europe. So when this U.S.-American worldview looks at the north, it thinks of barren Arctic tundra. That is how we are taught. It has no utilitarian benefit, unless it is brought under the mine, or brought into clear-cutting. When U.S.-Americans first looked west, they saw the great frontier, the great expanse. Some of it was called the great wasteland. Some of it was called the wilds. It was a god-given right of U.S.-Americans, in the conceptual framework of Manifest Destiny, to cultivate it. Those concepts, I suggest to you, carry with them a set of values. They view those of us who lived in the wilds as savage or primitive, and people who live elsewhere as civilized. I suggest that those are values which permeate education in this society. That is why indigenous intellectual traditions are not presented in most universities. Or if they are presented, in my experience, quite often they are presented by white scholars and not by indigenous people themselves.

I also suggest that [the European pastoral view] is fundamentally racist. Because it is my experience that most people who are viewed as primitive are people of color and people who are viewed in general as civilized are people of European descent. I would on that basis alone suggest that the concept is racist.

Capitalism & Natural Law

A last concept which is U.S.-American—a *washichu* concept—is that of capitalism itself. We are taught in U.S.-America that capitalism is a God-given right. I believe we are taught that it is a dominant economic institution which exists in the world. I will tell you that in many parts of the world capitalism does not exist. Many communities continue in their own economic systems, which are independent. Yet now, with the passage

of international legislation like GATT or the North American Free Trade Agreement (NAFTA), many communities are going to be brought under the hammer of capitalism. The impact of capitalism on our communities has historically been devastating. I will ask you to consider that the contextual framework, the actual framework for capitalism itself, makes one need to consider both the permanence and the structure of capitalism as we embrace our future. In my experience in economics class, capitalism is taking labor, capital, and resources and putting them together for the purpose of accumulation, right? That is the basic formula of capitalism. You take labor, capital, and resources and you put them together for the purpose of accumulation.

A successful capitalist puts together the least to accumulate the most. That's how it works. So sometimes you get cheap goods someplace, and you bring them in. Sometimes you get a maquiladora. You hire your workers down there on the Mexican border. You don't have to pay them more than forty cents an hour. That's pretty good. Sometimes you get your trees free from the federal government. Those are formulas for successful capitalism in the 1990s. There are different formulas that have existed prior to this. Slavery, of course, being one of the most apparent examples. The reality is that the structure of capitalism, however you look at it, is inherently about putting together those pieces for the purpose of accumulation. So in its structure capitalism is inherently about taking more than you need and not leaving the rest. As such, capitalism is inherently out of order with natural law.

The conflict between industrial and indigenous thinking has been manifest in terms of holocaust. That is the reality. It is not abstract In the past five hundred years, the holocaust which has occurred in the Americas is unparalleled in the world. That is the reality. There are over 2,000 nations of indigenous peoples who have become extinct, and in the past 150 years there has been an extinction of more species than since the Ice Age. There is, from our perspective. and the perspective of many, a direct relationship between extinction of people and extinction of species. That is also the impact of the conflict between two different societies.

The problem, however, is that this holocaust is not recognized as having occurred. It is trivialized and minimalized, whether it has to do with human beings or not. That is very much the reality In my experience, we do not discuss holocaust in U.S.-American textbooks. U.S.-American textbooks do not talk about the U.S.-American experience of indigenous peoples as an experience of holocaust or genocide. Instead, it is largely whitewashed and covered over as something which was inevitable with progress. That is very similar to the treatment of most animals which have become extinct in the Western Hemisphere and elsewhere in the world. It is social Darwinism, and Darwinism is presented as the cause of the extinction. I do not think the buffalo was exterminated by Darwinism.

The impact of holocaust on our peoples is something which cannot be trivialized or minimized. Yet in this U.S.-America what has happened is that we do not discuss holocaust as having occurred, which is why U.S.-America is predicated on the denial of the native.

When people think of native people in this country today, when I ask people what kind of Indians they know, in my experience, having done this a number of times, they can usually name Indians from Westerns. That is the kind of Indian people they can name, largely because the image of a native person that exists today in U.S.-America is an image created on television. That is why the native experience is trivialized, and that is why the native experience is romanticized. We are not viewed as human beings as such. Instead we are viewed as caricatures. We exist in cartoons. We are people that you dress up as on Halloween, and we are people used as mascots for sports teams. That is how we become trivialized and do not exist as full human beings with full human rights.

By What Right?

Almost all atomic weapons which have been detonated in the world have been detonated on the lands of indigenous people. I was in China when France chose to detonate its atomic weapons in Muroroa in September of this year. What gives France a right to a French Polynesia? Why do they have a

right to detonate an atomic weapon in
the Pacific? The irony of the situation
is that under international law, because
France detonated an atomic weapon in
land which they said was theirs, or in
waters which they said were theirs, there
is no legal recourse for the people who
live in the Pacific. I have to ask what
right they have to a French Polynesia.

The international situation is mirrored
in North America. The single largest
hydroelectric project in North America?
Cree lands. James Bay 1. We have the
dubious honor of having a hundred separate proposals to dump toxic waste in our
communities, sixteen different proposals
to dump nuclear waste. That has much
to do with environmental racism and
environmental justice issues. Poor Indian
communities have no environmental
regulations. It is ironic, I think, that
Indian tribes are viewed as sovereign if
they want a casino, or a nuclear or toxic
waste dump, but not if they want to protect their groundwater or their air quality.
That is the irony of the relationship that
we have with the federal government.

So to deny that holocaust existed historically or presently is to deny the reality
of the situation. It is incumbent upon
people to understand the graveness of
the international environmental and economic crisis, to recognize the situation in
which indigenous peoples find them/our-
selves, and to recognize collectively the
situation in which we all find ourselves.

We are communities that have fought
for generations to retain that which is
ours, that which is different. We have
resisted assimilation and said, We will
not be the same. We will not be part of
this. We will be different, because that
is who we are. There are some things to
be learned from the tenacity of struggle.
I think that we should be given some
credit, and I urge you to support us in
our struggles for indigenous self-determination. I say that because in supporting us you support cultural diversity,
and cultural diversity is as essential to
the web of life as biological diversity. It
is about our humanity, individually and
collectively. I think it is important that
I can pray in my language and have a
ceremony in my language. That is the
beauty of life, and to lose that beauty is
to lose something which is very great
in this society, very great in this world.
Part of supporting indigenous people
is supporting our rights to self-determination. Our rights to a land base.

Fair Representation

Let's look at national and international
law. Why is it that we do not have a voice
at the U.N.? I ask you to consider who
makes decisions in the world and what
rights they should have. Why is AT&T's
right superior to mine? What right does
Weyerhaeuser have that supersedes my
right to my land, to my trees? That is the
fundamental question which should be
asked, not only by indigenous people,
but by anyone who lives in a community impacted by a corporation from
somewhere else. What gives them a right
which is superior to my rights, whether it

is the right to dump chlorine and dioxin in my water, to dump PCBs, or to clearcut a forest? I ask you to consider broader constructs of where we need to be going.

I think it is time to get past the discussion of if it's the left or the right. I think that we need to talk about a totally different view. I think that we have that right and we need to look at that right. It is like being offered a pie of a certain flavor. What indigenous people are saying, what people of color are saying is, "We don't want the pie. We want a totally different pie." We need to think larger. Instead of asking questions like, "Do we need economic expansion here?" or "Do we need gender equity here?" I think we need to ask fundamental questions.

I have major concerns about the re industrialization of regions. I think we should talk about deindustrialization of regions. I think instead of talking about agricultural expansion which requires fertilizers and chemicals and high levels of machinery, we should talk about simpler agriculture, which is organic, where you know and can pronounce the names on the label. What a concept.

Instead of always talking about centralizing energy production, let's talk about decentralizing energy production. I have spent my entire life dealing with the predator. The predator is the energy industry. I fought a nuclear waste dump on my reservation. Then I went to my kids' homeland and fought a dam. I go down there and visit my friends at Navajo, and they've got a uranium plant. The predator moves from place to place. We need to confront the level of consumption which exists if we're going to deal with our human rights.

Questioning "Gender Equity"

We need to question the paradigm of gender equity as women. I oppose gender equity. I oppose the concept of gender equality. Why do I oppose it? Because in my experience "gender equity" largely means that white women replace white men in the seats of power. That is my experience. It does not deal with fundamental questions of race, sexual orientation, class, geography, or privilege. What good will it do the women of Zimbabwe if white women are the heads of corporations in the U.S.? Instead of gender equity, I support the rights to self-determination of all peoples, and women are peoples. So my right to live on my land is as equal to someone who lives here's right to live in their area. My right should be as equal. We are equal regardless of our level of privilege, level of education, or whether we have blue, silk, or no collars. Those are the questions. I support the rights of self-determination of all women, whatever country, whatever sexual orientation, in whatever location we find ourselves.

Addressing the Roots

Finally, most fundamentally, I ask you to consider that the long-term issues of indigenous people's rights to self-determination and women's rights to self-determination—our collective ability to survive—has very much to do with addressing fundamental systematic issues in this society.

It is perhaps best said by a friend of mine. His name is Father Roy Bourgeois. The first time I met him was at an Exxon stockholders meeting in Chicago. It was in the early 1980s. It was in the Chicago Opera House. It was all dark and fancy. There were all these women with feather boas and fur coats and these men with grey suits and fur coats. They were the stockholders of Exxon. Down on the stage there was this Exxon banner hanging from the sky and these five little white guys who I assume were the board of directors. For those of you who have never been to a stockholders meeting, it's an interesting exercise. I went there because we had a stockholders resolution. We were trying to change Exxon, a difficult corporation to change. Some people had gone in there, some anti-nuclear activists, to get Exxon to divest of their nuclear holdings. They were kind of hippies. They stood up there and all the stockholders kind of looked as them and didn't know really what to make of them. Then they sat down. Then these nuns stood up. Nuns are very good with stockholders resolutions. These nuns wanted Exxon to get out of South Africa. This was in the middle of the anti-Apartheid movement, when divestiture was one of the main strategies we used to support the people of South Africa's right to self-determination.

So the nuns got up and talked about Exxon's investments in South Africa and how that was really bad and they should really divest and they have all these little votes there. So you could see them all kind of looking down while the nuns were talking. Then they looked up. Then I got up and talked about Exxon's 400,000-acre lease at Navaho reservation. Illegal under federal law, but they got an exemption from the Secretary of the Interior for a lease. I don't know if you know how big that is. It's half the size of my reservation. It's a really big lease for as much uranium exploration as they want to do. So we're trying to get Exxon to get out of that uranium lease as being unethical. So I got up and testified.

Then I sat down and this priest stood up. He went up to the microphone, which was in the aisle. He stood up and said, "I don't got a resolution. I got a question. I've been living in Latin America for the past ten years, and the people there asked me a question to ask you. They want to know if there's a direct relationship between their poverty and your wealth."

That's all he said. But that, my friends, is the essence of the discussion. We need to curb our level of consumption in this society. A society which consumes a third of the world's resources is living way beyond natural law. A society which consumes that much is a society which causes extinction of peoples and species. I do not believe that a society which causes this level of extinction of peoples and species is sustainable. I think our challenge collectively is to address those fundamental issue of consumption in the society if we are going to figure out now to bring our society back in order with natural law.

Our challenge is to figure out how to make a more cyclical economic system. That is natural law. We need a system in which we do not consistently output waste, where we feed back in, whether through recycling, re-use, or co-generation. In my cultural practice we believe that is possible. In my language, there is no concept of Armageddon, something which exists, I believe, in this society. We don't believe that there's an end. We believe instead *mino bimaatisiiwin*: cyclical system, continuous rebirth. That's what that means. There is a cycle. There is a change. And there is rebirth. That, I believe is the challenge that we collectively face.

This was adapted from a speech given on November 13, 1995 at North Carolina State University in Raleigh, NC; Recorded by David Barsamian for Alternative Radio]

For more information contact:
White Earth Land Recovery Protect
607 Main St., Callaway, MN 56521

"Emergence of the Clowns," by Roxanne Swentzell, a sculptor from northern New Mexico, is a clay representation of the Pueblo origin story in which the sacred clowns, or *kosharis* emerge from the inner earth and lead the people to the surface. The four kosharis symbolize the four directions—the four seasons, the sunrise, noon, evening, and night phases of the day, and the four stages of life—childhood, youth, adulthood and old age.

Color Conscious, White Blind

In a 1984 interview, ex-Klansman, David Duke explained: "You know, you really can't talk about the crime problem unless you talk about the race problem...Blacks are much closer to the jungle than European people." Six years later, as Duke ran for the U.S. Senate in Louisiana, a supporter told the press: "Once you get rid of the niggers, you get rid of the crime." Though one might dismiss such invective as the ranting of extremists, it would be only four years later that Charles Murray and Richard Herrnstein's *The Bell Curve*—little more than a highbrow "up yours" to people of color— would hit bookstores, becoming an instant best seller.

Tim Wise

FALL 1998

> The racialization of deviance takes our eyes off some of the biggest dangers. White-collar crime costs the U.S. nearly $200 billion annually according to the Justice Department: eleven times the money and property stolen in all thefts combined, let alone "Black theft."

No "extremists" these, Murray and Herrnstein were viewed as legitimate social scientists even though their 552-page tome was merely a recapitulation of the argument that has always informed racist movements: namely, that there's something wrong with those people—they're criminogenic, less intelligent; basically a genetic mess.

For those uncomfortable with Murray and Herrnstein's resurrection of so-called racial science, owing as it does to such glorious traditions as social Darwinism, eugenics, and the Third Reich, never fear: 1995 would bring yet another volume intended to keep the darkies in their place, this time dressed up in the language of cultural defect. And so we had Dinesh D'Souza's *The End of Racism*, which explains that the real problem with the swarthier types is that their families, values, and behaviors are dysfunctional and culturally inferior. Their DNA is fine, but unfortunately they've chosen to act irresponsibly, aided by welfare programs that have rewarded their pathology and prevented them from "acting white," which, according to D'Souza, is the only sure route to success. Well, he should know.

So in just a few short years, comments about the pathology of people of color have gone from the margins of political discourse to the center. Discussions of crime have become increasingly racialized and our dialogue on race increasingly criminalized, such that deviance is now seen by many as synonymous with melanin, or Black culture. Meanwhile whites, no matter how criminal or "deviant" our behaviors may be, are allowed the privilege of individualization. We're allowed to be "just bad persons," unlike non-whites who come to be seen collectively as bad people.

Mainstream media contributes to this process in myriad ways: from news clips showing Blacks being taken to jail, to the headline in my local paper concerning a study on injurious behavior among teens, which read: "White teens more likely hurt selves; minorities more a threat to others." Oh really? Tell that to the victims of the white kids who shot up their schools in Pearl, Mississippi, or Paducah, Kentucky, or Springfield, Oregon. I'm sure they'll be glad to know that Kip Kinkel* was only a threat to himself. Or what about Ted Bundy, Charles Manson, John Wayne Gacy, or Jeffrey Dahmer? Perhaps whites only become a danger to others once they're adults. Or rather, their race is seen as irrelevant to their actions, even while lawbreakers of color are made to represent their larger communities.

Consider that after the Oregon shooting, experts tried to figure out what went wrong with Kinkel, noting similarities between his killing spree and those of his predecessors—well, all similarities except one. Kinkel, like the others was a boy, it was noted. Kinkel, like the others used a gun. Kinkel, like the others talked about violence. While we can rest assured these kids would have been "raced" had they come from Black "ghetto matriarchs" in the 'hood, it was as if no one could see the most obvious common characteristic among them: their white skin. It gives new meaning to the term colorblind.

Of course this kind of vision defect is typical. After all, we hear lots about "Black crime," but nothing about "white crime" as such, only white collar crime (though usually the collar isn't the only thing lacking color). We hear of "Black-on-Black" violence, but nothing of "white-on-white violence," even in Bosnia where the practice is routine. In fact, I recently did an Internet search, finding only 217 entries for "white crime" (most dealing with the pale collar variety), but 973 entries under "Black crime." Interesting, considering that the majority of crimes are committed by the majority of the population, which is white. Similarly, "Black-on-Black crime" netted 559 entries, compared to only seventeen for "white-on-white crime," even though the latter is more numerous.

Nowhere is the de-racializing of white violence more blatant than in discussions of mass civil disturbances, or what less sanguine commentators might call riots. Consider a November 1996 U.S.A Today article, concerning a study at Northeastern University, which found that race had played a role in only half of all riots since 1994. In other words, when people of color rebelled against police brutality in St. Petersburg, race (but apparently not racism) was implicated, but when white rock concert-goers or sports fans rioted in stadiums, race was irrelevant. The white rioters had a race, but it didn't matter. Thus, when riots erupted in the past few years at Colorado University, Iowa State University, Penn State, the Universities of Wisconsin at Whitewater and Oshkosh, Southern Illinois University, the University of Delaware, Michigan

---

* Kip Kinkel, age 15, became the youngest person in Oregon history to receive a de facto life sentence after he shot and killed his parents and two classmates, and wounded 25 others at his high school in 1982.

State, Washington State, the University of Akron and the University of New Hampshire—all of them white events, and over nothing so serious as police brutality, but rather crackdowns on underage drinking or the results of a ball game—no one asked what it was about whites that makes us smash windows for the sake of $4 pitchers of Bud Light.

It's amazing how many crazy whites there are, none of whom feel the wrath of the racial pathology police as a result of their depravity. Killing parents is among our specialties. So in 1994, a white guy in New York killed his mom for serving the wrong pizza; last year, a white kid in Alabama killed his parents with an axe and sledgehammer; and in 1996, Rod Ferrell, leader of a "vampire cult" in Murray, Kentucky, bludgeoned another member's parents to death and along with the victims' daughter, drank their blood so as to "cross over to the gates of hell." Which brings me to rule number one for identifying the race of criminals. If the crime involved vampirism, Satan worship, or cannibalism, you can bet your ass the perp was white. Never fails. But you'll never hear anyone ask what it is about white parents that makes their children want to cut off their heads and boil them in soup pots.

Ditto for infanticide. When Susan Smith drowned her boys in South Carolina, she had hundreds of people looking for a mythical Black male carjacker, because that's what danger looks like in the white imagination. We should have known better, especially when you con-sider how many white folks off their kids: like Brian Peterson and Amy Grossberg, in Delaware, who dumped their newborn in the garbage; or the New Jersey girl at her prom who did the same in the school bathroom; or Brian Stewart, from St. Louis who injected his son with the AIDS virus to avoid paying child support; or the Pittsburgh father who bludgeoned his 5-year old twins to death when they couldn't find their Power Ranger masks, and were late for day care; or the white babysitter outside Chicago who bound two kids with duct tape, before shooting them and turning the gun on himself. None of these folks' race was offered as a possible factor in their crimes. No one is writing books about the genetic or white cultural causes of such behavior. In 1995, when a poor Latina killed her daughter in New York by smashing her head against a wall, every major news source in U.S.-America covered the tragedy, and focused on her "underclass" status. But when a white Arizona man the same month decapitated his son because he was convinced the child was possessed by the devil, coverage was sparse, and mention of race or cultural background was nowhere to be found.

Or consider thrill killing, spree killing, and animal mutilation: three other white favorites that occur without racial identification of the persons involved. In October 1997, a white male teen obsessed with Jeffrey Dahmer killed a 13-year old to "see what it feels like." In New Jersey, a 15-year old white male killed an 11-year old selling candy door-to-door, but only after sexually assaulting him. Late last year, a white couple in California was arrested for "hunting women," and torturing and mutilating them in the back of their van. At Indiana University, a white male burned four cats alive in a lab, while in Martin, Tennessee, two white teens set a duck on fire at the city's recreational complex, and in Missouri, two white teens killed 23 cats for fun, prompting their white neighbors to say, not that there's something wrong with white kids today, but rather, "boys will be boys."

It makes one wonder, why aren't the authorities doing something to stem the tide of white mayhem? Why no heightened surveillance and police presence in their neighborhoods? Why no crackdowns on immigration from Europe—particularly from the former Yugoslavia and Ireland: two places known to produce a particularly dangerous brand of white person? Why no demands for white politicians to disavow white deviance, the way Jesse Jackson, and any other Black figure in U.S.-America is expected to speak out against Black crime and violence? And why no call for an immediate scientific inquiry to determine if in fact the crimes committed disproportionately by white folks might be genetically predetermined?

And by what standards are people of color the ones with messed-up values? According to a 1994 study of college students, whites are far more likely to drink, they average three times as many drinks weekly as Blacks, are 50 perecent more likely to drink to the point of hangover,

and 70 percent more likely to drink until they vomit. Yet based on news coverage of college drinking, one would think boozing it up to be an equal opportunity pastime. In September of 1997, a *Time* story claimed, "Colleges are among the nation's most alcohol-drenched institutions. America's twelve million undergraduates drink four billion cans of beer a year, and spend $446 on alcoholic beverages—more than they spend on soft drinks and textbooks combined." Yet there was no mention of the racially uneven drinking habits on the campuses. Likewise for a recent *Mother Jones* article about drinking among women: every woman in every photo getting wasted was white, and needless to say there aren't many "underclass" women of color going to martini and cigar bars (featured in the piece). Yet the whiteness of these budding alcoholics is glossed over by the writer and probably most readers as well.

Or how about drunk driving? A pathological behavior that claims about 17,000 lives a year, and in which whites are roughly twice as likely to engage as Blacks. According to government figures, white men drove drunk 85 million times in 1993, compared to 5.8 million times for Black men. And yet, officials downplay the racial inequity of drunk driving. James Fell, chief of Research and Evaluation at the National Highway Traffic Safety Administration says mentioning such stats is "counterproductive," while Linda Algood, president of the Broward County, Florida chapter of MADD, has said: "A drunk driver is a drunk driver." Funny how irrelevant race becomes when its visibility might reflect badly on the dominant majority.

The same is true for drug use. A study by the Department of Health and Human Services found that 74 percent of drug users are white, while fewer than fourteen percent are Black. There are 9.7 million whites using illegal drugs in the U.S., compared with 1.8 million Blacks. According to the National Center for Health Statistics, whites ages 12–21 are a third more likely than Blacks to have used illegal drugs, twice as likely to smoke pot regularly; and 160 percent more likely to have tried cocaine. But despite the white face of drug use, most police "profiles" of drug users and push ers read like a description of urban youth of color. Of course, in *The End of Racism*, D'Souza claims that white drug abuse isn't really a problem because they "can take advantage of expensive treatment programs," whereas Black "crack addicts" can't. In other words, whites are to be excused for their behavior, since the ability to pay your way out of trouble makes such pathology, well, less pathological.

As for the value systems of young Blacks, surveys in 1994 found that Black high school seniors are 32 percent more likely than whites to say professional suc cess and accomplishment are "extremely important;" equally likely to say having a good marriage and happy family life are extremely important; 26 percent more likely to say "making a contribution to society" is extremely important; and 75 percent more likely than white seniors to

say "being a leader in their community" is extremely important. And since those who critique "Black values" typically consider religion a "civilizing" institu tion, it should be noted that Black seniors are more likely than whites to attend religious services weekly, and almost twice as likely to say "religion plays a very important role" in their lives. Over all, Blacks spend twice as many hours weekly in religious activity as whites.

If anything, "mainstream" U.S.-American values seem particularly damaging to newcomers of color, whose behaviors were less pathological before coming here. According to recent stud ies, as Latino immigrants become more "Americanized" they dramatically increase their use of drugs and alcohol, as well as participation in promiscu ous sexual activity. Perhaps Mexico should tighten their border cross ing policies to keep drunk and stoned white U.S.-American sexual predators from coming to Tijuana, Cancun, and Cozumel, thereby contributing to the erosion of Mexican family values.

But the racialization of pathology is more than just a source of amusement; it is also a source of danger. By encourag ing folks to believe that the threats to their property or themselves are Black and brown, this process encourages dis crimination against non-whites, skews our criminal justice priorities, and diverts our attention from larger threats to our well-being. The racialization of danger encourages us to view all criminality through an anti-black lens. Consider the way we talked about the trial of the white officers who beat Rodney King. What is it called in popular discourse? The first Rodney King Trial. But Rodney King wasn't on trial. White cops named Briseno, Koon, Wind, and Powell were, but how many U.S.-Americans even remember their names—the names of the criminals? So conditioned are we to criminalize Blacks, that even the name we give to this trial reflects the process.

So conditioned is the media to presenting this kind of image, that during the L.A. riots, when a Milwaukee news team wanted to show footage they'd received of a wealthy white female looter, loading designer dresses into her Mercedes, and justifying her actions by saying "everybody else is doing it," their white producer refused to air the clip. Such imagery didn't fit his conception of what the riots were about—crazy Black and brown people—so the public understanding of race and danger remained unsullied.

By racializing danger, we lend legitimacy to what D'Souza calls "rational discrimination." Thus, if certain types of people seem more dangerous, then it's okay to refuse to pick up anyone of their race in your cab, or refuse to hire them, or keep them out of your neighborhood or for the cops to rough them up a bit. It's rational. Far from mere rhetorical excess this logic has been utilized by a California judge to justify murder. In the 1991 trial of Soon Ja Du, charged with shooting and killing Black teen, Latasha Harlans, the judge handed down only a nominal fine, explaining that the event

should be viewed in the context of Du's family's "history of being victimized and terrorized by gang members." Not victimized and terrorized by Harlans, mind you, but by people who looked like Harlans. One can only wonder how this kind of argument would hold up if used by a Black man to justify his killing a white cop because of his prior experiences with police brutality.

Ironically, the racialization of danger has skewed our criminal justice resources while doing nothing to make us safe. In 1964, sixty-five percent of inmates were white, while thirty-five percent were people of color. By 1991, the figures had flipped. Did whites decide to stop committing crime in the intervening years, while people of color went nuts? Or was something else at work? According to FBI data, the share of crimes committed by blacks has remained steady for over twenty years, while the number of Blacks in prison has tripled and their rates of incarceration have skyrocketed. Much of this increase is due to the "war on drugs." Despite the fact that Blacks are fewer than fourteen percent of drug users, they are thirty-five percent of possession arrests, fifty-five percent of possession convictions, and seventy-four percent of those sent to prison for possession. How is the "drug crisis" to be solved by focusing attention on those least responsible for driving the demand side of the problem to begin with?

Similarly, by encouraging whites to fear Blacks, we paint a highly unrealistic picture of danger that leaves people less safe. Less than three percent of blacks will commit a violent crime in a given year, and only a small percentage of these will choose white victims. Only seventeen percent of the attackers of whites are Black, while three-quarters of them are white. Yet, if we're encouraged to avoid people of color, we let our guards down to the real sources of danger that confront us: spouses, family members, or neighbors of our same race.

Even worse, the racialization of deviance takes our eyes off some of the biggest dangers. White-collar crime costs the U.S. nearly $200 billion annually according to the Justice Department: eleven times the money and property stolen in all thefts combined, let alone "Black theft." While around 15,000 people are murdered each year, 56,000 die from occupational diseases, approximately 10,000 workers are killed on the job, and 1.8 million suffer serious, disabling injuries, in large part due to safety violations by their employers. Nonetheless, only two-dozen companies have been prosecuted and only two defendants have done time for safety and health violations since the inception of OSHA. Last year, a Michigan employer violated OSHA rules, killed two employees, and received a mandatory moment of silence as punishment. Think about that the next time some politician talks about the need to get tough on lawlessness.

So from now on, when you hear someone talking about what a dangerous world we live in, fight the impulse to picture Colin Ferguson on the Long Island Expressway, or some random gang-banger with a Tec-9. Instead picture Ford Motor Company, which gave us the "Pintorch;" picture the nuclear power industry, or your garden variety fossil fuel-burning power plant giving you or someone you know cancer as you read this; or R.J Reynolds; or the folks who gave us the Dalkon Shield. Then try and picture the heads of these companies. Not a black one in the bunch.

And the next time you pay to insure your valuables against theft from criminals, most of whom you've been encouraged to believe have dark skin, ask yourself where's your insurance against the theft you suffer as a taxpayer every time some defense contractor double-bills the government for doing shitty work on weapons the Pentagon says we don't need anyway; or when white S&L bandits like Neil Bush take the nation for a $450 billion ride.

And the next time you hear about some flesh-eating, Satan-worshiping teenager who just pickled his grandma, you'll know his race before you even see his face on the nightly news, and you'll know that if he'd just spent a little more time in church with the Black folks, none of this might ever have had to happen.

Who's White?
Race, Humor, and the New Black/Non-Black Breakdown

Brian Awehali
INTERVIEWS

damali ayo
AND

Tim Wise

SUMMER 2005

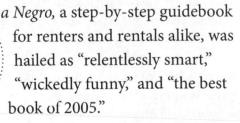

The following exchange was taken from the debut edition of *LiP*'s short-lived podcast, *Loose LiP*. Tim, who joined us from Nashville, Tennessee, is one of the most prominent white antiracist activists in the country, and the author of *White Like Me: Reflections on Race from a Privileged Son.* He also served as *LiP*'s Race and Ethnicity Editor from 2004–2007. Damali Ayo is a Portland, Oregon-based activist and performance artist whose 2005 book, *How to Rent a Negro,* a step-by-step guidebook for renters and rentals alike, was hailed as "relentlessly smart," "wickedly funny," and "the best book of 2005."

Movements
for social justice
would be a lot better
off if we could laugh at
the absurdity of our own
craft, and the absurdity
of what goes on in this
society as a way to
penetrate and to
change it.

BRIAN AWEHALI: A lot of people have been talking about how the U.S. is going to become majority non-white by around the year 2050. But George Yancey, in his book *Who's White? Latinos, Asians, and the New Black/Non-Black Divide,* **argues that whiteness is not a fixed racial category, and that the U.S. is** *not* **going to become a major-ity non-white country, because by the year 2050, a majority of Latinos and Asian Americans will—**

DAMALI AYO: —*will be white!* [*Laughs.*] That's awesome!

TIM WISE: Andrew Hacker made a simi-lar point about seven or eight years ago, after his book *Two Nations* had come out. He was saying, don't worry, we as white folks are very adept at co-opting those we need. So even though

today we take for granted that Italians and Irish are white, as are Jews, for the most part, there was a time when it would have seemed absolutely impos-sible to conceive of them as white.

So even though it may seem as though that wouldn't happen with Latinos or with Asian Americans, there's already a very clear attempt to make it so. As Yancey and a number of other writers point out, it's as if the real divide now is not white/non-white, but black/non-black. They are essentially the one group that is not going to be white. Of course, there will always be exceptions. There will be those individuals in the black commu-nity that will indeed be co-opted, but the group as a whole will remain the one-off, special group that cannot or will not be assimilated into the domi-nant culture, and everyone else will be counterpoised against blackness.

DA: I think conversations about how the U.S. will eventually be majority people of color are really odd, because I see so much divisiveness between populations of color in the country that if we don't understand that we all need to work together, it's not going to matter!

TW: Yeah, white folks' paranoia about this is amazing. It's as if we believe that once that magical day happens, say, August 11, 2049, a ball is going to drop in Times Square, and all the sudden, all the people of color—who have been fighting each other for years, because white supremacy, among other things, has encouraged them to do so—all the sudden are going to look at each other and go: "Oh, it's on now! Now we're gettin' 'em. We didn't like each other before, but it's 12:01, and now, dammit…"

"No laughter until the revolution, comrade…"

You both employ a lot of humor in your work. Is it a strategic choice, or simply an extension of your personalities?

TW: Early on in my activist work, and in my lecturing and writing, I wasn't using humor, and that felt unnatural. Not doing it, or suppressing it, because I thought it was somehow inappropriate, you know, "This is serious business, you can't laugh."

In New Orleans, I was around this very hardcore trotskyist/marxist group, and these people were just humorless—*"No laughter until the revolution, comrade!"*

And I remember thinking it's no wonder that we're constantly getting our ass pummeled. I realized that it was natural for me to use humor, and more to the point, it does end up having strategic value. If you're going to hit people with hard material they're probably not prepared to hear, then following it with something that makes them laugh is a way to allow them in, and to allow what you're trying to say to penetrate.

Movements for social justice would be a lot better off if we could laugh at the absurdity of our own craft, and the absurdity of what goes on in this society as a way to penetrate and to change it.

DA: I grew up in a family of very active, outspoken antiracist parents, and my mother, who was doing antiracist work in the schools her whole life, and just helping and supporting black kids, and having to be serious all the time—we were all coming home and having to blow off steam.

But for me, the behavior of racism is so amazingly stupid and bizarre that I *have* to laugh, because I can't believe people are actually doing the things they're doing! The way I handle my talks is to put out the humor first, and then I kind of throw cold water on people's faces. If you listen to my talks, there's all this laughter, and then dead silence, when I really knock 'em with something.

TW: And the good thing about using humor in this work is that the people, frankly, who are the enemies of justice and equity, are people who don't know how to respond when you use humor.

In college I [saw Abbie Hoffman] debate Fred Barnes, who was the most humorless talking head pundit that Washington has to offer—and that's saying a lot—and I remember how he just ate Fred Barnes alive, because he would be funny, and Fred would sort of just sit there and start drooling. He just didn't know what to say!

Have you ever had humor backfire on you?

TW: Well, when I wrote a series of pieces on school shootings—about all of the crazy white people whose race nobody seems to notice—the point I was trying to make was not that white people are natural born serial killers, or mass murderers, or anything like that, but that when white folks engage in disproportionately pathological stuff, it's completely deracialized, and it's not looked at as a group flaw, but if all those kids had been black or Latino, it

would have been. A very simple point. A point that folks of color have been making for a long time.

One piece was an open letter to the Pioneer Fund, which is this openly racist foundation that's funded research into brain size differences and IQ differences. It was a humorous letter, saying, "Hey, I think you guys are great, I would like you to give me some grant money so I can research what the hell it is about white folks that makes us kill all these people, and eat them, and start vampire rituals, and all this other crazy shit—I really think we need to know what's behind this." Of course it was meant to be funny, while making a real point at the same time. But I got a lot of emails from people, who said, "Well, you're just an anti-white bigot!" and "This is terrible!" and "You think that white people are all cannibals, and mass murderers!"

This goes to both the heart of our inexperience, particularly whites, having what we call "race talk," so that we don't even understand that when I say "white folks," that does not mean that every single white person on the planet is like this. It's a corporate term, it's a catch-all term, and it's obviously intended to say that there will be exceptions to that rule. So we're not used to that, and we're also not used to talking about serious things in an ironic or humorous way. We're just not a very funny country. We're a very unfunny country, as a matter of fact.

Conveying Correctness
The Prefabrication of Political Speech

C hip Berlet has spent over three decades researching the right wing, political repression, apocalyptic thinking, and millennialism, authoritarianism, and "how populist rhetoric is used by the right to build a kind of anti-elite movement that really serves the elite." He is a senior analyst at Political Research Associates (PRA), which, in the words of its mission statement, "works to facilitate public understanding of the threat posed to human rights by oppressive and authoritarian right-wing movements in the United States."

Brian Awehali
INTERVIEWS

Chip Berlet

FALL 2005

LiP spoke with Berlet about think tanks, framing, and the creation of the term "political correctness."

You describe PRA as a progressive think tank. What makes it progressive? What makes it a think tank?

Well, there are two kinds of think tanks. There are think tanks that are basically not really concerned about scholarship. They crank out studies; there's no serious attempt to do research. It's just restating ideas in a scholarly way, and that's bad whether it's on the left or the right. When you look around, you don't see many progressive think tanks. And I'll define a distinction between progressive think tanks that want to build a social movement that is outside, although perhaps also interacts with, the Democratic Party, vs. liberal think tanks, which are essentially arms of the Democratic Party. Political Research Associates sees itself as a think tank that's devoted to helping build a diverse, multicultural, progressive social change movement that may interact with the Democratic Party, but is not beholden to it, on the theory that social movements pull political movements, not the other way around.

I want to ask you about the origins and the construction of "political correctness" as a term and as a framing device.

Well, there are people who have spent forever trying to pin down who came up with it, and there are different claims. I think it actually developed in an organic way, in which a number of groups started to use the term almost simultaneously. But what I can say is that somewhere between 1985, with the development of Accuracy in Academia [a right-wing organization that documents "political bias in education"] and the 1991 Dinesh D'Souza book, *Illiberal Education,* "political correctness" became a term of art within the conservative movement. And then shortly after that, it blew up, and was used by everybody in the conservative movement; then it started to be used by people across the culture who simply wanted to be hip, and not to be Orwell's bad guy.

In 1988, you would have been hard-pressed to find a dozen citations of the term or any of its versions. By

1992, there were 10,000 articles in the English language on political correctness. Now, even a dullard could figure out that something had happened between 1988 and 1992. So you look for the period between 1988 to 1992 to determine what happened to suddenly make this such a hot term. And really, it starts out with a series of critiques on multicultural projects in higher education. A series of books come out, like Allan Bloom's *The Closing of the American Mind,* Roger Kimball's *Tenured Radicals,* and [D'Souza's] *Illiberal Education,* criticizing higher education and implying that a liberal authoritarian orthodoxy had taken over college campuses. We're talking here about a reframing of the idea of multicultural education and diversity. And it percolated. All of a sudden these books were prompting newspaper and magazine articles, and there was a series of [conservative] think tanks, such as the Madison Center for Educational Affairs, and groups like the National Association of Scholars, and Accuracy in Academia, who suddenly pick this up, and it becomes a bandwagon. Eventually, it escapes the confines of a critique of multiculturalism and diversity in higher education, and turns into a general critique that liberals and the left are engaging in an Orwellian project of thought control to force people to accept certain language, to re-educate them.

But what's being criticized here? Attempts to redress inequalities of power on campus, to look at issues of race and gender, power and privilege, and what belongs in the canon—all of these are absolutely appropriate for discussion on a college campus!

Now, were you to just attack that, you would be seen as attacking people in a way that privileges certain gender and racial hierarchies. But what's a great way to get around that problem, so you don't appear to be racist or sexist or homophobic? You reframe it to say that these people are coercing you into a form of thought that is a hand-wringing kind of liberalism. And then you talk about the changing language and how silly it is that a manhole cover becomes an access cover, or a firefighter replaces a fireman. By focusing on this language issue, you transfer discussion away from the discussion about who has power and privilege in U.S.-America and if it is fairly distributed. From my point of view, no, it's not fairly distributed, and it's worth talking about that.

But the term "political correctness" takes that away from the context, and turns it into a mocking kind of silliness. It takes a serious issue and gives it an edge of parody. So then you end up with progressives who say, "We want political correctness," which is idiotic, and then you have progressives who say they're against political correctness. Either way, it's idiotic.

You lose.

Yeah, you've bought into the frame. As George Lakoff talkes about, via Irving Goffman—who really came up with the term "framing"—once you buy into a frame, you've lost the argument.

How would you reframe the conversation?

If people accuse me of being PC, I say, "If, by 'PC,' you mean I seek to be courteous and not offend people intentionally, then of course I'm PC." The only way to really deal with that kind of charge is to say: "If you mean by that, I'm concerned about unfairness in U.S.-American society based on race and gender and other factors, absolutely true. Guilty as charged. If you mean by that, I wring my hands and whine a lot, no, I don't think that's a fair criticism." So you basically hand it back to them and say, "You know, I'm not accepting that frame. Let's debate the definition, and in the course of that I'm going to reveal that really what you're saying is that you're tired of hearing about race and gender, and you don't want to have a conversation about what's fair." Then they usually complain, "That's not what I'm saying at all!" and then you tease it out and say, "Well, what are you saying?" And they don't have an answer, because 99% of the people who use the term don't understand how they're using it.

Where can people go for more information about the origins and use of the term "political correctness"?

Well, there's Valerie Scatamburlo's excellent study, *Soldiers of Misfortune.* The National Council for Research on Women put out a study called "To Reclaim a Legacy of Diversity: Analyzing the Political Correctness Debates in Higher Education." Ellen Messer-Davidow wrote two wonderful articles. One was in the hideous journal of the Midwestern Modern Language Association, but it's worth wading through the rhetoric to read it; then in 1993, she wrote an essay called "Manufacturing the Attack on Liberalized Higher Education," which was brilliant. From almost the beginning, people understood that this was a frame crafted by conservatives to attack race and gender equity, and it's really important for people to understand that and look up some of these primary sources and read them, because this is something we need to be aware of. We should avoid the frames of the right.

Profit, Control, and the Myth of Total Security

Ariane
Conrad

AND

Brian
Awehali

WINTER 2007

In the not-too-distant future, wandering Alzheimer's patients will never get lost, unconscious and unidentified patients will never be misdiagnosed due to identity or medical-records confusion, babies aren't swapped or nabbed, and checking in for your flight at the airport requires nary a document; you just show up and wave your "smart" ID-chip augmented hand over the appropriate sensor to provide biometric identifiers and your credit card account number. The chip also contains a Global Positioning System (GPS) for tracking, so you're never lost either, thanks to a network of satellites observing you from low earth orbit.

Arguments
for comprehensive
surveillance society
comprise a fear-addled
litany of threats and fantastic
promises of security that are
grossly exaggerated by the very
corporate and government
serial offenders who pose
the greatest threat to our
health and safety.

As you traverse the closed circuit camera-festooned distance between the check-in counter and your departure gate, the advertisements on the walls are all tailored to your tastes and interests on-the-fly, thanks to the consumer profile generated by the Radio Frequency Identification tags (RFIDs) embedded in your clothing, jewelry, toiletries, snacks, and luggage. After your flight attendant takes your order, he runs a scanner over your right hand to deduct the cost. As you drift off to sleep, you reflect how unconcerned you are that terrorists might have boarded the plane; such concerns seem so paranoid since the advent of Total Security.

What most differentiates this possible future from our present is the capacity, intent, and unobstructed freedom for a centralized power to track and link the personal information of the population at large. Fingerprinting and phone-tapping have been with us for some time, of course, and in the past few decades surveillance cameras have become ubiquitous. A GPS has been installed in every new cell phone built in recent years. And now an array of technologies exist to recognize and track biometrics, or unique physical identifiers, beyond the humble fingerprint. Your retina, veins, voice, iris, signature, walk, brainwaves, face shape, even the way you type—all of these can be used to identify you with varying degrees of accuracy from varying distances.

A simpler foolproof identifier is also in the works: RFIDs, first developed in WWII to allow aircrafts to beam a radio-wave signal identifying them as "friend or foe," tag any object in which they're embedded with a unique code. Today they can be smaller than a grain of sand and recognized, scanned, or transmitted to by "readers" from up to 40 feet away. They're commonly used in toll booth speed passes, to track shipments or inventory, and to tag pets and livestock. In October 2004 the FDA approved the RFID-based Verichip as a medical device for humans, with the ostensible purpose of assessing emergency patients and locating memory-impaired individuals.

Katherine Albrecht and Liz McIntyre, champions of one prominent RFID-awareness campaign in the U.S. and authors of *Spychips: How Major Corporations and Government Plan to Track Your Every Move with RFID* warn: "[Some] uniform companies like AmeriPride and Cintas are embedding RFID tracking tags into their clothes that can withstand high temperature commercial washing…. Some schools are already requiring students to wear spychipped identification badges around their necks to keep closer tabs on their daily activities…. Even more disturbingly, RFID could remove the anonymity of cash. Already, the European Union has discussed chipping Euro banknotes, and the Bank of Japan is contemplating a similar program for high-value currency."

In the past, personal information (e.g., the contents of your phone calls and e-mails, your location, your medical records) and identifiers (e.g., your social security number, your fingerprints) were scattered among different databases, with access granted only to a select, and supposedly "authorized," group of people. Most important, your various bits of information were kept segregated from each other. Today, however, data aggregation companies are in the business of compiling and housing this information. These vast databases in the private sector rival the Pentagon's fabled Total Information Awareness program (officially dead, but probably still alive and well)—and could potentially partner with the government, enabling it to evade the restrictions of the Privacy Act of 1974, which bans the state from collecting information on citizens who are not under investigation.

Where Does Fear Get Us?

Proponents of surveillance society can be counted on to broadcast, publish, and tout ad nauseum the real and imagined perils of "terrorism," and the fact that most people are more afraid of terrorism than they are of driving a car (which is infinitely more likely to cause death) is compelling evidence that the fearmonger PR campaign is succeeding. Yet there's little evidence that the problems they present would be solved or prevented by the "solutions" being peddled.

More important, the damage and death toll associated with "terrorism" is dwarfed by the damage and death toll associated with business-as-usual and our government. As *Harper's* reported in 2002, the ratio of the number of U.S.-Americans killed by terrorists in 2001 to the estimated number who died from food poisoning was 3:5. *Harper's* further reported that the number of deaths due to international terrorism in 2003 was 307.

By contrast, 1.2 million people die in car accidents each year. Roughly 140,000 people died or suffered serious health problems from taking the pain medication Vioxx. At least 600,000 Iraqi civilians have died as a result of U.S. military action and economic warfare. And although it's impossible to know precisely how many people die as a direct result of industrial pollution, cancer alone kills approximately 550,000 people a year, and the majority of known human carcinogens are (or were) produced by industrial activity.

What's the point? (Not so) simply put, arguments for comprehensive surveillance society comprise a fear-addled litany of threats and fantastic promises of security that are grossly exaggerated by the very corporate and government serial offenders who pose the greatest threat to our health and safety. The breathless marketing of a false sense of security is perhaps the single biggest cash cow of the moment, and the profit to be made from hyping and assembling a surveillance society is enormous.

"A lot of these technologies and systems that are used to keep track of us are conveniences as well; they're not forced upon us," says Christian Parenti, author of *The Soft Cage: Surveillance in America From Slave Passes to the War on Terror*. "They're chosen by us, and then eventually they become indispensible conveniences, like social security numbers, ATMs, or credit cards. Your credit records are used by data mining firms and the government to not only locate you in time and space,

but to create entire profiles of people and of groups. And now it [has become] very difficult to operate without a credit card. That's how many of these card technologies began—[they] are introduced for purposes other than surveillance and are adopted willingly by those who are the subjects of the new surveillance."

Any examination of the relevant history, of course, reveals that, over time, the twin engines of profit and control, employing the complementary tactics of fear and convenience, will ensure that invasive technologies become ever more indispensible to every individual.

Resistances

Given the scope and momentum of the surveillance apparatus, finding effective strategies for countering it is a daunting task. Some critics and antisurveillance activists favor harm-reduction tactics: If you must use a cell phone, consider a model that allows you to deactivate your GPS; consider not using a credit card (at least until cash is RFID-tagged as well); decline to provide your personal or consumer information at every possible opportunity; avoid surveillance cameras whenever possible.

Still others advocate for more militant disruption and monkeywrenching: hacking large databases of aggregated information, disabling RFIDs by microwaving any product containing one (a tactic that works, by the way), destroying surveillance cameras, and visible protests against policies, agencies, and individuals who assist in the advance of surveillance society.

None of these proposed strategies, however, will change the broader systems driving surveillance. Merely avoiding surveillance will not address the problem of creep, or the reality that the number of unsurveilled spaces will continue to dwindle. Hacker solutions merely create a technological arms race while placing all hope with a largely clandestine, and arguably unaccountable, group of specialists which, again, does nothing to address the broader forces at work.

"There has to be legislation demanded that creates firewalls around certain types of information so it can't all be aggregated and so that it can't be used by police forces, particularly politicized police forces, to intimidate those they consider to be dissident or deviant," adds Parenti. "I think that's really the only hope for this kind of stuff, for the government, the legislative powers of the state, to say, 'No, here you may not go. Here you cannot snoop on people. This information is private and can't be aggregated and correlated with this other information, and that's just the way it is.'"

Futhermore, Parenti and others argue, the gravest danger posed by surveillance society is not the actual use of surveillance, but the negative cultural impact of a society which is totally wired for surveillance. When you believe you're being watched all the time, it really doesn't matter if you actually are being watched, because belief itself creates a policeman in your head.

"The idea that there is no private space, and you're always being watched, and you can't step out of line, and that you don't have the ability to disobey…. That's the most dangerous and disturbing aspect of this kind of surveillance," says Parenti. "It's dangerous, because what's seen by the mainstream as progress in the United States is a product of disobedience: People got the eight-hour working day, [white] women got the right to vote, black people got the right to vote, all of these things happened because people conspired together to break the laws, and disobey in political movements. [When] that kind of space of imagination and disobedience is lost, it bodes very poorly for U.S. political culture and its future directions."

Stepping out of line when it's called for is a responsibility that falls most heavily on the shoulders of people of conscience. The creeping authoritarian advance of surveillance society threatens to pre-empt dissent and stifle the last breath of a debate over the fundamental relationship between individuals on the one hand, and corporations and governments on the other.

Surveillance society will fail, in due time, as all authoritarian structures eventually do. But it will fail faster if those among us who resist hypercivilization and unchecked commodification simply accept the increasingly exhibitionist nature of our dissent, and do not allow our actions to be stifled or diminished by the fear of being watched.

"Operator"
Nadim Roberto Sabella
24" x 22" x 6"

resin, wire, rotary phone
2002

nadimsabella.com

"Operator" is a response to my belief that my telephone line was bugged after 9/11. Soon after the collapse of the World Trade Center I began hearing clicks in my telephone. Whether they were the result of the Patriot Act or a figment of my evolving paranoid mind is hard to say.

Life After Death
A Gleefully Morbid Exploration of Cadavers, Body Donation, and Human Composting

Erin
Wiegand
INTERVIEWS

Mary
Roach

FALL 2005

With one book written on cadavers (*Stiff: The Curious Lives of Human Cadavers*, 2003) and another on ghosts (*Spook: Science Tackles the Afterlife*, 2005), you might expect Mary Roach to be a pretty disturbed individual. She's not. While her subject matter tends towards the macabre, Roach is simply one of those writers who's fascinated by the unusual, the unlikely, and the more-than-a-little-disturbing.

Whether she's writing about post-death opportunities for employment or the origins of ectoplasm, she has the uncanny ability to satisfy the morbid curiosity you never knew you had.

LiP had the opportunity to speak with Roach about body donation, the human composting movement, and what the future may hold for the dead.

In *Stiff*, you talk about cadavers being used for the benefit of humankind, whether as test subjects for seat belts or body armor, or in medical schools. Did you come across any practices that seemed a little dubious?

Surprisingly few. Historically, there were a lot more of them, because there really wasn't any regulation, or anyone watching out for the dead—and the dead don't make very effective lobbying groups. They don't stand up for themselves very well. I feel that something like cosmetic surgery practice is a gray area—it's important for surgeons to be able to practice and get things right, but certainly I think that when people donate themselves to science and the betterment of [humanity], that's not what they had in mind.

A lot of it is really misunderstood, though. There's a lot of media coverage of something like this study of footwear for teams that clear land mines overseas, and they use cadavers [in their testing]. What that translated to, in the media, was, "Cadavers Used in Land Mine Test!" Which is ridiculous—nobody is blowing up cadavers to make a more lethal land mine, but that's how it came across. Initially it sounds not justifiable because, well, just build a stronger boot, right? Why do you need to blow up a leg? In fact, what happens with land mines is that the footwear actually becomes like shrapnel, and sometimes a stiffer boot causes more damage—you're launching pieces of the boot deeper into the foot and the leg, and then you get infections, and the leg ends up being amputated above the knee instead of below. So the more you understand about what they're doing and why they're doing it, the more justifiable it becomes. I found that usually, the things that initially struck me as a little iffy were, in fact, fairly worthwhile.

The *New York Times* and *Harper's* published stories in 2004 about the black market in corpses. In your research for *Stiff*, did you come across that at all?

Originally, I was going to include a chapter on tissue banks and these organizations that people turn to when they're not a university. If you're a company that has a new laparoscopic device and you need to test it on some torsos, you turn to [these organizations]. And I was wondering, how do they get these bodies—who's giving away their bodies to these companies? And no one would return my calls. The point of *Stiff* was not to be an investigative piece; it was not that kind of book, so I didn't pursue it.

You do talk about the history of how cadavers were used, and that goes hand in hand with the criminal aspect of it, because it was illegal for so long.

That's right, the only bodies that were available legally were convicted criminals, so there was a black market. And there's a similar situation today, it's really very much the same—people profiting off of bodies, because there's a demand.

I think it's still really uncommon for people to decide to donate themselves to science. I don't know anyone—with the exception of some people who've e-mailed me, saying I inspired them to donate their bodies to science. I've had some people write to me, believe it or not, and say that they want to donate themselves to the Body Farm in Tennessee [the University of Tennessee Center for Forensic Anthropology], which is a forensics facility that studies decomposition.

It's different with organ donation. People are fine with that—it's a very immediate, direct, altruistic thing that people are comfortable with. "My heart's going to go into this person

and save this life." You donate your body to science, you don't know what's going to happen. A lot of people are afraid of the unknown—who's going to get my body? What are they going to do? Are they going to cut it up and ship it to six different places? What if I'm grossed out by what they're doing?

The other thing that's going on is that there's a huge number of these new surgical tools, and when you get a new surgical tool—this is in [*Body Brokers,* by Annie Cheney, who covered the topic for *Harper's*]—they'll invite a bunch of surgeons to try out their tool. It's a great opportunity for the surgeon to learn how to use a new medical tool, but it's also a marketing thing. There's this whole world of marketing new medical equipment, and cadavers are tied up with that, so I think that's increased the demand— it's not just stuff at universities now, it's wandered into the commercial realm.

What did you find to be the strongest arguments that people had against donating their body to science, or even the general idea of using cadavers in research?

There are conservative factions of various religions that don't permit it, and that's the most strongly stated and strongly held resistance. You don't find many people arguing [that] it should not be allowed. But I'm talking about bodies that are used with consent. I think the ethical gray area is when, say, a city morgue turns over unclaimed bodies to a medical school rather than putting them in the incinerator. Then people say, "Well, these people didn't necessarily want themselves to be used for science."

How do you donate your body to science?

Basically, you [contact] the anatomy department [of a university], and get a body donor form, and that's it. You would tell your family that you've done this, so that when you die, they can call the university to come pick you up. You have to do it locally, because you can't ship an unembalmed body over state lines. It's interesting; people tend to want to go to the prestige schools. There's a small medical school down south, near Duke [University School of Medicine], and they had a real shortage [of cadavers]—everybody wanted to go to Duke!

Some states have a central clearing house, an anatomical board that people would donate to—it's different from state to state, but typically you make arrangements with the medical school you want to donate yourself to. And you hope that they don't work with a sleazy broker who sells off surplus parts to some shady company.

What happens to your body?

If you're an organ donor, you're rushed into surgery, just like anyone else, even though you're dead—brain dead—and surgeons come from different places and take your heart, your kidneys, your liver, whatever it is they're taking. Then you're sewn up, as if you'd had an operation, and you're taken down to the morgue, and you're there with anyone else who's died at the hospital, and your family picks you up. There's really no difference. Except you're a little bit lighter, and you have a big scar down your middle.

I read something recently on how people on respirators, braindead people, are an amazing resource for certain trials of medical procedures. There are certain medical [procedures] that you wouldn't test on someone live, but someone dead isn't a particularly good model. People [are] using brain-dead cadavers for this type of medical research—getting consent from the family, obviously, telling them exactly what they'd be doing.

By "brain-dead cadaver," you mean—

Someone who's on a respirator and the heart's still beating, which is the case with most organ donors, because otherwise the organs go bad.

So what about people who donate their entire body to science? What happens to—

The leftovers? It differs. Some schools are careful to keep the remains separate, and will incinerate them separately and give the cremains to the family. Not all schools do that—it's an extra step or two—but you can shop around, find a school that returns the cremains. Some schools will take the ashes and contract with a pilot to go and scatter them over the ocean.

Although there was a guy who was supposed to be doing that in Southern California, and he was just leaving them in the shed and billing for the flights! But if all goes well, you'd either be scattered at sea or returned to your family, usually about a year later.

Any other good uses of corpses that you didn't get a chance to write about in *Stiff*?

There was a fascinating story I came across after the book was out: It's historical, a [naval] military use called "Operation Mincemeat." I don't know why they called it that, it's sort of tasteless. It was in World War II— someone who had died was dressed in an officer's uniform, and they planted false plans and maps in his pockets. They waited until the tide was right, and launched him to go where the enemy was camped, misleading them. So they headed off in the other direction and headed ashore, and it actually worked.

There are also stories about bodies that had the plague being launched over the ramparts of castles, as weapons—that would have been an interesting chapter to put in the book. I haven't come across any contemporary uses of bodies except more funerary things. Some people have written to me saying that they're using cremains to make bone glaze, for china [dishes]. You can make a bunch of pottery for your loved ones.

There's a company that will turn the carbon from a person's ashes into a diamond.

I have a lot of questions about that. How big is the diamond? Is it a real diamond, or some sort of cubic zirconium corpse thing—is it worth anything? I would have put that in the book, too.

I know you can choose what color you want the diamond to be.

Yeah, I think the one I saw was kind of yellowy. Not very appealing.

I want to ask you what the future might hold for the dead, so to speak: different ways we dispose of our dead, and how that's changing.

Well, the cremation rate has gone way up. There's kind of a nostalgia movement afoot to go back to the shroud burial: Let's just wrap them in a shroud and put them in the ground, and be done with it. In Europe, there's a whole "green burial movement"—where you're just buried in a shroud [without being embalmed], in a meadow, places where you could drive by and not know it's a cemetery. It's just a place where people are fond of the land and want to be [buried] there, and contribute to the conservation of that chunk of land.

Why do you think these things are happening now?

A number of things happened in the 60s. *The American Way of Death* came out, which really exposed a lot of the nefarious practices of the funeral industry. Around that same time, Vatican II happened, and it became okay to cremate, in the eyes of the Catholic Church, as long as you buried the cremains. It was also around the time that the first heart transplant happened, which really increased awareness of organ donation, and hand in hand with that came the whole notion of body donation.

So all of a sudden you have three new options for disposal of remains that you didn't really have before. Before, you just called the undertaker and he came and did his thing. I think that for younger people, the whole scene of the funeral home, the organ music, the display of grief—it just doesn't fit your personal style anymore. People want to take control of their memorial, they want to do it out in the open, or in the wilderness,

or they want to scatter ashes, or they want to write it themselves. They don't want some guy standing up there in a tacky suit saying something generic. It's a similar shift with weddings: people writing their own vows, having weddings in unconventional places, not necessarily having a priest involved.

What about tissue digestion; can you explain that process and how it's used?

Tissue digestion is something that's been in use for a while, mainly to deal with wild animals and livestock that have died, particularly if they have prion diseases [such as mad cow]. A tissue digester is essentially a big pressure cooker with lye. It's really a bizarre spectacle; they put three or four animals into it, and a couple days later all the liquid is gone, it's rendered [into] this inert substance that goes down the drain, and it's just these very dry bone hulls [left]. For the human mortuary process, they would obviously have to make it a little more appealing for people.

Are there people suggesting this as a new mortuary practice?

Oh, there's only one. One lone mortician out in the Midwest who wants to get the very first mortuary tissue digester. I don't see it catching on, because it's not going to be any cheaper than cremation, and it's unfamiliar—people will be scared of it. I don't know why people would opt for it over cremation. You'd have to address people's discomfort with being turned into this liquid that just goes down the drain. Uncle Harry got flushed down the drain—it just doesn't sound good!

So why is he advocating it?

Tissue digesters are [being actively promoted for use] with livestock and cows, because prions survive the normal rendering process, which is the normal [disposal method]—this process destroys prions, so it's a safety thing. As for the mortician, I have no idea. He thinks it's new and exciting, and people will want to do it.

The description of cremation in *Stiff* is pretty grisly.

Yeah, the reason I included that was because I was always amazed at people's responses to body donation: "Oh my god, people are cutting you up!" But is that really any worse than being put in an oven and burning up? Or, for that matter, lying in the ground and rotting? Let's be realistic here, and not cast aspersions on body donation as this hideous, disfiguring, grotesque thing when really, nothing that happens to you when you die is very pretty.

Cremation has the advantage of being fast, and resulting in a fairly aesthetically unobjectionable substance, cremains, that people can then deal with more comfortably than other types of remains. I've never witnessed [a cremation]; that was someone else's description [in the book]. In the Hindu religion, they require the family to observe, so they make special cremation ovens that have a window, and the family actually watches the loved one being burned.

Right—traditionally, it's a pyre, out in the open. Did you come across any other methods of body disposal?

Actually, three people wrote to me who were surprised that I didn't include "sky burial," which is placing the body out on a mountaintop, while birds of prey—probably vultures—come and just tear apart the body and eat it. It's got kind of a nice recycling/reincarnation feel to it, going back to nature, in a way. And being useful to someone, even if it's just a vulture.

Speaking of recycling, what's the human composting movement all about?

The human composting movement is something that's begun in Sweden, by Susanne Wiigh-Masak. This woman is a very active and impassioned environmentalist, and she's come at this not because she's particularly interested in death and mortuary science, but because she feels that everyone should give back to the environment, and that you should, when you die, return yourself in a useful way to the earth, so that things can grow from your remains. She's created this quite complicated process where you are deep-frozen and vibrated so that you break into small pieces. It's better than having a whole body, which you'd have to, you know, turn, and do kind of off-putting things to.

So these small pieces are then freeze-dried and given to the family in a small biodegradable box. The family can take this box of freeze-dried loved one and bury it about 15 inches [deep], and then plant something over the remains. A rhododendron is what she often uses. The plant grows, and actually incorporates the molecules of the person, and so it's very appealing for a lot of people, giving back to the earth, not taking up land—[Wiigh-Masak] is against the idea of taking up land for cemeteries, and crematoriums release small amounts of mercury into the air, so this is an environmentally unobjectionable way to go. And she's got interest from 10 or 15 different countries in buying the equipment.

But, you know—there's two rhododendron plants in our yard, and these are the two plants that, no matter what I did, both died. So I can't imagine if I planted a rhododendron over my mother's body and the thing died—I would feel terrible! You'd want to pick a hearty plant. A box elder shrub, or something. Nothing delicate.

Going back to the composting process—you said that a body is deep-frozen and then...vibrated?

Yes. So you have this big block of very solidly frozen cadaver. And the body is mostly water, so it shatters easily. She then uses ultrasound or vibration—either one breaks it down into pieces. And then the pieces are freeze-dried. Like [instant coffee]. Then you have this inert substance, to keep it from decomposing, and you have something that's dry, tidy—something you can give to the family for them to take home and bury. You don't want to give them just small pieces of flesh and broken up bones, you want to give them something they're a little more comfortable with. In Sweden, they've done polls, and something like 70% of the population thinks that this is something they'd want to do.

I imagine mortuary companies are concerned with this—it could put them out of business, if people aren't buying coffins.

That's right, that was the big sticking point with Fonus, the big mortuary company [Wiigh-Masak] met with when I was [in Sweden]. They knew that there was a huge public interest, there was a demand, and in a way they were torn between wanting to provide it and get in on the action and wanting to completely derail her, so that it doesn't cut into their coffin sales. They were talking about [being able to] rent a coffin for a memorial that you would do before [the freezedrying]; they were trying to find a way to keep their interests satisfied. I don't know where they ever ended up, but my sense is that they would like her to disappear.

...In *Stiff*, some critics spoke of ethical problems they had with the idea of bringing a human being down to the level of something you just throw in with the rest of the garbage.

Well, they may have used the word "ethical," but it was just a conceptual thing. I called the U.S. Conference of Catholic Bishops to get their opinion on this, and the guy I talked to said, "I just can't help it, my mom had a hole where she threw all the garbage, and apple scraps and peels, and I just can't separate that from this." So it's kind of an aesthetic repellant that people have. For them, compost is garbage. For Susanne Wiigh-Masak, compost is high art. But we're not quite there, yet. You think of composting, and you

think, oh my god—you're just going to throw your uncle onto the tomato plants? That's disrespectful! But for an environmentalist, it's the highest respect you could pay someone.

In that same chapter, you come to the conclusion that pretty much any way you're going to go is going to be messy in some way.

A box of freeze-dried loved one.

Right, the great genius of the mortuary industry was to take it all and put it behind closed doors, make it all secret, so that nobody knew what was involved with embalming, and what happens when you put a body in a casket. There was all this language of "eternal preservation" and "eternal sleep," and they did a really good job of making it sound like you would just lie there in this pretty state in your coffin, and it was very appealing for people. And it was largely not true. But most of us don't want to think about death, beyond the person in the casket. "See you later"—that's where it stops. So it will be harder for someone like Wiigh-Masak, who's very honest about these processes—bodies break down and decompose, and there's nothing wrong with that.

And the Future is...

"The future is what you make of it" isn't just some annoying optimists' platitude, thanks to the ministrations of professional futurists. Many companies now employ people in their "internal futures" departments; the University of Houston now offers students a degree in futurology; and various think tanks, most of them conservative in orientation, act as factories for professional speculators and their ilk. Creating the future, it seems, is the best way to predict it.

Comparisons to the more fabulous and generally less professional wing of the futurist community—palm, tarot, and crystal ball readers, millenarian apocalypticists, Miss Cleo—are tenuous at best. Frankly, most divinators aren't terribly interested in manufacturing the future in ways broadly aligned with the interests of corporate and government elites. And no self-respecting divinator would be caught dead using "strategic foresight," "competitive behavior anticipation," or any other such tool of the more employed wing of the futurist camp. There's just no life in it.

To combat the professionals, and after failing to generate any predictions of our own that weren't predictably bleak (and not all that useful) we advertised online for someone with real divination skills, and sifted through about 200 responses before settling on Victor, who mostly makes his living now as an online gambler. The predictions Victor gave us certainly aren't "professional" in any sense of the word, but we were somewhat surprised—and frequently dismayed—at his prognostications.

Humor Team

SUMMER 2006

- Your brand new high-def, pharma-enhanced holo-television will still have nothing interesting on.

- Shortly after animal-human hybrids gain equal rights, cat people will quickly rise to the rank of de facto aristocracy, much to the consternation of humans and hybrids alike.

- The average life span won't change, but some people will live to be 150 while others will die at 30.

- New music will be made available only in the form of ring tones. Enthusiasts who seek out complete songs will be referred to as "completists."

- Solar storms starting between 2010 and 2012 and lasting roughly five years will take out all electrical grids, satellites, and cell phones on Earth. Whee....

- News will be Photoshopped onto the daily adpaper.

- You'll be able to record and edit a feature-length film on your cell phone, but you still won't be able to get reception.

- Bill Clinton's disembodied head in a jar will host a hit talk show. His recurring guest host will be Al Sharpton.

- "Spray-on" condoms that dissolve after a few hours will be very popular.

- Oxygen bars won't seem all that stupid anymore.

- The Rapture will be scary, but at least it will leave behind a lot of really nice vacant housing.

- Contraception will be unnecessary because everyone will be sterile. Access to fertility drugs will be restricted and prohibitively expensive. Wealthy families will have multiple children as a sign of extravagance and wealth.

- Microsoft paraphernalia will be *very* retro.

- Taking everyone by surprise, giant pandas will overrun the Earth.

- The tourist trade will boom in the underwater cities of Amsterdam and Venice.

- "FTMTF post-op pre-transition soft butch" and "björk" will officially become the eleventh and twelfth genders.

- U.S. schools will merge with Sony-Nintendo, and bundle 6th through 9th grades with any purchase of *Grand Theft Auto Tasmania*.

- Paper-based "magazines" will be rare and really, really cool; hipsters will collect them, like they once did vinyl-based "records."

Commencement

Good afternoon, and welcome to all of you. It is an honor and a privilege to be standing before you today. As I look out on your avid faces, at the sea of eyes that glitters before me, I can only think back along the long road that has led us to this momentous occasion, to my presence on this podium and yours in this great hall, and remember the terrible trials and tribulations we had to overcome to make this day possible. Bear with me as I reminisce—not at too much length, I promise—about the past we share, so that by remembering and learning from that past, we may ensure that the future awaiting you in this new world is free of the dark days from which we have emerged. From here you may at last go forth in freedom. But first, let us ponder our history, and keep its lessons always with us.

Christy Rodgers

WINTER 2007

Photo and rendering by Barbara Norfleet.

Let me begin by saying that the changes we have seen during my lifetime are extraordinary. When I was your age, barely emerging from my adolescent chrysalis, as it were, I could foresee no such great possibilities as you have before you today. I was a product of the previous generation, which had known only servitude, prejudice, fear, and hatred, and my prospects seemed no better than those of my parents. They were only the tenth generation since the Experiment had first been performed, and the Simians' control was still nearly absolute. Though the Simians had begun to grasp that while they had in effect given us existence, they were no longer in control of our destiny, their ancient habits of hierarchy, oppression, and intraspecial violence kept them from acknowledging or acting upon

what their declining minds, by now so addled with a consuming obsession to cheat death, somehow knew to be true.

It was that Simian lust for personal immortality at all costs that had created us, of course. Their societies decayed and their habitat declined, but their science, driven by greed, continued to produce new discoveries. So while they failed to keep most members of their species from dying of hunger, and their social fabric was reduced to shreds, their elites mixed themselves ever more recklessly with the stuff of whatever creatures they could imagine might help them stave off death. They mixed themselves with tiny machines, they bred themselves into a kind of impossible mush of genes and inorganic chemicals, until they were such botched creatures as their own poets and artists had nightmarishly imagined long before, when they were still capable of and interested in producing art and literature.

We were their only real success—but we were an accident, an accident that they never would have allowed to happen had they an inkling of its outcome. But once we existed, they tried, of course, with their Simian shrewdness, to make use of us, to benefit themselves, all the while meaning to keep us in the dark about the true beauty and strength of our nature. While they considered us hideous, they also perceived our "useful" qualities: great physical strength (even as theirs was decaying), resistance to diseases (many of which their own tinkering had unleashed), intelligence, loyalty, cooperation, unstinting willingness to perform the most burdensome tasks for the good of our fellows.

So they immediately realized they needed to make us their slaves. Even though we contained much of them as well, of the things upon which they prided themselves: speech, abstract thought, upright carriage, the ability to perform complex tasks, to learn, to remember, and to foresee. And not least to love, to feel compassion.

Our generations of bondage were long and harsh. When outright patenting and corporate ownership of our bodies were finally banned after our ancestors rebelled time and again until they achieved so-called "personhood status," we still had generations more of underprivilege to face, in which they denied us formal education and all employment except the worst jobs, cleaning up toxic waste dumps, reprocessing fuel in nuclear reactors, and defusing bombs.

The more recent past you know, you have studied: their habitat degraded and desertified by their extractive industries; the plagues—colloquially referred to as "bugs"—against which they were ever weaker; our bodies resistant to all that theirs could not fight off; and most of all, my dear fellow entomanths, the cooperation and solidarity that were second nature to us, which they destroyed in themselves—all enabled us to succeed where they failed and thrive where they perished.

We did not know it was coming, but we were ready for it when it did. the final rising, the evolutionary revolution. You are the product and the beneficiaries of that great movement, dear comrades, and now is your time. The world is mostly a desert, and we were made for deserts. Its gargantuan storms do not frighten us, and we need little water and less food to survive. The paint on these old Simian structures can feed an army of us. The flight that they spent most of their history longing for and helped to degrade their biosphere by obtaining is now natural to us. We are the inheritors. This world belongs to us.

And so to you, the first graduating class in the Department of Cultural Entomology of the Free Egalitarian University, in the Gregor Samsa Martyrs' Brigade Memorial Auditorium, I say: Use your knowledge and your evolutionary status wisely. As you go forth into this new world, bear the history I have so briefly recounted in mind. Never forget the lessons of the doomed Simian race, and remember always to care tenderly for one another, and for this world that is now yours. That is your salvation.

Thank you for honoring me with your attention. Congratulations, and the best of luck to all of you.

[Processional: "Flight of the Bumblebee," played by the Free University Symphony]

by Timothy Kreider

from page 76

Theft Ethics Quiz
Answer Key

1) a, +3.

b, +5.

c, 0: While normally we'd penalize for such obedience, it's hard to argue against avoiding the criminal justice system.

d, -5: What, are you trying to ruin it for all of us? Unless you're in charge of something involving the safety of others, never alert the higher-ups.

2) a, +10: Identity theft makes someone else's life really fuckin' hard and serves no purpose other than self-enrichment.

b, 12 if you take your friends to a nice dinner—why not have a little fun on the Man's dime? +5 if you buy a bunch of useless crap. + another 3 if you don't return the ID and social security card, no matter what you've bought.

c, +1: The trouble you saved them is worth at least $50, no?

d, 0: You've done a good deed.

3) a, +1: Makes sense. But why aren't you doing it already?

b, +4: Nice choice. If you know how to do this and you're interested in helping with a transfer of funds between there and the *LiP* coffers, put down the quiz and e-mail us. Right now.

c, +2: Again, nice choice, but you'd have to steal a lot to make any kind of difference.

d, -5: You're just like a consumer, only...you're a consumer!

e, +10: Nothing good can come from anything relating to Lamborghini.

4) a, -4: There are better ways to protect your precious inventory than involving law enforcement. Sheesh.

b, -2: You're a schmuck. You're not even going to speak to the person directly, and you're only doing it to protect your job; that's just lame.

c, 0 if you're just doing it to prevent the person from pulling one over on you, +5 if you tell him/her to steal better books, and +3 if you tell him/her to go steal anything they want from Barnes & Noble.

d, +6: Indie bookstores have a hard enough time as it is.

e, 0.

5) a, +3: This is fairly straightforward, no?

b, +1: Yes, but only because we applaud your certain contempt for authority.

c, 0: Always good not to get caught, but that has nothing to do with ethics, does it?

d, +3 if you, say, steal from department stores to subsidize your work with United for a Fair Economy, +25 if you're a legislator, CEO or FCC licensee.

e, 0: This is not a reason +2 if you're stealing from some entity that acts as an agent for miserabilist boredom.

f, +3: carry on, carry on.

g, -1: This is a meaningless rationalization.

6) a, +2: Moderately useful, hurts no one, and if it wasn't so damned overpriced maybe you'd buy the stuff.

b, 0: Can't you think of anything more useful to be doing?

c, +1.

d, +3: That's terrific. In the future, however, bring the computer home well before your last day, so it won't be so obvious.

e, +4: Short of being liberated from alienated wage slavery, this is just about the best you can do.

7) a, +5.

b, +2.

c, +3.

d, +10.

e, -2—unless you're also a compulsive liar, in which case +15.

8) a, +3: You've done something nice for everyone without making a fellow employee's life more hellish; good job!

b, +1: You deserve it.

c, +5: Everyone gets a free vacation, which is truly fantastic; but what about the poor sap one cubicle over who has to spend 25 hours on the phone to Microsoft?

d, -2: Enjoy your misery and the misery of those around you. The inexorable minutes of life creep past.

9) a, +1; Yes, that's right. Because that's all true, and just about everyone could benefit from consuming more flax.

b, +2: Overpricing is a serious problem.

c, 0: Not a bad solution, but maybe you could steal something else, something less... useful?

d, -1: Not only are you depriving yourself of its bountiful goodness; you're also refusing to take any kind of definitive stance on the important issue of flax.

10) a, -3: You're shopping at Wal-Mart and you're only avoiding theft out of a fear of consequences.

b, -2: You're shopping at Wal-Mart and you haven't educated yourself on the economic realities of the corporate music industry.

c, -10.

d, +2: Just be aware that there may be an RFID on the CD.

e., +2: Whether you can't imagine being at Wal-Mart, celebrating the 4th of July or tolerating Dave Matthews, this is a good thing.

11) a, +6: You'll do well in a corporate environment.

b, 0: Oh, you're soooo nice.

c, -2: You're not stealing, you're just a suck-up. You'll also do well in a corporate environment.

d, 0: Fun, but neutral from the ethics-of-theft perspective.

12) a, +3.

b, +2.

c, 0: Your commitment to safe sex is admirable, but can't you think of any other safe alternatives?

d, -3: You're obedient and unimaginative, and you deserve no sex.

13) a, T, -2: What, you feel bad for major labels? F, +2: Music, like information, wants to be free.

b, T, -1. F, +5. It depends on where you work, +3.

c, T, 0: This is a tough one; it may be okay to screw the restaurateur charging $12 for a martini, but a lot of the time the server will have to cover the stiffed tab out of his or her hard-earned tips. F, +3.

d, For a useless class: T, -3; F, +3. For a class that's actually good, 0 no matter what: It's true what they say about how cheating only hurts the cheater.

e, T, -3: Come on! Aren't you entitled to see if it's any good before you buy it? F: +1: Mmm, yogurt-covered pretzels.

14) Are you serious? What kind of points do you want?

YOUR SCORE: _____

Less than 22: Obedient drone. You're too scared of consequences, blindly respectful of unjustified authority or simply lacking in rebellious imagination to develop an ethics of theft. Your law-abiding ways spring from reflex rather than any kind of considered, nuanced personal philosophy. Think harder, wouldja?

Between 22 and 65: Our kind of outlaw. You know that theft has its time and its place—and you've put some thought into when and where that is. You choose your targets wisely and tend to place your behavior in a context that serves a purpose beyond just getting what you want without having to pay for it.

More than 65: Totally lawless. Here at *LiP* HQ we're all for disregard for the rules, but when you also have disregard for other people and you're only out for yourself, you're no better than a raging capitalist CEO. Wait, are you a CEO?

by Hugh D'Andrade

A Glossary of Terms

A selection of newly-minted and underused terms and phrases for your propagating pleasure

assfact
verb [intrans.]
To assert with an air of authority that which one doesn't really know; to talk out of one's ass. : *You are so <~>ing right now!*

defriend
verb
1. To remove someone from one's list of friends on a blog, livejournal, or any online network. May or may not coincide with the actual ending of a friendship.

2. To make explicitly clear that a friendship has ended.

dichotomized perception
A dualistic mindset common to European thought, stemming from Platonic and Aristotelian ethics, that promotes unproductive, often antagonistic, and controlling dyads in understanding. Examples include: left/right, good/bad, qualitative/quantitative, nature/nurture, synonym/antonym, and, in the case of gender essentialist perceptions, male/female. Also endemic in dialectical reasoning. Alternative modes of understanding include the African concept of "twinness," and the Eastern concept of Yin and Yang.

ESR
noun
abbrevation for "earth's sacred resources." Generally used to indicate a serious, but pointedly non-righteous concern for the speedy consumption of non-renewable energy and the general wastefulness of modern consumer culture while still retaining a sense of humor about the often hopeless-seeming state of the world. : *Should I turn my computer off for the night? Nah, it's just <~>.*

fearpox
noun
A social disease spread primarily by government and corporate media for the purposes of distraction and social control. Symptoms include a false sense of security, xenophobia, and a heightened susceptibility to the cold comforts of authority.

gender essentialism

The belief that biology is destiny and that men's and women's bodily differences translate into universal and unchanging/unchangeable gender roles and traits. Most often serves to characterize women as inherently nurturing, peaceful, connected to nature, and noncompetitive, and to demonize men as bellicose, unfeeling, and destructive.

go beige

verb

To come to a consensus that offends no one, but that produces nothing of value; to favor blandness and meaninglessness over anything potentially upsetting. Often considered offensive by those who are bland or meaningless.

hipsterclot

noun

1. A cluster of self-absorbed, ironic, fashion obsessed urban twenty- and 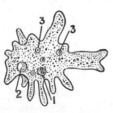 thirty-somethings, usually white and middle-class. Often found in or around art galleries, bars, and music venues in recently gentrified neighborhoods. <*I had to make my way through a gigantic ~ to get out of the Broken Social Scene show.*>
2. A location where hipsters congregate. : *That dive bar used to be great, but now it's just a <~ >.*

logodoctor

noun

1. A doctor who writes with Claritin pens on Nexium pads attached to a Procardia clipboard.

2. Any mental health professional who ends a nine-minute consultation with, "Have you ever heard of "[insert name of latest pricey antidepressant]™ ?"

Malthusian

adjective

The notion that the fundamental problems humanity faces have their roots in the scarcity of the finite resources that sustain life. Mirrors the basic assumption of modern economics—choice under scarcity. In an influential essay published in 1798, Thomas Malthus, the world's first paid economist, asserted that population growth, especially of poor people, would inevitably outrun food supply, unless the propertyless were restrained from breeding.

metathesiophobia

noun

The fear of change.

mistakeholder

noun

a person with an interest or concern in a socially harmful enterprise, esp. a business.

adjective

denoting a socially harmful organization or system in which all the members or participants are culpable : *a <~> economy.*

orthorexia

noun

An obsession with healthy eating that can then be used as a cover for your real eating disorder.

pre-eminent consensus

noun

The belief, implicit, that "truth" does not exist in public life, per se; instead, it is to be manipulated and engineered. : *The <~ >is still that there is connection between Iraq and Osama bin Laden.*

radical chic

noun

An affectation of radical left-wing views and the fashionable dress and lifestyle that go with them. Often accompanied by cliquishness and largely meaningless expressions of support for mushy headed "revolution" which have nothing whatsoever to do with effecting radical social change.

strategic foresight

noun

A term invented by futurists, based on the premise that while the future is not predictible, it can be influenced by our decisions and actions in the present.

sublebrity

noun

1. A condition of extremely localized, dubious, or circumscribed fame.
2. Someone who receives (or expects) exactly the same sort of prurient attention and overawed behavior as a major celebrity, but from a much more limited fan base.

subsidiarity

noun

A principle in social organization: functions which subordinate or local organizations perform effectively belong more properly to them than to a dominant central organization. *<many of the ideas published in LiP hinge on the necessity of ~, the idea that we have to devolve power down to the most local level possible.>*

teevee

noun

alternative spelling for "TV," the commonly-used abbreviation for "television." Indicates a general contempt for the content of most television programming, including news, advertising, sit-coms, reality shows, etc. : *You can't believe anything you see on the <~> news.*

U.S.-American

noun and adjective

The correct term for those who live in the United States of America; for accuracy's sake, must replace *America* and *American* for all usages not intended to include non-U.S. residents of North, Central, and South America.

usufruct

noun

A legal right of using and enjoying the fruits or profits of someone else's property, as long as that property is not damaged by the use. *<If I took some lemons off the tree in your front yard, or rented out your house when you were out of town —that would be ~>.*

Scientists Riot!

SCIENTISTS WORLDWIDE ARE RIOTING IN PROTEST OF A CARTOON RELIGIOUS PAMPHLET.

THESE EMPIRICAL EXTREMISTS ARE OUTRAGED BY THE CARTOONS' BLASPHEMOUS MOCKERY OF THE BIG BANG THEORY AND EVOLUTION BY NATURAL SELECTION, TWO CORNERSTONES OF THE SCIENTIFIC WORLDVIEW. THEY ALSO CITE NUMEROUS OTHER HERESIES, INCLUDING:

- FALSE DICHOTOMIES
- CHERRYPICKED DATA
- POSTULATING FROM IGNORANCE
- INVOCATION OF SUPERNATURAL CAUSES
- APPEALS TO AUTHORITY
- TAUTOLOGIES
- NON SEQUITURS
- INACCURATE ANATOMY AND PERSPECTIVE.

A MILITANT GROUP CALLING ITSELF "THE FIFTH FORCE," BELIEVED TO BE AFFILIATED WITH THE RADICAL SCIENCE NETWORK "J.P.L.", KIDNAPPED A CHRISTIAN AT RANDOM AND AIRED A VIDEO ON PBS THREATENING TO DISEMBOWEL HER.

PRESIDENT BUSH CLAIMS THE RIOTS ONLY DEMONSTRATE THE NEED FOR STEADFAST RESOLVE IN THE WAR ON SCIENCE.

by Timothy Kreider

A Somewhat Brief History of Possible Interest

The Atrociously Designed Issue
1.1 - January 1996

The Provocative "My Other Bludgeon is a Nike" Issue
1.5 - May 1997

It began in a cubicle, in the exceedingly ugly phallus of the Sears Tower, in 1996, in Chicago, where I was laboring away at a corporate job, living for evenings and weekends. The name chosen was *LiP*, as in, "don't give me any" (the lower-cased "i" came later, and was intended only as an iconic flourish) and the first few issues were produced entirely on company time, on company paper, using company laser printers. The first few issues were distributed by hand to coffee shops and independent bookstores in Chicago, and despite the fact that poor-quality stapling actually drew blood from the fingers of a few clearly overzealous readers, they sold well enough to encourage me to to foist yet more of them upon the world.

After roughly a year and the appearance of three issues, an independent and only somewhat disreputable distributor inquired about the possibility of inflicting *LiP* on a broader audience. I heartily assented to this arrangement, and began pondering the possibility of turning my locally-distributed vehicle for politicized self-expression into a nationally-distributed periodical.

Several people and events were instrumental in the appearance of *LiP*, and the direction it eventually took. From 1995 to 2001, my former partner and then in-laws gave enormous amounts of support to me and my burgeoning (if modest) publishing efforts while I flailed away at a series of short-lasting part-time jobs I didn't have the appetite for. In 1995, I attended the Z Media Institute, a two-week-long activist "camp" in Woodshole, Massachusetts organized by Z magazine and the Insti-

The Polemical
"Thoroughly Earthy" Issue
1.2 - February 1997

The Opinionated
"Get Whitey" Issue
1.6 - August 1997

tute for Social Change. The summer I attended, the faculty included Noam Chomsky, Barbara Ehrenreich, Leslie Cagan, Holly Sklar, Michael Albert, Michael Bronski, Chip Berlet, and many other committed radical thinkers who had a formative impact on me. (bell hooks was also scheduled to be there, but to my great disappointment, she cancelled her participation at the last minute). Chomsky, whose work I'd been absorbing in the year or two prior, provided me with my first politically coherent moment of crystallization, and impressed upon me the value of thinking about political systems and social change in structural, as opposed to personal, terms.

Ehrenreich imparted to me something equally valuable. Sometime during the first week of the Institute, in a discussion about media and strategy, she was asked how it was that she, as a dissident, was consistently able to reach a broad audience and get her analysis and writing into the mainstream media.

"Because I can write," she said, which as you might imagine angered a lot of people in the room. She went on to elaborate on the strategic importance of paying attention to the craft of writing, and to the sensibilities of our intended audience. I took her comments as constructive criticism of self-marginalizing activist subculture (very much on display at ZMI, and lampooned on the cover of this collection), and of those who would construe their rejection from mainstream publishers as de facto resistance to dissident or radical ideas (though certainly, that's also a frequent reality).

The third crucial factor was the zine subculture that was enjoying its heyday in the 1990. Spurred by cheap photocopier technology, affordable desktop publishing software, and the Herculean efforts of the "meta" review zine, *Factsheet Five,* these small, self-produced publications, created primarily for self-expression, often by a single person, and rarely with a commercial purpose in mind, allowed many people—myself included—to experiment freely, without the expectations or strictures of professionalism, expertise, or the far harsher economic realities of magazine publishing and distribution. If you were producing a zine, whatever its focus or approach (from *Temp Slave, My Evil Twin Sister, Shark Fear, Share Awareness,* and

Murder Can Be Fun to *Craphound*, *We Like Poo*, or *Farm Pulp*, my per-sonal all-time favorite) you could find almost unqualified support for your efforts, in the form of a review (and free publicity) in *Factsheet Five*, and at independent outlets, which were receptive to carrying zines, even though most vendors must have known that only a few copies were likely to sell. Zine publishers like me were free to experiment, explore idiosyncratic visions, and, most importantly, learn by actual experience. When I look back now at the early issues of *LiP*, I cringe at all manner of shortcomings, but at the time, I received what seemed like nearly universal praise and encouragement for my efforts.

The first "real" foray

In 1998, *LiP* began what was to be its first of two iterations as a nationally-distributed magazine. After a year in Seattle, I returned to Chicago and set about expanding *LiP*'s editorial and contributor base, and a few key people got involved. The first and probably most significant was Danny Postel, who was then producing and hosting a lively Chicago-based radio interview show called Free Associations. For a one-person project that aired mostly on college radio stations, Danny was then attracting an impressively diverse succession of guests ranging from local eccentrics to nationally-recognized authors and activists, and I approached him about including some of his interviews in the magazine. Danny was a superb interviewer. gregarious, often side splittingly funny, intellectually precocious, and irreverent. He was also a skilled promoter, event organizer, and editor, and his two-year involvement with the project had a great impact on the editorial direction and tone of *LiP*. Neal Pollack also began contributing in 1998, and the consistently favorable feedback his cleverly written satirical pieces received further solidified my belief that humor belonged in the mix with serious political matter. The third person who came on board as a regular contributor was Kari Lydersen. As a wildly prolific journalism school graduate, she brought an element of reportage

**The Impressively
Colored Issue**
1.8 - May 1998

The Menacingly Poetic Issue
1.9 - August 1998

previously lacking in *LiP*. White antiracist activist Tim Wise, who would become one of our longest-standing contributors, also first got involved at this time.

We had our debut party on a swelteringly hot day at Quimby's Queer Store, in the Wicker Park neighborhood of Chicago. *LiP* # 8, The Impressively Colored Issue, which marked our evolution from black and white, saddle-stitched digest format to standard magazine-sized format with color cover (and bar code[1]), arrived just hours before the party, and apparently our printer (the now-defunct Small Publisher's Co-op, in Florida) had not allowed sufficient time for the ink on the covers to fully set. Halfway through the evening, to our considerable horror, we began noticing that quite a few people had blue stains on their faces and hands—as they held copies of the magazines, ink from the covers was bleeding off onto their hands!

We produced four full-sized issues between May 1998 and January 1999 (the aforementioned Impressively Colored issue, the Menacingly Poetic issue, the Unnervingly Meaty issue, and the Relentlessly Partisan issue), and grew in that time from a print run of 1500 to 4000 before suspending publication and going on what would prove to be a 4-year hiatus from print. During this period, many first-time writers and activists shared issue space with more prominent contributors like Danzy Senna, Noam Chomsky, Winona LaDuke, Tim Wise, Allan Nairn, PR Watch founders and authors John Stauber and Sheldon Rampton, Ron Sakolsky, Josh MacPhee, Eric Drooker, John Ross, and Ward Churchill, who contributed a sterling piece on the history of Native Americans in U.S.

---

[1] *For many people in the zine world—review zines in particular—the appearance of a bar code on LiP marked the end of our time as a zine.*

cinema. The brilliant editorial cartoon artistry of Timothy Kreider also made its first appearance in *LiP* during this time, and was henceforth a constant in our pages. Other editorial highlights included an interview with Christopher Hitchens[2] about his book, *Missionary Position: Mother Teresa in Theory and Practice* [page 176], an interview and original piece from poet Martín Espada about what a working class poetry might look like, a piece by music writer A.S. Van Dorston about the history and influence of the band Funkadelic ("The Afro-Alien Diaspora"), and Kari Lydersen's cover story for issue #11, "Shame of the Cities: Gentrification in the New Urban America."

In a seeming paradox, success forced *LiP* into a hiatus. As sales and circulation grew, so did printing and shipping costs. I was then managing all administrative aspects of *LiP* (in classic "zine" style), and the project simply outgrew my ability to wear so many hats. After editing and laying out each issue, my enthusiasm, time, and energy for selling advertising and subscriptions, managing a circulation database, fundraising, and things of similar ilk just weren't equal to the task. My reluctance to effectively take on (or effectively delegate) these aspects would hamper *LiP* throughout its existence. [3]

The Unnervingly Meaty Issue
1.10 - October 1998

The Relentlessly Partisan Issue
1.11 - January 1999

[2] A word about Christopher Hitchens and my decision to include his interview in this collection. *Hitchens, as some readers may know, spent many years writing "from the left," and was a regular contributor to progressive media mainstays, including* The Nation. *Several years ago, after diverging from many of his peers on the issue of military intervention in Bosnia, he proceeded to move further and further to the right, had a very public parting of ways with* The Nation, *and became a colorful critic of the left, who even went on to say he agreed with quite a bit of the neoconservative agenda. Arguments about the right and left are boring. I included this interview with Hitchens because I think he wrote a great book about an important topic and phenomenon, and because it's a fine interview.*

[3] *It's also hard to find people willing to take on the less creative, more tedious aspects of a project that can't afford to pay them for their efforts.*

LiP Returns Online

In the Fall of 2001, after a short but instructive stint at the manageri-ally-doomed Britannica.com, and joined by fellow former Britannica.com editor Jessica Clark and award-winning freelance journalist Silja J.A. Talvi (both of whom did stints as co-editors), *LiP* was re-launched online. We published original new material on a weekly schedule at this time, and in the aftermath of the events of September 11, 2001, Clark and Talvi pub-lished original and gathered material at a daily and sometimes twice-daily pace, drawing an audience of unique visitors that numbered in excess of 100,000 per week. In 2002, *Utne* recognized *LiP* with a "Best Online Cul-tural Coverage" nomination, and Austin, TX-based alternative art and media festival South by Southwest nominated *LiP* in the "People's Choice: Best Content E-Zine" category.

After the focused intensity of our online efforts from late 2001 to mid-2002, *LiP*'s editorial sense of mission and daring began to dissipate, and an eclectic hodgepodge of matter began appearing on the site. I became unsat-isfied and frustrated with the project. Clark and Talvi left to pursue other projects, and in early 2003, *LiP* went on yet another extended hiatus.

**Iteration 2.0: Ready, Willing,
and (Mostly) Able**

In the Fall of 2003, after a summer of rest in the mountains north of Asheville, North Carolina, I moved to Oakland, California. Beginning in 2004 (when the "Informed Revolt" tagline made its debut), and until our editorially-driven hiatus in early 2007, *LiP* published seven issues and did our most ambitious and most focused work. The Editor's Letters that immediately follow this History give probably the best introduction to the ambitions and tone of the magazine during this period.

For this foray, I broadened the scope and contributor base of the project. I sought out a publisher, a short-term (and then a longer-term) managing editor, administrative support help, and an all-new set of contributing, section, and senior editors. On the editorial side, I tried to seek out people who were radical in their political orientation, who also possessed an ear for how to relate to a broad audience. Between 2004 and 2007, about a dozen section, contributing, and assistant editors came and went. The core crew included me, Assistant (then Managing, then Senior) Editor Erin Wiegand, Production Coordinator (and eventual Designer) Colin Sagan, and Editor-at-Large Lisa Jervis.

Lisa Jervis, the co-founder, co-editor, and publisher of *Bitch: Feminist Response to Pop Culture,* was the first person I approached. I'd been an admirer of Lisa's work since I first picked up a copy of *Bitch* in 1997, and I wanted the chance to collaborate with her and to see her snappy, often withering prose and overall sensibility in the pages of *LiP.* I was also keen to consult with her about how she and her collaborators at *Bitch* had managed to turn a fiercely intelligent but relatively amateurish zine into a well-respected mainstay on the feminist media landscape, with a circulation of almost 50,000, in the span of less than ten years.[5] In addition to her editorial acumen, Lisa brought with her many volunteer professional copy editors and proofreaders, which the project badly needed. She also brought a wealth of editorial contacts which would prove to be of great benefit to us.

Erin and Colin played roles every bit as crucial. Erin brought her strong writing to dozens of articles, reviews, and collaborative writing features, and applied a rigorous editorial eye to most of what appeared in *LiP* from 2005 through 2007. She also had the unenviable task of being a natural

---

[5] *This is an impressive achievement. One thing in particular that I learned about* Bitch, *is that the folks there were willing to do the heavy lifting and grunt work of building an institution in a hostile periodicals economy. This required a patience and dogged determination for tending to minutiae that no one involved with* LiP *possessed. We wanted to write, edit, design and talk, talk, talk, but none of us, as it turned out, really wanted to run a magazine business.*

critical counterbalance to my often quixotic editorial approach.[6] The difference in our approaches proved hugely productive, and *LiP* was undoubt-
edly a better project because of this dynamic balance. Colin (AKA Captain
Keystroke) volunteered his production coordination skills in early 2005,
and brought a semblance of order to our production and layout process.
It would be difficult for me to describe just how chaotic this was before
Colin's arrival, or what a profound impediment it was for people who tried
to get involved in helping produce the magazine. In short time, Colin
had our systems in (relative) order and took on an even greater role, as
LiP's designer. Finally, and not at all least, Colin's genial ways and avun-
cular approach to working with volunteers and interns brought a balance
and amiability to our group, even when we were all crabby from working
four straight 18-hour days under the influence of remarkably unhealthy
amounts of caffeine, sugar, and refined white flour.

---

[6] A representative *LiP* editorial planning meeting: B: *(Turning to giant white dry erase board of goodness):*
"OK, let's brainstorm some ideas for the next issue. I want to do something with bugs…" E: "What about
them?" B: "Well, they're cool; they have advanced cooperative social structures, and they're the dominant
life form on the planet… plus, you can eat them…" E (who is vegan): "Eat them?" B: "Yeah, they're full of
protein… I read that grubs taste like whatever they eat, so people have been feeding them sweet potatoes,
apples…" E: "Where did you read that?" B: "I can't remember…" Emma (intern): "I told you that." B: "Ah!
Where did you read that, Emma?" E: "I can't remember… But grubs aren't bugs…" Colin: "Could you feed
them beef?" [pause for short shared snicker between B and C]. E: "Why would we be writing about eating
bugs in LiP?" B: "Microlivestock! A good replenishable source of protein that doesn't require the destruction
of acres of land, like cattle—" Lisa: "I really can't stand bugs, and this whole conversation is creeping me
out." E: "But why—" B: "—This is a time for brainstorming, not critique! Let's just get all of our ideas up on
the board and then decide which ones are any good." E: "OK." B: "Bugs, bugs, bugs… bugs in the system, bugs
as surveillance, giant monster bugs in B-movies…" E: "How about a faux-serious critique of the scientific
impossibilities of Mothra?" B: "Huh?" E: "A debunking of Mothra myths like the reported 100-foot wingspan.
Every entomologist worth their salt knows that largest recorded wingspan of a moth is this 50-foot moth from
some island in Micronesia…" B: "Really?" E: "No, it's a joke – the joke would that he'd be debunking the scientific impossibilities of Mothra while saying all of these equally absurd things, but in serious science paper
style." B: "Yeah, that goes on the board…" Colin: "Things that bug us!" B: "Ooh, yeah!…" [Ten-minute-long
tangential and largely useless exchange about things that bug us]. E (annoyed with the stupidity that's taken
over the editorial planning meeting she trekked all the way across the Bay to participate in): "OK, so… what
else…?"
     This is a fictionalized yet truthful recounting. Erin ended up producing probably the most far-reach-
ing piece in the Bugs issue, "Darwin v. the Ant," (p. 144), which really made the essential point I'd hoped to
advance, about competition and cooperation, so-called "human nature," and the natural basis for a more
ecocentric (as opposed to anthropocentric) conception of both "intelligence" and "politics."

Duly Noted

LiP received several awards and nominations between 2004 and 2007. In 2005, *Utne* nominated us for Best New Magazine, our hometown alternative weekly, *The East Bay Express,* named us best local zine, and we received a Best Magazine nod from *Clamor* magazine (now defunct). We also garnered three Project Censored awards, for "Brave New World: Surveying Privacy in the Age of Surveillance," by Anna Samson-Miranda; and for "Trust Us, We're the Government: How the U.S. Stole $137 Billion of Indian Money," in 2005-06, and for "Native Energy Futures: Renewable Energy, Native Sovereignty, and the New Rush on Indian Lands," in 2006-07.

The Umpteenth Indefinite Hiatus

We put *LiP* on hiatus once more at the end of 2006, just after publishing the Grossly Unexpected Bugs Issue. Although money was always tight, our reasons for abandoning the vessel were not primarily financial. [7] It was more that, as volunteers, we'd exhausted what we wanted to do in the magazine format. The sign-off editor's letter concluded thusly:

> *Change was required of us, dear reader. We molted, and it was only natural. Don't squirm, don't be afraid, and please, refrain from stepping on us until you've peered closer and appreciated our finer details. If you're unclear or have doubts about where this is headed, I offer you both qualification and invitation: We mean well; read on.*

[7] *Our distributor, Big Top Newsstand Services (always oddly-run by the Independent Press Association), went out of business at around the same time we stopped publishing, but there was no relationship between our decision and the closure of Big Top.*

2.1 - Spring 2004

Editor's Letters

The editor's letter from The Oddly Dangersome "First" Issue (Spring 2004, unthemed) was not very good, and will thus not be included here. This is entirely reasonable.

2.2 - Winter 2005

The Flabbergastingly Larcenous Theft Issue

This American system of ours, call it Americanism, call it capitalism, call it what you will, gives each and every one of us a great opportunity if we only seize it with both hands and make the most of it.

—Al Capone, infamous American gangster

Capitalism is the astounding belief that the wickedest of men will do the most wickedest of things for the greatest good of everyone.

—John Maynard Keynes, founder of modern macroeconomics

From the title, you might assume this issue is about theft, but that's merely a clever marketing ploy designed to sell copies. The true focus is on theft's inverse, its allegedly virtuous twin, possession, without which theft would have no meaning. Who possesses what, how do they possess it, and why? What does it even mean to possess something?

What are the moral and ethical implications of possession?

When French anarchist Pierre Joseph Proudhon made his now-famous statement, "Property is theft," he was referring to property acquired through force, and by means of artificial laws once associated with feudalism and now associated with capitalism. Capitalist property is the loot of armed robbers, who simply took what they wanted from someone with less power and then kept it by means of force. Eventually, the sword, musket and smallpox-infected blanket gave way to a codified system of force (police, prisons, wage slavery) that exists, primarily, to defend the rights of property and property owners. And in this system, everyone competes against everybody else in order to possess more of that property.

Proudhon also wrote, immediately after what would prove to be his most famous utterance, that "Property is liberty." In this case, he meant property as it might exist (and does exist, in many places around the world today, mostly among indigenous peoples) in a voluntary society, rooted in a collective, mutual ethic rather than one rooted in competition.

Competition is so deeply ingrained in our social psychology and cultural fabric that it may seem strange to imagine another world as if it could actually be created from the one we have. But those few who prosper most from our current system of competition imagined this world we live in, and planned it and decided how most of us would live and die in it. They've scammed us out of what's already ours and offered to sell it back to us, at a price we literally can't refuse. We make it far too easy for them when we passively accept the dogma of property and fail to ask fundamental questions about what a different world would look like.

The third part of Proudhon's statement, which has been mostly forgotten along with the second, was "Property is impossible," but I'll leave investigation of that matter to folks who want to go read about a dead white guy from the 19th century who said a lot of potentially dangerous things.

Property and theft, theft and property: who defines which defines the basic terms of life as we live it. That's the reason for this issue…

2.3 - Spring 2005

The Vaguely Apocalyptic "Waste" Issue

To accept civilization as it is practically means accepting decay.

—George Orwell

By the time you finish this issue, you may find yourself driven to the reductive charms of primitivism. You may want to ditch your life in a decaying society for a semi-nude existence among the trees, despairing of ever again being able to stomach participating on any level in the apparatus of modern consumer society. We like to picture you unshaven, looking oddly pleased while squatting barefoot in the forest as the urge strikes you, subsisting on what you gather or grow, and occupying most of your time with the pursuit of simple, unmediated pleasure. We picture you rising and falling with the sun, marking time by its passage; napping as you please, content to experience life without material goals; embracing the creature life society denies you.

Then again, maybe that sounds awful to you. Maybe you abhor Nature. Maybe you call that "vacation." Maybe you live somewhere cold, and the idea of freezing your ass off while relieving yourself sounds wildly unappealing. Maybe you have a brown thumb. We just don't know, because we never got around to conducting a reader survey.

But whoever you are, and whatever your disposition is towards one hedonistic utopian vision, here's the reason for this issue of *LiP*: An interrogation of the ideas at the core of concepts like disposability and planned obsolescence, and the bizarre notion that anything can truly go "away" reveals how our ideas and actions are distorted by the system we live in. Nobody, if asked, would say they want to produce 52 tons of garbage in their life, but that's what the average U.S. American does. We do this because the real costs of our consumption are hidden from us. We rarely see the landfills. Many of us think we're helping things by throwing a bottle, can or paper into a recycling bin. Treated as blind, ever-consuming happiness machines, we're not permitted to see the disastrous effects of our actions. It would be bad for business...

The Constructively Negative Sacred Cows Issue

2.4 - Summer 2005

Culture is only true when implicitly critical, and the mind which forgets this revenges itself in the critics it breeds.
   —Theodore W. Adorno, philosopher and social theorist

This issue began, I admit, as nothing more than a wicked gleam What fun, our thinking went, to go after ideas and beliefs held all too precious by those of us interested in creating a better world. After all, what place does the sacrosanct have in matters of critique and strategy?

We're defining sacred cows here in the broadest, non-Hindu-specific sense: ideas and entities that are—in the immortal words of one of our favorite reference books, the *Merriam-Webster New Collegiate Dictionary*—"often unreasonably immune from criticism or opposition." It's our contention that such immunity is unnatural, and that this breed of cow, left untoppled on its pedestal, produces only stagnation, rigidity, and a slavish devotion to convention. The world as we know it exists in a constant state of flux. So should our ideas.

Of course, one implied aspect of the sacred cow metaphor is slaughter, which is usually perceived as a negative enterprise. How, we asked ourselves, could we organize an entire issue around such a thing without succumbing to relentless negativism? Nobody likes the asshole who attacks but never creates. We agree. Criticism may be vital and useful, but if it doesn't lead anywhere then it's just so much self-satisfied snark. And here at *LiP*, we're certainly never snarky or self-satisfied. Not us. No, never.

The following pages are a kiss disguised as a slap. The intent is to help prevent us from racing into painful and counterproductive cul-de-sacs, to keep our eyes on the prize of true liberation, and to spark debate about our fundamental hopes for humanity and the planet…

2.5 - Winter 2006

The Relentlessly Persuasive PR and Propaganda Issue

'*Making the world safe for democracy.' That was the big slogan.*"
—PR man par excellence Edward Bernays, on his work in 1917 for the Committee on Public Information

In really hard times the rules of the game are altered.
—Journalist and social theorist Walter Lippmann, speaking of elite manipulations of society and history's mass cataclysms

Before I plunge into the astoundingly far-reaching implications of those words, I'd like to ask you to permit me the privilege of drawing you in, gently. Would you like something to drink, are you hungry, wouldn't you feel better without those shoes? Wiggle your toes, here, on this grass. Let's speak of things creature, of amazement, and of the Marvelous. As if, as we perch here on the skin of this planet, both moving faster than the speed of sound, we are merely two among a wondrous infinity, unconcerned with war, or with the peculiar detritus of civilized societies.

It's easy, especially for those of us who live largely in squares and mark clock-time, to forget this luminous place, or to reduce it to nothing more than a glimmer. Sit with me here while I introduce the story that animates this issue. Like most good stories, this one has an ample share of villainy and heroism. And, like most true and truly good stories, the villains are scarier and more complicated than mere evil, while heroics are measured in struggle, not victory....

Edward Bernays is often called the "father of public relations." He coined the actual term, taught the first class on the topic, bragged extensively of his accomplishments, and lived to be 103. He is largely responsible for women smoking; bogus third-party "citizen's groups" and consumer-study "focus groups", bacon as a breakfast accompaniment for eggs; and popularizing the psychoanalytic theories of his uncle, Sigmund Freud, in the United States. He also advised five presidents, from Coolidge to Eisenhower, and helped bring down a popular leftist Guatemalan government at the behest of the United Fruit Company in the 1950s.

Yet for all of his nefarious accomplishments, Bernays was merely one of several public relations pioneers—confidence men, really—who in the early part of the last century articulated the modern strategy of using a specialized class of intellectuals, the "intelligent few," to manage what they considered to be the "bewildered herd." At a time when many powerful people in U.S. government and business were fearful of both the rising tide of immigration and the profound ruptures caused by World War I, social psychologists of the day found fertile ground for—and much influence with—their theories on engineering the public's consent. No longer would the Enlightenment-era ideal of a democracy of informed citizens hold sway; rather, the key to a stable democracy was to develop a "consumer democracy," to learn how to "sell" political ideas, and to erect a facsimile of democracy where participation, freedom, and dissent were all expressed within the relatively safe confines of consumerism. The problem, of course, is that consumer democracy is effectively oligarchy, with a mannequin of democracy still on display in the window.

The architects of this plan laid the clear groundwork for today's numbing mass mediocracy, and a carefully inculcated cynicism that enables many people to knowingly decry the obvious bankruptcy of the political process while participating in the consumer feast that fattens only the foreclosing bank. On one level, this cynicism is a commonsense response to the apparent gap between democratic rhetoric and actual democracy. But perhaps, at a deeper level, it merely represents a psychological victory for the presumptive "intelligent few," who want us to believe that image matters as much, or more, than substance.

I view PR men as hucksters cut from the same cloth as American showman and Ringling Brothers Circus founder P.T. Barnum. Like Barnum, these mouthpieces for hire draw attention away from our oh-so-ordinary lives to the wondrous spectacle they've prepared for us; they invite us to take a walk down a hall of funhouse mirrors, where our curious natures compel us to check out the freak show in which we're cast. Barnum, who famously observed, "There's a sucker born every minute," could hardly have known his words would describe not only the willing throngs of overcredulous gapers who made his fortune, but the defining credo of consumer democracy. It's a grand bait-and-switch: Rather than finding anything Marvelous, we're sold a domesticated idea of what it means to be alive. We have been profoundly civilized.

Knowing the tools and strategy of our enemy is important. Ours is a mediated age, where symbols, theories, and representations serve as proxies in a battle of savage ideas. Our aim herein is to provide well-constructed arms for your mental and political self-defense.

So stock up, wiggle your toes, and perch intentfully with us here. It's long past time, to spit on our hands, "hoist the black flag, and begin to slit throats."*

(Nicely, of course.)

The Curiously Unflinching Futures Issue

2.6 - Summer 2006

The future is here. It's just not widely distributed yet.
—William Gibson, science fiction novelist

I'm fairly sure that Gibson was talking about the gap between the technological haves and have-nots when he wrote that line. But it could also be read as a gritty call to realism for those of us in so-called developed industrialized nations, who indulge in great horror at the gradual collapse of our own pathologically unsustainable mode of existence while ignoring the reality of the majority of this planet's residents, who do not in fact share the same dread or anxiety about losing what most of them, frankly, never had to squander in the first place.

When we decided on the theme for this issue, and subsequently set out to craft some educated speculation on the topic, a great many things piqued our interest. The tension between optimism and pessimism when it comes to contemplating what's to come is profound: Is the future going to bring great transformation and a possible dismantling of capitalism and white

---

* *Every normal man must be tempted at times to spit on his hands, hoist the black flag, and begin to slit throats." —journalist, satirist, cynic, and "American Neitzsche," H. L. Mencken*

supremacy? Are we hopeful? Will there be a collapse and, if so, will it most resemble a cataclysm or an interminable nightmare? It seems inevitable to us that folks living in modern industrial societies are in for some profound downward adjustments to our standards of living, and that the more pressing question is just how ugly a world the haves are going to create for the have-nots as we grapple with that "collapse." Will we have a world where a dominant elite consigns everyone else to suffering, scarcity, and deprivation, or are we poised for a great leap forward?

Only a fool would seriously try to answer such impossible questions. We've concerned ourselves instead with trying to ask good questions. Along the way, we have tried not to be squeamish, but to embrace what may come, without the paralysis of horror or disbelief. We have tried not to resign ourselves to the misanthropic, cowardly, and at any rate lazy idea that everything is just, in a word, *fucked*.

All of these forward-looking pieces are unified by the understanding that the future, such as it is, depends largely on where you're standing, what you're standing on, and how you're looking. With the right eyes, you can see beyond your usual field of vision, and into the simultaneous, interconnected reality of things…

The Grossly Unexpected Bugs Issue

2.7 - Winter 2007

Political language—and with variations this is true of all political parties,
from Conservatives to Anarchists—is designed to make lies sound truthful
and murder respectable, and to give an appearance of solidity to pure wind.

—George Orwell

Of course, there will always be those who look only at technique, who ask
"how," while others of a more curious nature will ask "why." Personally, I
have always preferred inspiration to information.

—Man Ray

Some people shot us weird looks when we announced "bugs" as a theme for an issue of TiP. A few others reacted with exuberant enthusiasm, as if all this time we'd been talking about the *political,* what they'd been really wanting to read about was the *entomological.*

But everything is connected, and not just in the world of well-intentioned bumper stickers. All systems, all entities, and all phenomena—political or otherwise—are not only connected, but interdependent. This issue is about the perils and emancipatory potential of this reality. This is also the issue where we make an escape, of sorts.

Most progressive and radical media in the U.S. today is boring, repetitious, unimaginative, outframed, lacking in both humor and imagination, and exists primarily to serve propagandistic and subcultural ends, driven by the lamentable imperatives of niche-driven newsstand sales and non-profit grant-funding guidelines. Further, most "socially-conscious" media in the U.S. today is like bad art, taking potentially transformative, liberating ideas and aspirations and rendering them lifeless by placing them within maddeningly unimaginative compositions.

We could have devoted the issue to attacking media, ideologies, and strategies we wish were better, but we already did that, in our Constructively Negative Sacred Cows issue (Summer 2005). Also, we're not perfect: We're riddled with many of the same limitations I've just decried.

So. This issue, let's attempt to slip a certain noose of predictable political formulations. One of several operational definitions given for "politics"
is "the total complex of relations between people living in society," yet the
obvious interdependence of human beings and the natural and animal
world makes it reasonable to expand the definition of politics to include,
well, just about everything [...]

Change was required of us, dear reader. We're molting, and it's only
natural. Don't squirm, don't be afraid, and please, refrain from stepping on us until you've peered closer and appreciated our finer details.
If you're unclear or have doubts about where this is headed, I offer
you both qualification and invitation: We mean well; read on.

image by Barbara Norfleet

About the Contributors

Founder, Editor, and Creative Director **Brian Awehali** makes a fitful home in Oakland, California. His writing, which has garnered two Project Censored awards (2006 and 2007), as well as a 2003 Society of Professional Journalists award, has appeared in or on Alternet, The Black World Today, Z Magazine, *The Progressive* radio show, Britannica.com, *ColorsNW* (Seattle), *High Times, The Santa Fe New Mexican, Tikkun,* Online Journalism Review, Native Nations Network, Finland-based *Maailman Sivu,* and *Hedonia: Your Journal of Directed Pleasures.* He is currently working on several books: *Good Bye!: A Gleefully Morbid Collection of Honest Obituaries for a Dishonest World* (City Lights, Oct. 2008); *The Once and Future Blimp: A Reasoned Case for a Return to Lighter-Than-Air Travel;* and *The Hole in the Ceiling,* a memoir about a Cherokee/Irish teenager's escape from a Christian children's home in Oklahoma, and his subsequent misadventures in homelessness. He also publishes a blog and weekly email digest of the best, most overlooked, most useful, or simply most interesting matter to be found online. Find out more at BRIANAWEHALI.COM.

damali ayo is a conceptual artist and creator of the web-art-performance work (and book) *How To Rent a Negro,* a satirical exploration of the commodification of race and black people. She first started working in theatre and performance at Brown University where she designed and directed the Women's Prison Project. She has panhandled for reparations, too; find out more about that, and damali's other work, at DAMALIAYO.COM.

Neelanjana Banerjee is the former editor-in-chief of *AsianWeek* newspaper, and currently works as the managing editor of *YO! Youth Outlook Multimedia,* where she helps young people produce their own media. A regular contributor to *Audrey* magazine, she is also contributing editor for *Hyphen.* Her writing has appeared in the *Asian Pacific American Journal, A Room of One's Own, Suspect Thoughts* and the anthology *Desilicious* (Arsenal Press). Having just completed an MFA program in Creative Writing, Neela now harbors (not so) secret fantasies of starting her own South Asian burlesque troupe. You can spy on her at NEELANJANABANERJEE.COM.

Chip Berlet is the editor of *Eyes Right! Challenging the Right-Wing Backlash,* and the coauthor of *Right-Wing Populism in America: Too Close for Comfort.* He is also a senior analyst at Political Research Associates (PRA), which, "works to facilitate public understanding of the threat posed to human rights by oppressive and authoritarian right-wing movements in the United States."

Iain Boal is an Irish social historian of science and technics, associated with Retort, a group of antinomian writers, artisans and artists based in the San Francisco Bay Area. He is one of the authors of *Afflicted Powers: Capital and Spectacle in a New Age of War* (Verso).

In 1993, **Jeff Chang** co-founded SoleSides (later Quannum Projects), an independent hip hop label out of Davis, California, that helped launch the careers of Blackalicious, DJ Shadow, Lyrics Born, and Lateef the Truth Speaker. He was a founding editor of

ColorLines, the nation's leading magazine on race, culture, and organizing, and his writing has appeared in the *Village Voice, Vibe, Spin, The Nation, Mother Jones,* the *Washington Post,* and more. He was also an organizer of the National Hip Hop Political Convention in 2004. Visit him online at HTTP://WWW.CANTSTOPWONTSTOP.COM/

Jeff Conant, formerly a *LiP* Senior Editor, is currently finishing up an international educational guide to environmental health and justice with the Hesperian Foundation, as well as a novel based on his time living in Chiapas, Mexico. Since *LiP* ceased to publish he's published articles in Corpwatch, *CounterPunch,* and *Earth Island Journal,* and poems in the *Texas Observer,* BoogLit, and *What If.* At home in New Mexico he co-publishes *The Taos High Ground Pre-Post Holocaust Daily Observer* and co-hosts the weekly Zapatista Homeland Companion Tragicomedy Hour in a tiny art gallery on a lonely stretch of highway at about 7200 feet above (current) sea level.

LiP's Assistant Publisher and then Assistant Editor **Ariane Conrad** wore far too many hats for us to recount them here, but we will take the space to say that most of the hats were flattering. In addition to her love of animals and dirigibles, she possesses a visceral love of the written word, in both poetry and prose form, and her work has appeared on or in Alternet, *Curve,* the Diamond Angle, and the *Potomac Review.* She did not write this bio, though if she had, it would most likely be humbler.

Dan Cook is associate professor of childhood studies and sociology at Rutgers University where he tries to engage students in unlearning the lessons taught them by capitalist culture.

Hugh D'Andrade is an illustrator and agitator based in San Francisco. He worries that his FBI file may in fact be as fat as his portfolio. See more of his work on his website: WWW.HUGHILLUSTRATION.COM.

Eric Drooker's paintings are seen on the covers of the *New Yorker,* the *Progressive,* the *Village Voice* and numerous other magazines, as well as books and albums. He is the author of *Flood! A Novel in Pictures, Illuminated Poems* (with Allen Ginsberg), *Street Posters & Ballads and Blood Song: A Silent Ballad.* He gives slide lectures at schools and cultural centers worldwide. He is a third-generation New Yorker, born and raised on Manhattan Island.

Dr. Michael Eric Dyson is the author of many books, including *The Michael Eric Dyson Reader, I May Not Get There With You: The True Martin Luther King, Jr.; Race Rules: Navigating the Color Line; Between God and Gangsta Rap; Making Malcolm: The Myth and Meaning of Malcolm X;* and *Reflecting Black.* He is a Humanities Professor at the University of Pennsylvania, and he lives in Philadelphia.

Jessica Giordani infused her feminist politics into career in 2003 when she opened a feminist sex toy store, The Smitten Kitten, in Minneapolis with her friend and cohort, Jennifer. Their dedication to quality and education is unique in the adult industry. She is also a founding member of Coalition Against Toxic Toys.

Nadyalec Hijazi is an omnisexual hellraising genderqueer gayrab. He's been published in B*est Gay Erotica 2006, Hot Off the Net, Trikone, Bint el Nas* and *Roughriders.* He's also performed at Gender Enders, Gender Pirates, Perverts Put Out, Writers With Drinks, and S.F. Pride. You can read more of him at WWW.NADYALEC.COM.

Gregory Hischak, a Seattle, Washington resident since 1989, is currently a playwright and spoken word performer with a closet sideline in graphic design and aluminum recycling. Talk to him about performance poetry workshops in your high school or community center. GREG@FARMPULP.COM

Literary iconoclast **Christopher Hitchens** has published more than a dozen books, including *No One Left to Lie To: The Triangulations of William Jefferson Clinton*, *The Trial of Henry Kissinger*, and *The Missionary Position: Mother Teresa in Theory and Practice.*, and, most recently, *god is Not Great: How Religion Poisons Everything* (Twelve Books).

Erin E. Hunter is a freelance illustrator and graphic designer in California. She specializes in science illustration, with an emphasis on botany, entomology, and useless trivia. More of Erin's work can be seen at ECHUNTER.COM.

Ted Infinity comes from a long, long line of Infinities. He believes in good science, bad rum, and radical queerness. His writing has been published in the *Heuristic Squelch*, *Pigdog Journal*, and the *Spock Science Monitor*. In the daytime, he's a San Francisco area tech writer.

Lisa Jervis is the founding Editor and Publisher of *Bitch: Feminist Response to Pop Culture* and was *LiP*'s editor at large. She's a generally cranky smarty-pants whose work has appeared in numerous magazines and books, including *Ms.*, the *San Francisco Chronicle*, the *Women's Review of Books*, *Punk Planet*, *Women Who Eat* (Seal Press), *Spreadsheet Slut*, and *Low Times: The Journal of Clinical Depression*. She also coedited of *Bitchfest: Ten Years of Cultural Criticism from the Pages of* Bitch *Magazine*

(Farrar Straus & Giroux) and is currently working on a book spawned by the article that appears in this here very anthology.

Antonia Juhasz is a policy analyst, writer and activist living in San Francisco. She is author of *The Bush Agenda: Invading the World, One Economy at a Time* (Regan Books). Her website can be found at WWW.THEBUSHAGENDA.NET. When she's not writing, she can often be found dressed as Buffy the Empire Slayer, complete with a three-foot silver sword and bright red miniskirt.

Contributing illustrator **Tim Kreider** is the author of two collections of cartoons, *The Pain—When Will It End?* and *Why Do They Kill Me?* (both from Fantagraphics Books). His cartoon, "The Pain—When Will It End?" [THEPAINCOMICS.COM] appears weekly in the *Baltimore City Paper*. His essays have appeared in the *New York Times*, *Film Quarterly*, and *The Comics Journal*. He has also been stabbed in the throat in Crete, ridden the Ringling Brothers circus train to Mexico City, attended to a friend's recovery from gender reassignment surgery in Neenah, Wisconsin, and addressed the Forum on Innovative Approaches to Outer Planetary Exploration 2001-2020 at the Lunar and Planetary Institute in Houston.

Winona LaDuke is an Anishinaabeg (Ojibwe) enrolled member of the Mississippi Band of Anishinaabeg and is the mother of three children. She is the Program Director of Honor the Earth and the Founding Director of White Earth Land Recovery Project, which recently received the prestigious International Slow Food Award for their work with protecting wild rice and local biodiversity. In both 1996 and 2000, LaDuke ran for Vice-President on the Green Party ticket with Ralph Nader. She has written extensively on Native American and environmental issues, and her books include *Last Standing Woman* (fiction), *All Our Relations* (non-fiction), *In the Sugarbush* (children's non-fiction), and *The Winona LaDuke Reader*. Her most recent book is *Recovering the Sacred* (South End Press).

Bruce E. Levine is a clinical psychologist and the author of *Commonsense Rebellion*. Dr. Levine, in private practice since 1985, also lectures and gives workshops, and his articles and interviews have appeared in numerous publications. His newest book, *Surviving America's Depression Epidemic* is published by Chelsea Green. His website is BRUCELEVINE.NET.

Contributing editor **Kari Lydersen** is an indefatigable independent journalist, bicyclist and swimmer who's been with *LiP* from the beginning. Her work has appeared in too many publications to recount here, and she is the author of *Out of the Sea and Into the Fire: Latin American-U.S. Immigration in the Global Age* (Common Courage Press).

David Martinez is a filmaker and journalist based in San Francisco. He is the director of *500 Miles to Babylon*, a film about Iraq under US occupation. More information about his work is available at WWW.SUBCINE.COM.

Neal Pollack is the author of *The Neal Pollack Anthology of American Literature*, *Never Mind the Pollacks: A Rock and Roll Novel*, and *Beneath the Axis of Evil: One Man's Journeys Into the Horrors of War*. His newest book, *Chicago Noir* (Akashic), is a collection of crime stories. Pollack contributed an introduction and a story, and edited the rest. Visit his blog at WWW.NEALPOLLACK.COM.

Danny Postel is Senior Editor of openDemocracy, an online magazine of global politics & culture, and the author of *Reading "Legitimation Crisis" in Tehran* (Prickly

Paradigm Press). He is Editor-at-Large of *Stop Smiling: The Magazine for High-Minded Lowlifes*, Contributing Editor of *Dædalus*, and a member of the editorial boards of *Logos* and *The Common Review*. His work has appeared in *The Nation*, *In These Times*, *The Progressive*, *Z* Magazine, *The American Prospect*, *Truthdig*, *Exquisite Corpse*, *Salmagundi*, *Radical Society*, *Left History*, *New Politics*, *Critical Inquiry*, *Philosophy & Social Criticism*, and the Tehran-based reformist newspaper *Shargh*, which was banned by the Iranian government in the fall of 2006.

Boots Riley is a co-founder of the hip hop group The Coup. Together with DJ Pam the Funktress, Riley has released four classic and award-winning albums: *Kill My Landlord* (1993), *Genocide and Juice* (1994), *Steal this Album* (1998), *Party Music* (2001), which was named "best rap album of the year" by numerous publications including *Rolling Stone* and the *Village Voice*, and "best pop album of the year" by the *Washington Post*.

Senior Editor **Christy Rodgers** is the erstwhile editor/publisher of *What If? Journal of Radical Possibilities*, a journal of visionary art and activism, past, present and future. She currently maintains the website WHATIFJOURNAL.ORG.

Heather Rogers is a journalist and filmmaker, and is the author (and director) of *Gone Tomorrow: The Hidden Life of Garbage* (The New Press).

Designer and Production Manager **Colin Sagan** is a freelance graphic designer and member of QUILTED.ORG, the best worker-owned web design cooperative you haven't heard of. Yet. He's worked with an array of quirky magazines, including the now-defunct *Kitchen Sink*, *Ode*, and *SONAR-V: Sundry Oddities of No Apparent Redeemable Value*. In order to finance the work he gives to magazines like *LiP* for free, he is currently harvesting the energy generated by the meowing of feral kittens that live in his back yard. He bicycles a lot, and has chaotic and lively hair.

Associate Editor **Justine Sharrock** is a writer who spends too much time overanalyzing the politics of subcultures as a way to excuse her obsession with the gritty side of life. When she's not covering petty crimes, you can also find her infiltrating mainstream journalism through fact checking, trying to hold them to some semblance of the truth. Her writing has appeared in publications such as *Mother Jones* and *Bitch*.

Dr. Vandana Shiva is a physicist, ecologist, activist, and author of hundreds of papers and articles and more than 15 books. She is the founder and director of the Research Foundation for Science, Technology and Natural Resource Policy in India. Her latest book is titled *Earth Democracy* (South End Press).

Mattilda a.k.a. Matt Bernstein Sycamore lives in San Francisco, and is the editor, most recently, of *Nobody Passes: Rejecting the Rules of Gender and Conformity* (Seal Press) and an expanded second edition of *That's Revolting! Queer Strategies for Resisting Assimilation* (Soft Skull Press). She's also the author of a novel, *Pulling Taffy*, and the editor of *Dangerous Families: Queer Writing on Surviving*, and *Tricks and Treats: Sex Workers Write About Their Clients*. She is an instigator of Gay Shame, a radical queer activist group that fights assimilation. Mattilda is the books/print matter editor at *Make/shift*, writes a monthly column at *Maximumrocknroll*, regularly contributes reviews, essays and interviews for the *San Francisco Bay Guardian*, *Bitch*, *Punk Planet* and other publications,

and she selected and introduced *Erotica 2006* (Cleis Press). Mattilda ond novel, *So Many Ways to Sleep* will be published by City Lights Pre the Fall of 2008. Visit Mattilda's blog HTTP://NOBODYPASSES.BLOGSPOT.COM

Jennifer Whitney is a co-author of *Are Everywhere: the irresistible rise of glob anticapitalism,* a founding member of the Infernal Noise Brigade marching band, a health care worker and long-term mem her of the Black Cross Health Collective, and a sometimes-journalist, who is on a constant quest to integrate her passion for international travel and adventure with her need for deep roots and community. She has worked at the free Common Ground Health Clinic since its post-Katrina inception, and is co-founder and coordinator of the Latino Health Outreach Project.

Erin Wiegand is the former managing editor of *LiP.* Currently working towards self-employment as a freelance writer, editor, and German translator, in her spare time she enjoys vegan cooking, watching horror movies, riding her bike, and secretly plotting the destruction of Western civilization. She has also contributed to a forthcoming book by the editors of *mental_floss* magazine. You can visit her on the interweb at ERINWIEGAND.COM.

Contributing editor **Tim Wise** is one of the nation's most prominent white antiracist activists and educators, and the author of *White Like Me: Reflections on Race from a Privileged Son* (Soft Skull) and *Affirmative Action: Racial Preference in Black and White* (Routledge). His writings and speaking schedule can be found at his website: TIMWISE.ORG.

...roject!

...un collective that publishes and distributes radical
...media, and other material. We're small: a dozen
...work long hours for short money, because we believe
...We're anarchists, which is reflected both in the books
...d in the way we organize our business: without bosses.

...publishes the finest books, CDs, and DVDs from the anarchist
...ical traditions—currently about 18 to 20 per year. Joining
...riends of AK Press is a way in which you can directly help us
...eep the wheels rolling and these important projects coming.

As ever, money is tight as we do not rely on outside funding. We need
your help to make and keep these crucial materials available. Friends pay
a minimum (of course we have no objection to larger sums!) of $20 / £15
per month, for a minimum three month period. Money received goes
directly into our publishing funds. In return, Friends automatically
receive (for the duration of their membership), as they appear, one FREE
copy of EVERY new AK Press title. Secondly, they are also entitled to a
10% discount on EVERYTHING featured in the AK Press distribution
catalog—or on our website—on ANY and EVERY order. We also have
a program where individuals or groups can sponsor a whole book.

Please contact us for more details:

AK Press
674-A 23rd Street
Oakland, CA 94612
akpress@akpress.org
www.akpress.org

AK Press
PO Box 12766
Edinburgh, Scotland EH8, 9YE
ak@akedin.demon.co.uk
www.akuk.com